D1713390

"No one has done more to rescue Scripture from centuries of skeptical assault and restore it to its proper place as the inspired, inerrant Word of God than Scott Hahn and the St. Paul Center for Biblical Theology. In this carefully researched book, Dr. Hahn teams up with Dr. Wiker to lay bare the sorry history of skeptical Scripture scholarship and reveal its bankruptcy. Nothing is more important for the challenges the Church is facing today than restoring Sacred Scripture to its proper place. We all owe a deep debt of gratitude to the mighty labors of Dr. Hahn, Dr. Wiker, and their growing number of collaborators."

Ralph Martin

Director, Graduate Theology Programs in the New Evangelization, Sacred Heart Major Seminary

"We are living in a world where nearly every aspect of life has been politicized, resulting in a less-than-truthful understanding of what it means to be human. But what if the Bible has also been politicized over the centuries? Could it be that our understanding of Sacred Scripture is less than God intended it to be? Drs. Scott Hahn and Benjamin Wiker do a brilliant job of taking us down a long and winding road into the past, pointing out where Scripture scholars took philosophic detours resulting in a flawed way of approaching the Bible. The good news is that Hahn and Wiker instill in the reader a renewed hope and confidence in the book of all books."

Jeff Cavins

Founder and Creator, *The Great Adventure* Bible Study

"There are few topics more important in Catholic theology and apologetics than the inspiration and inerrancy of Scripture. The latter necessarily follows from the former, but both of these essential and infallible teachings of the Catholic Church are under attack and have been for centuries. What riveted me to *The Decline and Fall of Sacred Scripture*, however, was more than just an apologetic defense of Scripture. That's been done before. Hahn and Wiker masterfully demonstrate in remarkable detail the devastation that follows in the wake of the abandonment of the inspired text. Essential doctrines of the historic Christian faith are jettisoned. The foundations of Western Civilization so integrally interwoven with these essential truths go with it. But perhaps most dangerous of all, we see the prophetic words of Psalm 11:3 incarnated: 'If the foundations are destroyed, what can the righteous do?' Catholics are gravely mistaken if they believe they are immune from the chaos because we have Sacred Tradition and the Magisterium. And these are blessings to be sure. But there is a reason why CCC 95 says 'in the supremely wise arrangement of God, sacred Tradition, Sacred Scripture and the Magisterium are so interconnected and associated that one of them cannot stand without the others.' For Scripture's part, Scott Hahn and Benjamin Wiker show you why this is so in a manner truly prophetic."

Tim Staples
Senior Apologist, Catholic Answers

"Scott Hahn and Benjamin Wiker have written a very readable explanation of what has gone wrong with modern biblical scholarship. How did it get to be such an incoherent mess? Surprisingly, as they answer this question, they end up explaining a great deal of what has gone wrong with the entire modern world."

Cy Kellett
Host, *Catholic Answers Live*

"Clearly written and persuasively argued, *The Decline and Fall of Sacred Scripture* explains how the Bible went from being revered as the very Word of God and the font of Western Civilization to being denigrated and dissected by so-called experts on TV and in the classroom. Hahn and Wiker's text should be read by anyone entering college, who has a child or grandchild going off to college, or who is interested in why politicians, teachers, and even clergy have been able to voice public doubt on the Bible with confidence. Hahn and Wiker teach the reader to be skeptical of the skeptics. This book does the important work of clearing the ground of the scholarly rubble that has sown the seeds of doubt so that the Bible can once again be turned to as the source of authentic theology and as God's great love letter to all of us, His children."

Jeff Morrow
Coauthor, *Modern Biblical Criticism as a Tool of Statecraft (1700–1900)*

THE DECLINE AND FALL *of* SACRED SCRIPTURE

THE DECLINE AND FALL *of* SACRED SCRIPTURE

How the Bible Became a Secular Book

SCOTT HAHN & BENJAMIN WIKER

Steubenville, Ohio
www.emmausroad.org

Emmaus Road Publishing
1468 Parkview Circle
Steubenville, Ohio 43952

Library of Congress Control Number: 2021931203
ISBN 978-1-64585-099-1 (hard cover) /
978-1-64585-100-4 (paperback) / 978-1-64585-101-1 (ebook)

Cover design by Patty Borgman
Layout by Emily Demary
Cover image: *Ecce Homo* (1896), Mihály Munkácsy,
Déri Museum, Hungary

TABLE OF CONTENTS

PART I

Chapter One

THE GREAT DIVIDE

Scripture died a quiet death in Western Christendom some time in the sixteenth century. . . . For over a millennium, Western Christians read and revered the Christian Bible as Scripture, as an authoritative anthology of unified, authoritative writings belonging to the Church. The scriptural Bible was neither reducible to a written "text" nor intelligible outside a divine economy of meaning. It was not simply the foundation of the Church's academic theology; it also furnished its moral universe, framed its philosophic inquiries, and fitted out its liturgies. It provided the materials for thought, expression, and action, becoming what Northrop Frye famously called the "great code" of Western civilization. As the book at the center of Western Christendom, the Bible functioned scripturally.

—Michael C. Legaspi, *The Death of Scripture and the Rise of Biblical Studies* (Oxford University Press, 2010), 3–4.

Why should anyone worry about the history of Scripture scholarship, especially reaching all the way back to the early fourteenth century?

The simple answer is that our peculiar situation today—in which priests, preachers, and people in the pews study the Bible as the inspired Word of God and academic Scripture scholars in universities study the Bible as an ancient book of mythology—is the *result* of the history of Scripture scholarship. We are searching for the reasons for this Great Divide, and that means searching for its ultimate origins.

It is a far greater divide than most lay people may realize. It's no exaggeration to say that (setting aside a few outlier colleges and universities like Franciscan University of Steubenville) the last place one should go to study the Bible *as* the inspired Word of God is a Biblical Studies department at a university. Indeed, that's the first place to go to have one's Christian faith destroyed, for nearly the entire curriculum is defined by the assumption that the Bible is an entirely human artifact cobbled together in a "prescientific age."

This assumption and the method built upon it define the academic study of the Bible today. For the great majority of the academy, the Bible is no more a guide for our lives than Homer's *Iliad*, Hesiod's *Theogony*, Icelandic sagas, or a collection of fairy tales from primitive Teutonic tribes. It might be interesting as a form of ancient literature, but then, so is Ovid's *Metamorphoses*. Modern science has replaced ancient faiths and the stories based upon them, the Bible included.

By invoking the authority of modern science, academic

biblical scholars seem to have history on their side. What *could* Moses, who lived well over three thousand years ago, know about anything—a man who had no idea either of the age or size of the universe, who had no inkling of the existence of the molecular structure of DNA and couldn't name even one chemical element on the periodic table, whose grasp of geography was limited to a very small region around the southeastern edge of the Mediterranean, and who understood nothing of the causes or cures of leprosy or the glories of modern astronomy? For that matter, do we even have demonstrative proof that Moses existed? But whether he did or not, no one living over three thousand years ago had a clue about the real world as revealed by the efforts of science over the last three centuries.

On this view, modern science would seem to provide *the* justification for how modern Scripture scholars tend to treat the Bible. If you ask such a scholar why he or she approaches the Bible as a work of mythology—or, variously, an ancient Jewish tribal propaganda piece written or at least edited by the priestly class, or a hodgepodge of histories turned into legends, or a great work of ancient literary fiction, or anything but the inspired Word of God—the answer will generally boil down to "That is the *scientific* way to approach the Bible."

Fleshed out, this reply means something like this: "Modern science has demonstrated that the assumptions of the biblical actors and authors are simply wrong. The world wasn't created in seven days. Evolution is the real cause of the fish of the sea, the birds of the air, and the animals of the land, including the two-legged animal, the human being. Furthermore, there are no such things as angels, good or bad, although it is likely that there are aliens. And most important of all, miracles cannot happen because they violate the known laws of physics. Therefore, seas do not part, walking sticks do not turn into snakes, lepers are not spontaneously healed, virgins do not give birth, a man cannot walk on water, and dead people do not come back to life. Scripture scholars must proceed accordingly and treat such stories in the Bible in exactly the same way as classical scholars treat the various fantastic stories in Greek and Roman mythology."

Readers may now realize the importance of our argument that the historical origins of modern Scripture scholarship actually stretch back to the early 1300s, almost four centuries *before* the advent of modern science.

Modern Scripture scholars assert that their treatment of the Bible is the *result* of the victories of modern science and *rests upon* their authority. A sign of this is that almost all histories of modern Scripture scholarship begin in the 1700s, the century after the publication of Isaac Newton's *Principia Mathematica* in 1687. They then move on to nineteenth-century Germany, whose universities represent the intellectual paragon and pinnacle of the proper scholarly method that defines nearly all that follows in the twentieth and twenty-first centuries.

But if we are right, and the assumptions of modern Scripture scholarship can be traced back almost four centuries *prior* to Newton, then the effect would seem to precede the cause.

If such is the case, there must be other, more fundamental, nonscientific (even "prescientific") reasons for the assumptions of modern Scripture scholars and their consequent methods. While the history is quite complex, we believe that we have recovered one of the most important: the *politicization of the Bible*—that is, the bending of Scripture to very earthly, political ends, the fundamental assumption being that there are no other ends but those of this world, and these are purely material ends.

We have argued this thesis in great detail in our academic work, *Politicizing the Bible: The Roots of Historical Criticism and the Secularization of Scripture, 1300–1700* (Crossroad, 2013). In the present work, we wish to set out those arguments for a more popular audience, adding new material and reflections that significantly strengthen and enrich the thesis and make it available to a wider readership.

Our goal in doing this is not primarily to "win" an academic argument, but to contribute to a critical revival of biblical scholarship that supports (rather than undermines) the Christian faith of priests, preachers, and people in the pews.

For those interested in greater detail, we invite you to read *Politicizing the Bible* along with, or after, the present work. (Note: we will not interrupt our narrative in the present work by constant footnotes to scholarly sources already contained in *Politicizing the Bible*; rather, we will assume that those who wish to explore these sources may readily find them there, and we'll footnote only direct quotes and new sources in this work.)

Since the present work is aimed at those who may not be fully aware of the assumptions and conclusions of contemporary Scripture scholars, we now provide the following typical representation of contemporary biblical scholars, followed by an illuminating miscellany of other like-minded advocates. It is not difficult to see how corrosive their scholarly results are to Christian believers.

CAUGHT UP IN A FUNK

In his *Honest to Jesus*, biblical scholar Robert Funk maintains—based on his own spiritual progress—that our "youthful convictions" rooted in belief in the Bible as revealed must be let go.[1] As the intellectually mature realize, modern scholarship reveals that, in the Bible, there are two Jesuses, the one an actual historical man as understood by academic scholars, and the other the divinized, mythological God-man as worshiped by churchgoers. Scholars have gotten to the historical man by peeling away all the mythological elements of the Bible that violated the canons of modern science.

This new "revelation" has a direct effect on the understanding and practice of Christian faith—or, declares Funk, it *should* have. For almost two millennia, Funk explains, churches have based their creeds, dogmas, and worship upon the "traditional" belief in the God-man and defined both their spiritual questions and answers accordingly. "Traditional answers to theological questions no longer completely satisfy," Funk informs readers. "We can no longer simply repeat the old creeds and *pre-Enlightenment* [emphasis added] shibboleths and expect thinking

[1] Robert Funk died in 2005.

people to regard them as illuminating and persuasive."[2]

Those who want to wind the clock back to our intellectual, prescientific infancy prior to the Enlightenment (the 1700s), Funk declares, are doing no service to those in the pews, especially if the motive is the pastoral protection of "the faith of simple believers, as though the suppression of knowledge can somehow advance the faith."[3] The only way is forward, with scholars leading the way. We must leave behind the God-man of myth and set our sights on the "search for the Jesus of history," which Funk claims "is the quest for the holy grail of truth."[4]

Funk thus illustrates the basics of what is generally called "historical criticism." We need to get a bit of a deeper grasp of both aspects, the historical and the critical, beginning with the latter first. (And, for the sake of avoiding confusion, we will provide further clarification at the end of this chapter concerning the important distinction between the *historical method* and the *historical-critical method*, as related to historical criticism.)

According to the tenets of historical criticism, to be *critical* means primarily to understand that modern science has forever removed us from the mythological world of our ancestors, the "enchanted" world of gods, goddesses, and god-men, as well as fairies, demons, magicians, and miracles. The Bible itself is the last text, historically, to be disenchanted: last because, long after belief in Greek and Roman gods had been historically discarded, the institu-

2 Robert Funk, *Honest to Jesus: Jesus for a New Millennium* (San Francisco: Polebridge, 1996), 27.

3 Funk, *Honest to Jesus*, 27.

4 Funk, *Honest to Jesus*, 29.

tional and cultural spread of Christianity ensured that the Bible maintained its hold on Western culture. The "simple believers" are the last holdout.

Funk would certainly seem to be correct that the advent of modern science brought an end to this mythological spell, and (simple believers aside) the result has been the increasing de-Christianization of Western culture since the 1800s (though outside the West, e.g., in Africa, the trend appears to be the opposite). The historical criticism was a crucial instrument in loosening the formative hold of the Bible on Western culture, at least as a revealed theological text—although as Funk notes, its work is not yet fully done.

So much for the "critical" part. The *historical* aspect follows upon the critical assumption that modern science demands that miracles reported in the biblical text could not have occurred. Since the reports are untrue (and reveal only the ignorance of the ancient Jews and first Christians about how nature really works and what its laws allow and forbid), the scholar's focus shifts to what *really* happened historically.

In this shift, the scholar has no theological work to do except to discredit the mythological claims of the Bible that for so long formed the foundations of theological claims. But the main goal of the scholar is reduced to studying the historical sources and literary parallels of these mythological biblical beliefs, ferreting out what historical persons or events might remain once demythologizing has occurred. Since nothing *super*natural could ever have occurred historically, the scholar may then provide a merely natural explanation of how and why the particular mythological elements got into the text to begin with.

And so, as Funk declares, *critical* scholarship tells us that Jesus wasn't a God-man, and so there was, *historically*, no divine birth, no resurrection, and hence no miraculous post-resurrection appearances of Jesus. Something else must have actually occurred historically.

For example, behind the story of the angel visiting Mary and the virgin birth, Funk (following other scholars) opines that "an illegitimate conception seems a plausible explanation of Mary's condition."[5] The virgin-birth story was a cover-up, hiding Mary's shame and cleaning up Jesus's pedigree.

Likewise, the "story of the women discovering an empty tomb on Easter morning . . . was undoubtedly a literary creation of Mark," repeated in variations in the other, later Gospels.[6] What really happened was that "after the crucifixion Jesus' disciples fled to Galilee and resumed their previous lives." Distraught and disappointed, they later "came to the conviction that Jesus was not dead but alive." So it was that a dead man became, in the minds of ignorant fishermen, tax collectors, and tentmakers, the resurrected God-man of Christian mythology.[7]

Jesus's ignorant followers were therefore the source of the false deification of Jesus the man, and so they were perpetrators of what Funk refers to as the "reverse enhancement" of Jesus's life, adding in elements to his various biographies (a.k.a. the Gospels) that befitted

5 Funk, *Honest to Jesus*, 288.
6 Funk, *Honest to Jesus*, 221.
7 Funk, *Honest to Jesus*, 280.

his newly attributed divine status (such as birth from a virgin somehow united to a god, the very stars aligning to announce his entry into the world, and the capacity to do miracles). All these elements, Funk informs readers, are just what one finds are added to other notable figures in ancient Greece and Rome.[8]

Since, for Funk, the son of Mary was merely a man, however exceptional a man he might have been, "Jesus himself should not be, must not be, the object of faith. That would be to repeat the idolatry of the first believers."[9] Christianity needs to be reinvented by recovering its real, historical roots, revealed not by God but by scholars, a reinvention somehow based upon the diligent, scholarly recovery of the religious vision of the real historical Jesus, who was (Funk assures the reader) merely a "humble Galilean sage," a man who never claimed to be divine.[10] The lay faithful must step aside and step in line: only "scholars and experts" are qualified to lead the way.[11]

Where will they lead us? While the goal may not be clear, Funk is certain that the scientific approach to Scripture results in very practical political and ethical effects of a certain kind. As Funk informs readers, it undercuts fundamentalism, and that's a good thing. "It is no accident . . . that fundamentalist groups have the highest racial bigotry ratios among religious bodies in the United States. They are also the most vigorous supporters of a military solution

[8] Funk, *Honest to Jesus*, 281ff.

[9] Funk, *Honest to Jesus*, 305.

[10] Funk, *Honest to Jesus*, 306.

[11] Funk, *Honest to Jesus*, 25.

to world problems. I want to know what the right-to-lifers have done for the starving children here and abroad before I listen to their theories about the beginning of life."[12] Also among his desiderata, "We must divorce the abortion issue from the concept of sex as sin. We should endorse responsible, protected recreational sex between consenting adults."[13]

Clearly, for Funk, once the mythology is removed from the Bible, historical criticism ends up at least indirectly reaffirming what is generally acknowledged as a liberal or left-leaning political agenda. To put it succinctly, there is a *politicizing* connection between his scholarship and his agenda.

This is a very important connection, one we will treat throughout this work. Our aim is not to show that modern scholarly methods invariably end in supporting the Left, since we'll see them supporting other political persuasions, such as buttressing absolute monarchs in England or the pretensions of Germany's unification efforts in the late 1800s. Our aim is to make readers aware of the connection between the historical criticism in biblical studies and the politicization of the biblical text—or, more accurately, to make readers understand how the politicization of the Bible *led to* the creation of historical criticism and its various methods, a "development" that began, as we've noted, seven centuries before Funk (and in much different political circumstances).

[12] Funk, *Honest to Jesus*, 29.

[13] Funk, *Honest to Jesus*, 314.

MISCELLANEOUS KINDRED VOICES TODAY

Before we turn to our main analysis, we need some further indications that Funk's approach is typical so that readers unfamiliar with contemporary biblical scholarship have a representative sample of other academicians (and some of the variations on the typical theme as well).

We would be remiss in not presenting the assumptions and some of the conclusions of the Jesus Seminar, not only because of its notoriety but also because Robert Funk was himself one of the many scholarly members. The Jesus Seminar produced its own considered version of the "authentic words of Jesus" in *The Five Gospels*, which they dedicated to "Galileo Galilei who altered our view of the heavens forever, Thomas Jefferson who took scissors and paste to the gospels, and David Friedrich Strauss who pioneered the quest of the historical Jesus."[14]

This list is instructive. Galileo ushered us from the prescientific to the scientific era in the early 1600s, thus allowing us to shed biblical mythology for modern cosmology. In the early 1800s, Jefferson, acting as his own historical-critical scholar, famously and quite literally cut everything out of his copy of the New Testament that smacked of the supernatural. While Jesus Seminar members contend that the scholarly search for the Jesus of history began with Hermann Samuel Reimarus (1694–1768), it was D. F. Strauss who

[14] Robert Funk, Roy Hoover, and the Jesus Seminar, *The Five Gospels: The Search for the Authentic Words of Jesus* (New York: HarperCollins, 1993), dedication page.

brought scholarship to its paradigmatic peak in his *Life of Jesus Critically Examined* (1835), in which Strauss famously declared that the real Jesus of history must be divided from the imagined Jesus of mythology.

Such is the historical-critical scholars' view of history: modern science provided the justification; those who were enlightened realized the implications for the study of the Bible and so removed the detritus of miracles and mythology, some as enlightened amateurs, some as highly educated professional biblical scholars (generally from nineteenth-century Germany).

The Great Divide, according to the authors of *The Five Gospels*, is therefore between the non-miraculous Jesus of history (a man), and the Christ of the churches, theologians, and creeds (a God-man). That assumption, they claim, is the first "pillar of modern biblical criticism."[15]

Readers perusing *The Five Gospels*—the fifth is the Gospel of Thomas—will discover that the words of Jesus are color coded. In ironic deference to red-letter editions of the Bible, the Seminar scholars put what they deemed, after much sifting, to have been actually said by the historical man Jesus in red letters. Less likely words attributed to Jesus are colored pink. Those not likely at all to have been uttered by the historical Jesus but perhaps instructive in giving us some idea of him are colored gray. Finally, in bold black letters we find what Jesus could not have said and ought to be jettisoned as misrepresenting him.

[15] Funk, Hoover, and the Jesus Seminar, *The Five Gospels*, 2–3.

Unsurprisingly, there's not much red, since most of what Jesus says in the four Gospels (especially John) pertains to him being a God-man messiah who can perform miracles and who expects to be crucified and resurrected.

For example, in Mark only one short sentence makes the red grade. In their translation of Mark 12:17, we have the following: "Pay the emperor what belongs to the emperor, and God what belongs to God."[16] In Matthew 6:9–13, the only words of the "Our Father" that are authentic are the first two, "Our Father."[17] As noted, anything smacking of the miraculous or messianic is printed in bold black so as to warn readers of its dubious origins. Thus everything Jesus said in the Gospel of John is blackened, the only exception being a single pink phrase (in their gratingly contemporary translation, "A prophet gets no respect on his own turf").[18] The real Jesus, who is only a "human sage"[19] from Nazareth, most decidedly did not say, "**I am the way, and I am truth, and I am life**" (John 14:6).[20]

The Jesus Seminar deigned to publish its findings to the unacademic because the "level of public knowledge of the Bible borders on the illiterate," the public being "poorly informed of the assured results of critical scholarship, although those results are commonly taught in colleges, universities, and seminaries." And indeed, the "scholarship represented by the Fellows of the Jesus Seminar is the kind

[16] Funk, Hoover, and the Jesus Seminar, *The Five Gospels*, 102.

[17] Funk, Hoover, and the Jesus Seminar, *The Five Gospels*, 148.

[18] Funk, Hoover, and the Jesus Seminar, *The Five Gospels*, 412.

[19] Funk, Hoover, and the Jesus Seminar, *The Five Gospels*, 7.

[20] Funk, Hoover, and the Jesus Seminar, *The Five Gospels*, 450.

that has come to prevail in all the great universities of the world."[21]

Quite so. And its adherents sit on the enlightened side of the Great Divide with evident disdain for the biblically illiterate priests, pastors, and believers who squat intransigently on the other.

More recent biblical scholar Bart Ehrman has, it would seem, a similar biography to the late Robert Funk, as he reveals in his *Misquoting Jesus* (2005). In his Introduction, Ehrman relates that he "was born and raised in a conservative place and time—the nation's heartland, beginning in the mid 1950s." Although his own family was not particularly religious, Ehrman himself had a "born-again" experience while in his teens, noting that beforehand he had a feeling of "emptiness inside that nothing seemed to fill." This religious experience occurred as the result of "attending meetings of a Campus Life Youth for Christ club," which convinced him, at its leader's promptings, that only Christ could fill the void. And so, Ehrman reports, "I . . . asked Jesus into my heart, and had a bona fide born-again experience."[22]

As he now took the Bible with the utmost seriousness, he went to the conservative Moody Bible Institute to study Scripture intensely. His goal: to become an evangelical scholar who could act as "salt" to the secular biblical scholars who undermined devotion to the Bible. From Moody, Ehrman went on to Wheaton to get a degree in English,

[21] Funk, Hoover, and the Jesus Seminar, *The Five Gospels*, 34–35.

[22] Bart Ehrman, *Misquoting Jesus: The Story Behind Who Changed the Bible and Why* (New York: HarperOne, 2005), 1–3.

but in studying Greek while he was there, he became more aware of the twin difficulties of translating from the original language of the New Testament. First, the Greek had nuances and meanings that couldn't be translated into English. Second, and even more perplexing, there was no copy of the "original" New Testament but only a significant number of copies made by a multitude of later, nameless scribes wherein there were variations in regard to the actual Greek.

Ehrman then set sail for Princeton Theological Seminary to study with eminent New Testament scholar Bruce Metzger so that he could reconcile these difficulties by working with a first-rate historical-critical scholar. Soon enough, he began to doubt that the New Testament was the inerrant Word of God because of significant conflicts and seeming contradictions he found in the various Greek manuscripts, added to the fact that we don't have any original documents. How could the Bible be the inspired Word of God? "We don't even have copies of the copies of the originals, or copies of the copies of the copies of the originals." If God was truly the God of miracles, he could have preserved the originals. "And if he didn't perform that miracle, there seemed to be no reason to think that he performed the earlier miracle of inspiring those words."[23]

"This was a seismic change for me," declares Ehrman. "Just as human scribes had copied, and changed, the texts of Scripture, so too had human authors originally *written* the texts of Scripture. This was a human book from begin-

[23] Ehrman, *Misquoting Jesus*, 10–11.

ning to end."[24] Ehrman had crossed the Great Divide:

> It is a radical shift from reading the Bible as an inerrant blueprint for our faith, life, and future to seeing it as a very human book, with very human points of view, many of which differ from one another and none of which provides the inerrant guide to how we should live. This is the shift in my own thinking that I ended up making, and to which I am now fully committed.[25]

As Professor of Religious Studies at the University of North Carolina at Chapel Hill, Ehrman now takes his students through the same process by which he lost his faith. Beyond the academy, Ehrman has been quite successful in reaching over the Great Divide and evangelizing the biblically illiterate: many of his books have ended up on the *New York Times* bestseller list.

Ehrman's efforts are (at the very least) implicitly secular and therefore lead to a de-Christianized view of the public political and moral realm. If God has not provided the inerrant blueprint for how we should live, then the Bible should not in any way determine how we live out our lives today. Historical-critical scholarship demonstrates this, in part, by showing that we have no original texts but are instead peppered with innumerable variations in multiple Greek copies.

John Dominic Crossan is another critical scholar

[24] Ehrman, *Misquoting Jesus*, 11.

[25] Ehrman, *Misquoting Jesus*, 13.

who hit the bestseller list, in his case with his *Jesus: A Revolutionary Biography* (1994). In it, Crossan gives his "own reconstruction of the historical Jesus derived from twenty-five years of scholarly research on what actually happened in Galilee and Jerusalem during the early first century of the common era" (the first century AD), a work he dedicated to Robert Funk and the Jesus Seminar.[26]

As many other critical scholars assume, Jesus is not a God-man but a "Mediterranean Jewish peasant." For Crossan, he is best defined as a Cynic—that is, as someone with beliefs akin to the philosophical sect originating in the Greek Diogenes of Sinope (ca. 400–320 BC), a sect that was skeptical of theories and theologies, and moreover, whose proponents were flouters of "ordinary cultural values and civilized presuppositions"[27]—much like historical-critical scholars themselves.

For his cynical efforts, which upset both Jews and Romans, Jesus was crucified. He was not resurrected, however. Such a thing is, we all know, scientifically impossible. What really happened, then? What is the source of the resurrection stories? Differing from Funk, Crossan suggests that the notion of the resurrection was imposed by later, more educated Christians who wanted Jesus to fulfill Jewish prophecies about the messiah.[28] In fact, the burial and the resurrection were later conjured up to cover the brutal truth that Jesus's body was actually eaten by dogs.[29]

[26] John Dominic Crossan, *Jesus: A Revolutionary Biography* (New York: Harper, 1994), xiii.

[27] Crossan, *Jesus: A Revolutionary Biography*, 129.

[28] Crossan, *Jesus: A Revolutionary Biography*, 163–172.

[29] Crossan, *Jesus: A Revolutionary Biography*, 174.

A conjecture impossible to prove, but such is the latitude enjoyed by scholars in telling us what actually happened.

The Jesus of history was therefore a "peasant Jewish Cynic" whose primary aim was political, to foster "religious and economic egalitarianism that negated . . . the hierarchical and patronal normalcies of Jewish religion and Roman power."[30] The Jesus of Easter, for Crossan, was a later creation of those who founded the institutional church. After the conversion of Emperor Constantine to Christianity in AD 312, this institutional church, *using political power*, finally succeeded in changing Jesus the man into Jesus the God-man, thereby transforming Christianity into a patriarchal, imperial religion of emperors and bishops.[31]

Crossan's account of Jesus is even more overtly politicized than Funk's. Crossan's "real" Jesus was an anti-establishment radical, championing religious and economic egalitarianism, and striking out at hierarchical and patriarchal powers—much like those on the Left side of the cultural and political spectrum today. The false Jesus, the divinized Jesus of politicized mythology, supports the very structures that the real Jesus opposed (and so, coincidentally, does the Left).

In a similar manner, scholars Richard Horsley and John Hanson assure us that Jesus was really only a "Jewish prophet from the remote district of Galilee," that is, a peasant, which explains why in the beatitudes and elsewhere, he's so concerned for the poor, as against the rich.

[30] Crossan, *Jesus: A Revolutionary Biography*, 222.
[31] Crossan, *Jesus: A Revolutionary Biography*, 225–226.

The great difference with Jesus is that while the other peasants "were largely illiterate," and so left us no evidence of their struggle, we have the sayings of, and stories about, Jesus, "which were remembered and developed in oral form until written down in the New Testament Gospels." Unlike the other peasants of the time, Jesus therefore was able to become "the focal figure for what has developed into Christianity and become the dominant religious faith and established religious institution in the West."[32]

As a peasant, Horsley and Hanson claim, Jesus represented just one kind of reaction of the poor to oppressive Roman rule in the mid-first century AD (a rule that was aided by the Jewish upper class). Jesus was one of a number of prophets at the time, as was John the Baptist. But there were two other reactions beyond the purely prophetic, the first being the messianic movements looking for another King David to overthrow Rome, and the second being the swarm of bandits who roamed the hills attacking Roman society (in somewhat the same way as the much later Robin Hood tradition). This last group formed a significant number of those who rose in direct revolt against Rome in the mid-60s AD. In partial confirmation of their thesis, Horsley and Hanson assert Jesus was arrested as if he were a kind of bandit (Mark 14:49) and was crucified between two bandits (Mark 15:27).[33]

The assumption of their study is, of course, that Jesus was not God incarnate but represented a particular type

[32] Richard Horsley and John Hanson, *Bandits, Prophets, and Messiahs: Popular Movements in the Time of Jesus* (Minneapolis: Seabury, 1985), xi–xiii.

[33] Horsley and Hanson, *Bandits, Prophets, and Messiahs*, 256.

of political reaction by the poor to the oppression of Romans and elite Jews from above. The reason their study is relevant and hence significant, they inform the reader, is quite *political*: we have a growing awareness today of the importance of peasants in revolutions against political oppression, one advanced even beyond Marx, an awareness that allows us finally to see what is actually going on underneath the mythological surface in the New Testament.[34] (And, we assume, allows at least some relevance and inspiration to arise from the mythological text for us today—absent the mythology, of course.)

Barbara Thiering, also a member of the Jesus Seminar, penned a bestseller, *Jesus the Man* (1992), purportedly demonstrating that the Great Divide between the mythological and the factual, the miraculous and the historical, is real—a common theme in nearly all works of historical criticism. But Thiering adds that the division has another quite interesting source: the divide is really between (on the one hand) a carefully crafted mythological and miraculous *exoteric* surface meant for the uneducated, and (on the other) the underlying *esoteric*, rational message meant for the philosophically initiated. The latter know that there are no miracles and Jesus was a mere man. The mythological and miraculous aspects of the Bible are not, then, due to the ignorance of the writers but rather to the cleverness of these first-century-AD philosophers in embedding a modern-scholar-friendly message in a mythological veneer.

Using the Dead Sea Scrolls as the key to cracking the

[34] Horsley and Hanson, *Bandits, Prophets, and Messiahs*, xvii–xviii.

interpretative code, Thiering claims to be able to discern that Jesus was conceived by Mary and Joseph during betrothal, and therefore counted (according to the rules of the day, as some interpreted them) as illegitimate.[35] As a result, he was a kind of social outcast.[36]

Based upon the noncanonical Gospel of Philip, Thiering assures us that Jesus was actually married to Mary Magdalene, with whom he had three children.[37] Moreover, Jesus didn't die on the cross. The vinegar given to him during his crucifixion actually contained a poison that rendered him unconscious. He "recovered from the effects of the poison, was helped to escape from the tomb by friends, and stayed with them until he reached Rome, where he was present in AD 64," hence accounting for the resurrection appearances.[38] So the historical Jesus's life continued even after the crucifixion. Alas, during this period Mary Magdalene divorced him, but he was married again, this time to a woman named Lydia, who was also a female bishop in a Hellenistic religion.[39] Who would've known?

While critical scholars generally frown upon Thiering's efforts (even though, as we'll see in later chapters, she resembles in pedigree one of the grandfathers of modern biblical scholarship, John Toland), *Jesus the Man* received popular acclaim, which was magnified a thousandfold in helping to inspire Dan Brown's fanciful mega-bestseller, *The Da Vinci*

[35] Barbara Thiering, *Jesus the Man: Decoding the Real Story of Jesus and Mary Magdalene* (New York: Atria, 1992), 45.

[36] Thiering, *Jesus the Man*, 74.

[37] Thiering, *Jesus the Man*, 87–89.

[38] Thiering, *Jesus the Man*, 115–116.

[39] Thiering, *Jesus the Man*, 146–148.

Code. The politicized take-home of Thiering's work should not escape us: the real Jesus "fought against oppressive structures, moral and political," be they the Church or the State.

For yet another variation, we have the arguments of Morton Smith, who famously claimed that Jesus was actually a magician, effecting natural cures in a way that made them seem miraculous—an argument much more acceptable to scholars. According to Smith, the attribution of the miraculous to Jesus is too thoroughly attested to have been made up whole cloth by the disciples after the resurrection. Therefore, the alleged miraculous events must have been the result of conjuring.

To demonstrate his thesis, in his *Jesus the Magician* (1978), Morton parallels miraculous aspects of Jesus in the Gospels to ancient accounts of magical rites and practices, thereby vindicating the charge made by the early enemies of Christianity that he was not the Son of God but a mere magician.[40]

Clearly, then, Jesus was not, for Smith, a miracle-working God-man. But, against other biblical scholars, Smith maintains that as a magician, the Jesus of history really was the "miracle-working" founder of Christian faith, whose very success as a magician swelled the ranks of his devotees.[41]

We've had enough examples from contemporary biblical scholars to understand the effects of modern biblical historical criticism in creating the Great Divide between faithful Christians and demythologizing scholars. The

[40] Morton Smith, *Jesus the Magician* (New York: Harper, 1978), esp. chapters 6–7.

[41] Smith, *Jesus the Magician*, 5–10.

miscellany, by its very nature, was not exhaustive, but illustrative—something to give those outside of academia a good idea of what scholars have been all too busy doing for generations.

Those familiar with the state of biblical scholarship today will immediately recognize that we did not include "developments" in biblical studies that go beyond the mainstream of modern biblical historical criticism—such as Feminism, Marxism, Queer Theory, or any of a number of postmodern approaches to the Bible, almost all of which deem themselves to have left behind the assumptions and goals of the historical-critical method, which have, for so many years, defined the academy (even though, interestingly enough, they are even more fervent politicizers of the text). It is beyond the scope of this study to venture beyond the mainstream, however important and fruitful that might be.

The mention of the historical-critical method reminds us that we have a bit more clarifying work to do before we launch into our main analysis. There is a fair amount of confusion in regard to the terms *historical method*, *historical criticism*, and the *historical-critical method*. We hope to provide some clarity by making the following distinctions.

To recall a point made above in sorting out the meaning of *historical criticism*, we noted that what is meant by "critical" is definitive: "critical" refers to the skeptical attitude toward the supernatural that defines what can happen in history. *If* miracles are impossible, *then* Jesus couldn't have cured lepers, walked on water, or risen from the dead; therefore, the historical-critical scholar must provide his or her own entirely natural account of what actually happened. As we'll see in the chapters that follow, this skeptical attitude began to exert cultural influence in the early 1500s, before the scientific revolution.

While many use the term *historical-critical method* to mean whatever kind of exegesis that flows from the critical assumption that supernatural beings and events cannot exist, technically speaking the historical-critical *method* refers to three specific academic approaches to the biblical text: *source criticism*, which developed in the late 1800s; *form criticism*, which developed in the 1920s; and *redaction criticism*, which developed after World War II. Source criticism attempts to argue for the existence of hypothetical literary documents that are alleged to be the real foundation of extant biblical texts; form criticism tries to make the case for hypothetical oral traditions and sources that are alleged to be the real foundation of biblical texts; and finally, redaction criticism focuses on some alleged editorial process that brought about the biblical texts.

There is a good reason why many simply associate these developments with the "critical" assumption that modern science has eliminated the supernatural: most academic scholars who engage in the use of source, form, or redaction criticism accept the historical-critical assumption uncritically, and make use of source, form, or redaction criticism accordingly.

But, we must stress, there is no intrinsic relationship between the "critical" assumption and the legitimate inquiry about preexisting literary documents or oral traditions, or about editorial processes. To take an important illustration, I (Scott Hahn) made extensive use of source criticism in my *Kinship by Covenant* to show how an understanding of the types of covenants in the Old Testament contributes to a much deeper grasp of the way that the overarching theme of covenant unites the Old and New Testament.[42] My use of source criticism therefore illuminates rather than undermines the faith because canonical criticism (in the words of the Pontifical Biblical Commission) "aims to carry out the theological task of interpretation . . . within an explicit framework of faith: the Bible as a whole."[43]

Speaking more broadly, it is quite possible to analyze in the greatest scholarly detail biblical texts and manuscripts, and make intelligent *judgments* about their authenticity, integrity, and credibility without the assumption of skepticism about the supernatural inherent in historical criticism. In other words, we can subtract the peculiar identification of "criticism" with skepticism, and call such an approach simply the *historical method*. This method is *critical* in the original etymological sense, coming from the Greek word *krinein*, meaning "to judge." Understood in this way, the historical method can make well-grounded judgments about the authorship and dating of texts, whether they are genuine or forged, whether there has been interpolation, and so on, all without adopting an attitude of complete skepticism about the possibility of the supernatural.[44]

If we can take out the assumption of "critical," defined

[42] Scott Hahn, *Kinship by Covenant: A Canonical Approach to the Fulfillment of God's Saving Promises* (New Haven and London: Yale University Press, 2009).

[43] "Interpreting the Bible in the Life of the Church," 118, quoted in the context of my account, *Kinship by Covenant*, 24.

[44] See the cogent analysis of the historical method in Gilbert Garraghan, S.J., *A Guide to Historical Method* (New York: Fordham University Press, 1946).

by the rejection of the supernatural, then we can rightly ask, "How did this sense of 'critical' enter into biblical studies in the first place?" *That* is a rather long, complex story, one which (as we've noted above) begins in the early 1300s. To that story we now turn.

Chapter Two

MARSILIUS AND OCKHAM

IN DEFINING the ultimate headwaters of any river, one must work one's winding way back through much unfamiliar territory to get to the first rivulets, and such is the case in any attempt to trace the earliest historical origins of later intellectual developments. When we work our way backward through the centuries to get to the headwaters of the modern historical-critical method, or more exactly, its assumptions, we find ourselves in the calamitous fourteenth century.[1]

This is the century in which the Black Plague swept through Europe, killing at least a third of the population, if not twice that. Even more important for our purposes, it's also the century of the Avignon Papacy (1309–1376), where the papal court was transported from Rome to Avignon (located in the south of modern-day France).

[1] To borrow a famous phrase from historian Barbara Tuchman's *A Distant Mirror: The Calamitous 14th Century*. The details of this chapter are in Hahn and Wiker, *Politicizing the Bible*, ch. 2, "The First Cracks of Secularism: Marsilius of Padua and William of Ockham."

At Avignon, the popes lived as prodigal princes of the Church under the political control of the French kings. The end of the so-called Babylonian Captivity of the Church in Avignon only brought further degradation to the papacy, ensuring that it would sink even lower in people's estimation. At the urging of St. Catherine of Siena, Pope Gregory XI brought the papacy back to Rome in 1377 but died soon after. Rather than a smooth transition to a new pope, rival claimants backed by rival kings each vied to be the rightful heir to St. Peter's throne, resulting in the Great Schism (1378–1417).

It was in this historical context that modern biblical scholarship was born, or to be more accurate, that the deep politicizing of the Bible would—along with other key developments—prepare the way for modern biblical scholarship. Since our concern is the politicizing of Scripture, we've got to have a firm grasp on the often confusing political situation of the time.

The central figures in our story are Pope John XXII, the would-be Holy Roman Emperor Ludwig of Bavaria, the political philosopher and imperial advocate Marsilius of Padua, and the Franciscan friar William of Ockham. The political disputes between the pope and the emperor, as well as the theological and philosophical disputes surrounding Ockham, defined the particular way that politicizing the Bible took place.

While the details of the wrangling between emperor and pope are dauntingly complex, the simple beginning point of the conflict is not overly difficult to grasp. In Western Europe, two figures had grown to claim universal prominence, the pope over the Roman Church and the

Holy Roman Emperor over the empire.

In a bare theoretical sense, one might think that there would be no conflict since the pope should oversee the care of souls on their journey to heaven and the emperor should oversee the temporal political realm and keep things running smoothly in the meantime.

The problem was that Rome wasn't theoretical, but an actual city *within* the Holy Roman Empire. Moreover, the Roman pontiff was also a very worldly prince of the Papal States, which took up the middle of the boot of Italy. As a result, the popes of the time were sometimes acting more as rival political rulers to the emperors (or other kings, dukes, or princes) than shepherds of souls. Even worse, they were often using the spiritual powers of the Church for the evidently secular, political ends of providing for and protecting the Papal States.

Corruption went both ways: the emperors wanted both the power and the wealth of the Church under their control for their own political designs. Holy Roman Emperors were (as the dig goes) neither holy nor Roman, nor really even emperors, but rather lesser German kings trying to slip into the glories of previous emperors like Constantine and Charlemagne.

There was not, to begin with, really an empire stretching across the known world. The Holy Roman Empire, such as it was, covered a bit more on the map of Europe of what we think of today as Germany (plus Austria, Switzerland, and part of Northern Italy). Even within his alleged territory, the emperor had to deal with powerful and recalcitrant Germanic archbishops, kings, dukes, and princes, seven of whom were responsible for electing him to his exalted office (and none of whom were interested in supporting him financially, hence his desire to secure control of the coffers of the papacy). This alleged empire sat ominously north of the Papal States, the emperor brooding southward, mulling over ways to absorb the pope's rich temporal holdings so that he could better secure his imperial claims.

Such was the larger political context in the conflict between Pope John XXII and Ludwig the Bavarian. But, we remind ourselves, the pope at this time, Pope John XXII, was not in Rome but Avignon, and Ludwig was still struggling to become the emperor.

Ludwig's immediate problem was that, because of a rivalry between the various German emperor-electors and dynastic conflicts, *two* emperors had been elected in October of 1314, Ludwig and Frederick I. In response, Pope John XXII issued a papal bull paternally instructing them both to step down, and informing them that *he* would rule Germany until things got sorted out.

Ludwig ignored Pope John, which resulted in a papal warning of excommunication. Unamused, Ludwig threatened to call a council to question the necessity of papal approval for imperial election (approval signified by the pope's crowning of the emperor), and added to this a public call for the investigation of the pope for heresy.

That brought Pope John to excommunicate Ludwig formally in 1324. Keep in mind that excommunication was a spiritual tool with direct political implications: it immediately removed all authority to rule of the excommunicated and released subjects from obedience. Ludwig's response to this challenge was to march into Rome in

1328, have himself crowned emperor, and then put his *own* pope on the throne of St. Peter (Nicholas V). Unsurprisingly, Pope Nicholas used his newfound powers to confirm Ludwig as rightful emperor.

At Ludwig's side in the Roman expedition was Marsilius of Padua, who also had been excommunicated by Pope John XXII for heretical ideas launched in his political treatise, *Defensor Pacis* (*Defender of the Peace*). As Ludwig didn't have enough political or monetary support to stay in Rome for long, he soon enough headed back north to Germany with Marsilius. On the way, he was joined by William of Ockham, another unhappy recipient of John's powers of excommunication. Marsilius and Ockham were both bent on cutting down the power of the papacy, and hence both were very welcome in Ludwig's imperial court.

As noted above, this messy political conflict is the context for the birth of modern Scripture scholarship, wherein the Bible comes to be treated as a non-revealed, largely mythological ancient text rather than the revelation of God. But this same political conflict also provides the context for the birth of modern *secular* political philosophy, which redefines humanity's highest aim as entirely this-worldly and subordinates religion to the state as a useful political tool.

How are the two related? Simply put, in order for modern secular political philosophy to use religion as a political instrument of secular state, it had to deflate or deflect the claims of the Bible to be the revealed Word of God. The Bible points to the next life as the only worthy goal of our earthly endeavors. It is therefore a text that judges all the kingdoms of the world in their earthly glory to be so much dross by comparison to eternal life in the Kingdom of God. Consequently, that makes it a religiously authoritative text that could be used by popes and bishops against emperors and kings.

Marsilius was the first great secularizer of political philosophy, and so he carried this aim into the conflict between pope and emperor. As the title of his *Defensor Pacis* indicates, he believed that earthly political peace is the *highest* goal (in his words, it is "the greatest good of man"), and so the state must keep the papacy from upsetting "the tranquility or peace of civil regimes."[2] The Church, and the pope in particular, cannot be allowed to quote the Bible against secular power.

Marsilius no doubt had in mind well-worn biblical passages that had become the mainstay of the pope's assertion of power over the temporal political realm such as found in Pope Innocent's decretal *Novit* (1204), where the pope declared that he has the power "to rebuke any Christian for any mortal sin and to coerce him with ecclesiastical penalties if he spurs our correction." The Christian in Innocent's mind in the decretal was the king or emperor. "That we can and should coerce" these political rulers "is evident from the pages of both the Old and New Testaments," Innocent continued, quoting from Jeremiah 1:10, "Lo I have set thee"—the prophet, and hence the pope—"over nations and over kingdoms to root up and to pull down and to waste, and to destroy, and to build, and to plant." He then quoted Matthew 16:19, that the "Lord

[2] Marsilius, *Defensor Pacis*, I,1.1.

gave the keys of the kingdom of heaven to blessed Peter" and therefore the pope can lock heaven against the access of a recalcitrant king.[3]

On Innocent's behalf, these scriptural texts were often used to block efforts by the emperor to capture and use the Church for his own purposes. But since this was also done to protect the Papal States as well, the political and ecclesiastical aims were confused. By the time we get to the Avignon Papacy, the political seems to have been clearly primary.

For Marsilius, that meant that the pope *and* scriptural interpretation need to be subordinated to the emperor. Here we have the first instance of the modern *politicizing* of the Bible (which was, in a way, a reaction to the papal politicizing of Scripture). As we'll see, it will occur in several variations over the next centuries.

In Marsilius, it's not mere Caesaropapism, as would occur in the Eastern empire, where the emperor *as* a Christian rules the Church, whose ultimate aim is eternal salvation. Rather, it's a revival of the pagan notion—held by certain ancient philosophers and historians—that there is only one life, life in this material world, and therefore the supernatural claims of all religions are false and belief in them mere superstition. However, if these religious beliefs are properly understood and used by clever philosophers, they can be very helpful political instruments of thoroughly *secular* political rulers.

3 Pope Innocent III, *Novit*, in Brian Tierney, *The Crisis of Church & State 1050–1300* (Englewood Cliffs, NJ: Prentice-Hall, 1964), 134–135.

We need to understand Marsilius's revolution very clearly *as* secular. Affirming that there is only one life in this material world, Marsilius set out a new political philosophy that, unlike Plato and Aristotle, jettisoned the concern for the soul and focused only on bodily nourishment and comfort, and the peace to enjoy them (in short, treating human beings as if they were mere political *animals*, and nothing more).[4] This purposeful stunting of political life to mere bodily existence marks the beginning of modern philosophy's entirely materialistic foundation, and modern political philosophy's entirely secular aims.

But if there is only material existence, then what of religion? Again, if materialism is true, then all religions are false and superstitious. While the "enlightened" pagan philosophers realized this, they also believed that even though religion isn't true, it's useful as a kind of myth contrived to control the ignorant and unruly masses politically. In the revival of this pagan belief by Marsilius, Christianity is the religion historically at hand, and in accordance with pagan wisdom, the Bible must be turned into a useful religion of the state. Holy Scripture therefore must be politicized accordingly.

As should be evident, putting forth such a bold doctrine in the deeply Christianized society of the early 1300s would quickly lead to persecution and most likely death. Therefore, Marsilius had to be discreet in his presentation, so we must read his *Defensor Pacis* carefully.

In the *Defensor Pacis* he sets out this pagan view of religion in a very long passage *as if* he's merely describing

[4] Marsilius, *Defensor Pacis*, I,2.3 and I,4.1–3.

rather than prescribing it. The reader is informed that even though ancient "philosophers" such as Hesiod, Pythagoras, and others didn't believe in the gods, they set forth "divine laws or religions" for the sake of maintaining political peace. "For although some of the philosophers who founded such laws or religions did not accept or believe in human resurrection and that life which is called eternal, they nevertheless feigned and persuaded others that it exists and that in it pleasures and pains are in accordance with the qualities of human deeds in this mortal life." The reason for the ruse? Rulers cannot punish all evil deeds, but vengeful and vigilant invisible deities can. Heaven and hell provide divine backup for the rulers' laws and hence serve to bring tranquility to the political order, "which was the end intended by these wise men laying down such laws or religions."[5]

In other words, religions were invented by philosophers to control the ignorant masses; they are useful myths, stories designed to rule the unruly. Some of the "others" who held this view (or at least wrote about it) in antiquity were Critias, Polybius, Livy, and Plutarch (whom we'll treat in a later chapter). This view obviously counsels the most blatant politicizing of pagan religion. The big difference in the early fourteenth century is, of course, that Marsilius is recovering this political use of religion within the context of the cultural dominance of Christianity.

But ancient pagans aren't the only source of Marsilius's revolution. He was also heavily indebted to the twelfth-century Islamic philosopher Averroes (or Ibn Rushd). Averroes noted that there were actual contradictions between what reason pro-

[5] Marsilius, *Defensor Pacis*, I,5.11.

claimed (for him, through the philosopher Aristotle) and what revelation declared (for him, in the Koran). Rather than simply dismiss the Koran—a very dangerous alternative in his time—Averroes argued that truth is indeed known through natural reason by the few philosophers. Most people, however, are not capable of such difficult reasoning but only of rhetorical persuasion that appeals to the imagination. These latter are best controlled by religion—that is, by the Koran.

Of course, it is clear who should rule whom in this scheme: the rational philosophers should rule the ignorant, using the religious stories of the Koran. So Averroes famously sets up a "double truth," reason and revelation, rational philosophy and the irrational or sub-rational Koran, but only one truth really counts, the philosophical.

We can see the connection between the ancient writers referred to by Marsilius above and Averroes: for both, religion is an instrument of the enlightened state. As an Averroist in Christian Europe, Marsilius substituted the Bible for the Koran, and that is the ultimate reason why he wanted to subordinate Christianity to the emperor. The great Thomist philosopher Étienne Gilson rightly calls the *Defensor Pacis* "as perfect an example of political Averroism as one could wish for."[6]

But, in setting out his version of political Averroism, Marsilius well understood that he must be circumspect or he would suffer persecution in his Christian-dominated culture. Thus, after the suggestive passage about philosophers inventing religion, Marsilius soon enough prudently

[6] Étienne Gilson, *History of Christian Philosophy in the Middle Ages* (New York: Random House, 1955), 526.

avers that Christianity is, of course, the only true religion,[7] but only after having planted seeds of doubt in his readers.

For some readers of Marsilius this would likely result in posing forbidden questions to themselves, such as, "Maybe Christianity isn't *the* true religion, but only one more religion designed by crafty rulers—or priests!—in order to gain power over others? If we compare religions, don't we find resurrection stories in Greek, Roman, and Egyptian mythology? Promises of heaven and Hades? Every kind of miracle? Perhaps we should compare what we find in the Bible to other ancient religions and see how many parallels we can discover?"

It will not be too very long, historically, until such secret thoughts turn into published treatises in the 1500s and 1600s, and the questions are applied directly to the study of the Bible itself.

Let us return, however, to Marsilius's situation. For Marsilius, the problem was that the pope—and not the philosopher or his king or emperor—had all the interpretive cards. Not only did faith trump reason, and the eternal good of the soul trump all temporal goods, but the pope and the Church over which he resided claimed sovereignty over biblical interpretation.

Marsilius's strategy for dealing with this was as ingenious as it was devious. He asserted that the revelation of God is so far above reason that the acceptance of revelation is entirely the result of irrational fideism, fideism

[7] Marsilius, *Defensor Pacis*, I,10.3.

resting upon the Bible alone (*not* the pope).[8] Sounding eerily like the future Protestant reformers, Marsilius declared that "for salvation it is necessary for us to believe in . . . the certainty or truth of no statements or writings except those which are canonic, that is, those which are contained in the volume of the Bible."[9] No papal bulls, decretals, letters, or other ecclesiastical pronouncements or writings. No convoluted and self-serving papal interpretations using elaborate biblical allegories. Just the Bible alone, *sola scriptura*.

To ensure that the Bible itself could not be used by the pope or other bishops against secular power, Marsilius argued that the authoritative interpretation of any contested aspects of Scripture must be settled "by human legislators," or more exactly, by "priests and non-priests" appointed by human legislators.[10] Marsilius also noted that human legislators should have the power to appoint both priests and bishops.[11] Obviously, the appointees will decide debated scriptural passages on the side of the secular power to whom they owe their position, a sure recipe for politicizing the Bible.

So as not to leave his future protégés without examples, Marsilius provided his own politicized exegesis of the Bible. Since the Old Testament proved fertile grounds for popes claiming ecclesiastical control over kings—think of Moses, Samuel, and the prophets—Marsilius declared that the advent of the New Law made the Old Law irrelevant

[8] Marsilius, *Defensor Pacis*, I,9.2; II,19.1–3 and 10.

[9] Marsilius, *Defensor Pacis*, II,28.1 and 19.1.

[10] Marsilius, *Defensor Pacis*, II,20.2.

[11] Marsilius, *Defensor Pacis*, II,17.8–9.

and nonbinding.[12]

In the New Testament Jesus Christ himself tells us, "Render unto Caesar the things that are Caesar's," and St. Paul declares in his Letter to the Romans, "Let every soul be subject to the higher powers"—that is, the governing authorities, which have been instituted by God himself. And so, Marsilius assured the reader, "From all these [passages] it is quite evident that Christ, the Apostle, and the saints held the view that all men must be subject to the human laws and to the judges according to these laws."[13] Connecting to what we outlined above, all men must be subject to the human legislators' interpretation of Scripture—*including the pope*.

But Marsilius was not finished clipping the pope's ecclesiastical wings. As we noted above, Pope John XXII was not in Rome but in Avignon, immersed in an embarrassment of riches (but, apparently, without the embarrassment part). As historian Heather Para notes, "Considered to be the 'Midas pope,' John dressed in gold cloth and slept on ermine fur, continuing to prosper even more through simony, the sale of indulgences, and the collection of taxes."[14]

This allowed Marsilius, using Scripture, to attack an exceedingly weak point in the papacy. Christ did not preach riches for his followers, but poverty and contempt for the world and worldliness, asserted Marsilius, as he pounded away with passage after passage—Matthew 6:21,

[12] Marsilius, *Defensor Pacis*, II,9.10.

[13] Marsilius, *Defensor Pacis*, II,9.9.

[14] Heather Para, "Plague, Papacy and Power: The Effect of the Black Plague on the Avignon Papacy," *Saber and Scroll* 5, no. 1 (April 2016): 10.

13:22, 19:16–21; Mark 10:17–21; Luke 6:20, 9:23, 14:33, 18:18–22.[15]

Marsilius was correct. On nearly anyone's account, the riches and luxuries of the Avignon Papacy were a disgrace, an affront to Christ's own life and words. We must keep in mind, however, that Marsilius's call for apostolic poverty was not fueled by genuine desire for reform of the papacy or the Church but by the political desire to undermine the temporal power and prestige of the papacy and subordinate Christianity to the state.

Yet, on the surface, there appears to be a confluence of the two strange and unlikely bedfellows: those who desire to politicize the Bible and those who genuinely desire to reform the Church. In the present case, the pair is (respectively) the neo-pagan Marsilius and (as we'll now see) William of Ockham, a Franciscan friar. Let us bring Ockham into our account.

Again, Marsilius and Ockham had much in common, beginning with the fact that they (along with Ludwig) were excommunicated, Marsilius for his daring *Defensor Pacis*, and Ockham for leaving Avignon without permission. Ockham had been summoned there for investigation of potential heresy in his writings. But the reason Ockham fled Avignon—and ran to the protection of John XXII's archrival, Ludwig—was not the threat of a heresy trial but a bitter dispute about poverty, or more exactly, two disputes.

The first and most obvious echoed the criticisms of Marsilius and many others. The riches of the Avignon Papacy were not only a scandalous affront to Christ's call

[15] Marsilius, *Defensor Pacis*, II,11.2; 13.22–27.

for apostolic poverty evident in Scripture,[16] but were also, he argued, *the* cause of political turmoil. For Ockham, "all the dissensions, wars, fights, and battles and the destructions and devastations of cities and regions and countless other evils which have occurred in Italy for many years past, and still do not cease, have resulted from the riches of the Roman Church"; therefore, "it would have been beneficial for the whole Church of God if the Roman Church had in fact and deed imitated the Apostles' poverty and their way of living."[17] Marsilius's sentiments exactly! And the state would be quite ready and willing to receive the Church's divested riches.

But there was another dispute about poverty boiling over at the time, one that is so intricate and counterintuitive in its convolutions that we almost hesitate to mention it. We must, however, at least in outline, because it bears directly on the origin of the modern biblical exegete.

As we've mentioned, William of Ockham was a Franciscan. As everyone knows, the founder of the Order of Friars Minor, St. Francis himself, was adamantly devoted to absolute poverty, both in his life and in his preaching.

Ironically, St. Francis was a victim of his own success, gathering great numbers of disciples after him, some of whom held tenaciously to the founder's absolute poverty (the Spirituals) and some of whom (the Conventuals) believed that preaching the gospel required education, and hence books and buildings with libraries to house them, as well as other accoutrements. The rivalry was bitter.

[16] William of Ockham, *The Work of Ninety Days*, I.3; II.93.
[17] William of Ockham, *A Dialogue*, III:I.2.2.

The popes before John XXII settled things by taking the side of the Conventuals, declaring that all the things that the more lax Franciscans seemed to own were actually owned by the papacy, and the Franciscans were only *using* them. Furthermore, these same popes forbade any further discussion of the contentious issue.

And then along came Pope John XXII. He not only opened up discussion again, but after critics pointed out that previous popes forbade further debate, he declared that he had the power to overrule them. To prove his point, he rejected the rather questionable notion that the pope owned everything that the Conventuals used. The luxuriating pope thereby took the side of absolute poverty.

Both Marsilius and Ockham proclaimed that John XXII was, in overturning previous papal pronouncements, a heretic, and Ockham thereby joined the opposition party. In Ockham's own words, "I gladly left Avignon to devote myself, in my small measure, to attacking that heretic and his heresies."[18]

There is no doubt that his new companion, Marsilius, was only too willing to influence Ockham, as they sheltered together under Ludwig's protection. So we find that Ockham marshaled Scripture to show that kings can rule over priests, and hence emperors over popes, especially in times of dire emergency (e.g., when there is a heretical pope), a prime example being King David appointing "several highest pontiffs" in 1 Chronicles 24:5.[19]

We also find Ockham taking the power to interpret

[18] William of Ockham, *A Letter to the Friars Minor*, 8.

[19] William of Ockham, *A Dialogue*, III:I.2.20.

Scripture out of the hands of the papacy. He does not (with Marsilius) put this power in the hands of the secular ruler, but in a cadre of exegetical elites, academic scholars, or in his words, "experts" (*periti*) who know "the true meaning of what has to be interpreted."[20] Whatever he may have intended, Ockham doesn't seem to have demanded any qualifications of his experts other than expertise. He mentions neither personal holiness nor adherence to orthodox tradition as prerequisites. The *periti* sound strikingly like modern academic biblical exegetes.

And here's another twist. We recall that Marsilius asserted a doctrine of *sola scriptura*, rooting the faith in the Bible alone in order to nullify extra-biblical papal pronouncements, bulls, and so on, and that Marsilius declared that this faith was fideistic, a pure act of the will with no intellectual support. Following the "strange bedfellows" pattern noted above, Ockham also declared his own version of fideism, in his case, to defend the faith against the pretensions of rationality put forth by philosophers (ironically, philosophers like Marsilius).

To deepen the irony, William of Ockham famously invented a philosophy, Nominalism, to destroy the pretentions of philosophy. For Ockham, philosophers look at the world and discover that there are "universals," such as "cow," "pig," "bird," or less generically, the Hereford cow, the Sardinian pig, and the sparrow. According to previous philosophers such as Aristotle, these universals aren't mere names, but are actually existent universal *forms* in each particular animal. When we know these forms by our

[20] William of Ockham, *A Dialogue*, III:I.2.24.

human reason, we thereby know necessary and universal truths that can provide the foundations of our reasoning. And if these truths are necessary and universal—so argued or implied some medieval devotees of Aristotle—then just as God is constrained by the necessary truths of mathematics, so God is also constrained by the forms, both in creating them and in his actions toward them.

To Ockham, all that sounded as if mere human reason could plumb the depths of God's wisdom and that philosophers could therefore fathom the unfathomable mind of God. Even more, they were asserting that God's power was also limited rather than omnipotent. To safeguard God from the pretensions of mere human reason, Ockham argued that there are no universals, but rather, *everything is particular*. All cows may *seem* to be similar in some fundamental way, just as all crows *look* alike, but that is mere surface similarity. Underneath it all there are no common forms; each thing is a unique individual, a particular rather than a member of a real species. Such universals as we capture in names like cow and crow, then, are not really universal or necessary, but *mere names*—hence nominalism from the Latin, *nomines*, names.

But that was not the only way that Ockham sought to protect divine omnipotence. He also argued that God could have made creation, nature itself, any of a number of ways. Consequently, there is nothing about nature that either constrains God's actions or even gives us a clue about his wisdom or nature. For Ockham, this deflated the claims of philosophers who asserted that, because nature is *this* way, then God must be or act *that* way, or who argued that through nature, mere human reason can understand the mind of God.

Ockham would have none of that. For Ockham, since God's power was absolute, he could have created nature an infinite number of other ways—*nothing* constrains his power. Nature therefore gives us no clue about God, and there is no natural philosophical way to make any claims about him, such as in, for example, St. Thomas's Five Proofs of the Existence of God, which reason from effect (creation) to cause (Creator).

Ockham was not yet finished defending God's omnipotence. He gave the same treatment to morality and revelation itself. There are no universal, absolute moral rules, either written into nature or ordained by God, because if there were, then God would necessarily have to affirm them, and even abide by them. God *could* have made murder of the innocent moral, but he just *happened*, by divine decree, to do the opposite. Likewise, God *could* have chosen another means of incarnation to save the human race—Jesus Christ could have been incarnated as a stone, a block of wood, or even a donkey—but he just *happened* to choose incarnation as a Jewish man. There is no *reason* for particular moral rules, nor any *reason* for any aspect of revelation except that God arbitrarily chose to do it that way. The holy Scriptures record what God has in fact ordained, but it all could have been otherwise.

The effect of Ockham's nominalism was to reaffirm Marsilius's assertion that faith was entirely irrational fideism, which in turn supported Marsilius's efforts to subordinate religion to this-worldly political aims, thereby allowing the politicization of Scripture.

We should also note that, in reframing the Christian

God as a kind of absolute, arbitrary, and irrational deity, Ockham was preparing the way for a kind of rational rejection by a new wave of this-worldly philosophers that would arise in the Renaissance when pagan philosophy was rediscovered and embraced.

All of this was not confined to some kind of a local dispute. The thought of both Marsilius and Ockham spread quickly all over England and Europe in the 1300s and 1400s, deeply influencing intellectual and political life for generations to come.

Enough has been said to give readers an understanding of the distant origins of the modern politicizing of the Bible. We'll witness in the next few chapters an interesting and important pattern conforming to the main characters and the circumstances we've just examined. Let's set down the basics of that pattern.

First, there is the need for ecclesiastical reform, one that is often blocked by a pope, cardinal, bishop, or other Church official who uses his office for political gain—in this chapter, Pope John XXII and the Avignon Papacy.

Second, we have a political ruler at odds with the papacy or some other Church authority, whose own political ambitions conflict with the ecclesiastic—here, Ludwig.

Third, we have a religious reformer who sincerely wants the Church to shed its corruption and return to its pristine or intended purity, but is thwarted by the papacy—in this case, William of Ockham.

Finally, we have the philosopher who, having seen the hypocritical corruption of the Church in lurid detail, is convinced that the ancient pagan philosophers were right, religion is a sham, a ruse to control the ignorant masses. The problem for this philosopher is not, as such, the hypocrisy of the Church hierarchy but the fact that it has taken this instrument of control from the state, where (as the pagans maintained) it rightly belonged. Such was Marsilius.

The interaction of these characters will itself follow a pattern. The sincere religious reformer will argue that the ecclesiastical hierarchy is so hopelessly corrupt that full power must be given to the state to make the Church holy again, stripping the Church of its riches and subordinating it to the reforming state. As a Christian, this reformer will interpret Scripture to justify both actions against the Church, thereby politicizing the Bible. Unfortunately, the sincere religious reformer's program will fit exactly into the plans of the political ruler and the neo-pagan philosopher, both of whom will further politicize Scripture to enhance their own agendas.

We'll see this pattern quite clearly in the next set of chapters that cover the latter 1300s through the 1500s. The Church and papacy will still be in need of reform, as the Avignon Papacy gives way to the Great Schism, where rival popes lay claim to rule of the Catholic Church. Then follows the dominance of the Renaissance popes, such as the infamous Alexander VI. There will be new rulers, such as England's Edward III, the German Elector Frederick the Wise, and Holy Roman Emperor Charles V. Different religious reformers will appear, most notably John Wycliffe in England and Martin Luther in Germany. We'll meet the most cynical and political of philosophers, Machiavelli, who will set the stage for the return of pagan philosophy as a weapon to reassert the power of this-worldly politics over religion, that is, over Christianity. Finally, we'll examine the first great modern tyrant in whom all these strands come together, Henry VIII. All will carry forward the politicization of the Bible, laying the deep foundational assumptions and methods of modern historical-critical scholarship.

We began on the Continent in the ecclesiastical and political struggles in Italy and France. The story now takes us to England with the great (and somewhat ambiguous) reformer John Wycliffe.

Before embarking on the next leg of the journey, we bring before the reader an important but obvious point—at least obvious once it is explained. The fundamental assumption of the modern historical-critical method that miracles are impossible is implicit in the ancient pagan assessment of religion by Critias, Polybius, Livy, and Plutarch; that is, one doesn't need modern science to embrace this assumption. To be applied to Christianity, all that was needed was to adopt this ancient pagan assumption, as Marsilius did, and apply it to the Old and New Testaments. To put it perhaps too sweepingly, but perhaps not, the demythologizing treatment of the Bible by modern historical-critical scholars could be gotten entirely from pagan sources predating the Enlightenment by fifteen to twenty centuries.

Chapter Three

THE MORNING STAR OF THE CHURCH OF ENGLAND

John Wycliffe (ca. 1330–84) is often known as the "morning star of the Reformation" for his advocacy of making the Bible available in the native tongue, in his instance, English.[1] That is the Wycliffe of legend.

The actual man might be better called the "morning star of the Church of England," because it was he who first brought the kind of arguments made by Marsilius to England—for reasons of reform, not for Marsilius's own. In that, he was more like Ockham, a sincere reformer who passionately believed that the Church could only be saved by the state—except for the interesting wrinkle that Wycliffe *hated* Ockham and his nominalism. Setting aside that little irony, we can say that in reaffirming Ockham's arguments for reform, Wycliffe thus prepared the way for the actual thought of Marsilius to deeply penetrate England during

1 For our deeper analysis see Hahn and Wiker, *Politicizing the Bible*, ch. 4, "John Wycliffe."

the reign of King Henry VIII, thereby helping to create the politicized national church entirely under the king's control.

As we'll see in a later chapter, Henry VIII is the first significant modern king who forcefully subordinated the church to the state along Marsilian lines. Since it was still a Christian church, that meant politicizing the Bible in the service of the crown, which will have long-term effects not only in England but on the Continent. We may hint at these effects here by saying that the modern historical-critical method is far more indebted in its origins to England than Germany. We'll leave Henry VIII and later developments in Scripture scholarship in England for now and concentrate on Wycliffe.

John Wycliffe's place in the history of Scripture scholarship is best understood in terms of the national political contest between England and France in the Hundred Years' War (1337–1453), a war that was entwined with rivalries between the English king and the popes in Avignon under control of the French kings.

We must remember that the Protestant Reformation is about a century and a half in the future. At this point, the Church in England was Catholic, and like the Church elsewhere, it needed reform, not the least in regard to its rich holdings seemingly at odds with Christ's own poverty. John Wycliffe, an ordained priest of the Catholic Church, was eager to do just that.

Wycliffe's solution—which should sound strikingly like that of both Marsilius and Ockham—was that the political ruler should forcibly disendow the clergy, thereby restoring the Church to its proper apostolic poverty that we find in the New Testament.

"I have adduced from Scripture," Wycliffe asserted, using 1 Samuel 2:12–36, 1 Kings 2:26–27, and Ezekiel 34:1–10 for support, "that the priests of Christ should humbly minister to the Church by means of the sacraments, the sacramentals, and the teaching of the gospel of peace." And so priests "should live a poor life, devoid of property, thereby imitating Christ in this way."[2]

Importantly, according to Wycliffe, if a cleric "fails notoriously in this task, the layman has the right to lay claim to such property" as the cleric has accumulated in contradiction to Gospel-mandated poverty.[3] For Wycliffe, this was a divine command to kings, not a suggestion, for (according to his reading of Scripture) God made kings the stewards of the Church. It is not only lawful to disendow the clergy. Indeed, in some cases rulers "are in fact damned and excommunicated by heavenly justice if they fail to exercise the power the Lord has bestowed upon them."[4] No small incentive to the king, buttressed by the happy fact that the Church's riches would be transferred to the state's coffers.

Wycliffe's arguments for disendowment (set out in various works, such as *On Divine Dominion*, *On Civil Dominion*, *On the Duty of the King*, and *On the Truth of Holy Scripture*) were not penned in a political vacuum. As noted, the context was the Hundred Years' War between England and France, and his account was immediately

[2] John Wycliffe, *On the Truth of Holy Scripture*, I, vii, 114–115.

[3] Wycliffe, *On the Truth of Holy Scripture*, II, xxv, 307.

[4] Wycliffe, *On the Truth of Holy Scripture*, II, xxvii, 320.

attractive to an English king who did not want English money siphoned off to a Church whose pope was under the control of a French king.

Because of his writings, Wycliffe was hired by King Edward III, through his son, to make the king's case against the pope (in the immediate context, to stem the flow of money out of England to the papacy). As historian Michael Wilks succinctly puts it, "what Edward III needed was a justification of his right to act as a supreme ecclesiastical overlord on a Biblical basis . . . and that was what Wycliffe gave him."[5]

In this capacity, Wycliffe identified himself as the special "cleric of the king" (*Regis clericus*) and set about fervently preaching disendowment. Obviously, he couldn't help but politicize Scripture in his dutiful efforts, bending the Bible to the king's cause by providing exegetical justification. Wycliffe's attacks against the corrupt clergy in pursuit of this political aim would fuel anti-monastic animus in England right up through Henry VIII.

At this point it would be helpful to step back a bit to take a look at the bigger historical picture. In the conflict in which Wycliffe was an essential participant, there is a great political shift, the political focus moving from the Holy Roman Emperor to the kings of England and France. We are witnessing in these events something monumen-

[5] Michael Wilks, "Royal Patronage and Anti-Papalism from Ockham to Wyclif," in Anne Hudson and Michael Wilks, *From Ockham to Wyclif* (Oxford: Basil Blackwell, 1987), 147–148. Note: Wycliffe's name has a multitude of variant spellings, which scholars use variously; thus, we "correct" the spelling to Wycliffe so as not to confuse the reader.

tally important for history: the *rise of modern nationalism*, where territorial rulers struggle to assert their "national" sovereignty against universal claims of both the emperors and the popes.

Wycliffe's call for ecclesial reform through disendowment must be understood in terms of the rise of nationalism—that is, of the English king asserting full rights over his own territory. For Wycliffe, the English king (in this instance, Edward III) is not an ordinary political ruler but a king in line with Old Testament kings, like David and Solomon, who, as God-appointed rulers of the land, govern the priests as well. On this view, reducing the Church in England to poverty for the sake of reform was a biblically grounded divine mandate (just as the Levite priests had no land but only God as their inheritance), one that would happily return clerics to conformity with the poverty of the early Church.

There was a deep strain of nationalism in these assertions. Wycliffe firmly believed that the earliest Church in England, founded and watched over by its legendary kings, was a poor and holy Church *just like the apostolic Church*, and was *in fact* the providential heir to God's plans reaching back to the ancient Israelites.

So Wycliffe wasn't merely drawing scriptural parallels from Jewish to English kings. He was convinced that England was the actual, historical, providential heir to Israel—and he wasn't the only one making such bold assertions. Both in England and in France, the notion of the Holy Nation had taken hold of the imagination, where the king supposedly reigned over the New Israel, taking the mantle from the apostolic Church as the providential political vehicle of Almighty God. The difficulty, one that no doubt fueled the Hundred Years' War, was that *both* England and France claimed the divine mantle, and so both used the Bible to support their dynastic claims. A French joke circulating at this time whimsically captures the struggle: "the pope has become French and Jesus has become English."[6]

This entanglement of Scripture with nationalist state aspirations—"messianic nationalism" we might call it—was not confined to England and France. Again, from Wilks: "In the course of the fourteenth and fifteenth centuries this equation of *ecclesia* and *terra*, church and land, spread to most parts of Europe. . . . The result was that the Reformation became a virtual inevitability as Europe came to accept this territorial doctrine of the Church as being essentially a collection of 'lands', of independent Israels." As Wilks further notes, "this new—or rather, very old—conception of a church as a territory, as a defined geographical area, was bound to be inherently anti-papal."[7]

Consequently, the pope's universal claims, buttressed by Scripture, clashed with various kings' nationalist claims, also buttressed by Scripture. Politicizing on both sides was inevitable, and the situation in England with Wycliffe is an early, very important example. Wycliffe proved immensely helpful in using Scripture to support the English king's

[6] Quoted in J. W. McKenna, "How God became an Englishman," in *Tudor Rule and Revolution: Essays for G. R. Elton from His American Friends*, ed. D. J. Guth and J. W. McKenna (Cambridge: Cambridge University Press, 1982), 30.

[7] Wilks, "Royal Patronage and Anti-Papalism from Ockham to Wyclif," 152.

claims to sovereignty over both his state and the Church *in* England—which would soon enough, with Henry VIII, become the Church *of* England.

Wycliffe therefore attacked the pope, declaring in his *On Civil Dominion* that the Roman pope was not the universal ruler of the Church but merely "the head of a particular Church," that is, of Rome,[8] and so had neither temporal nor ecclesiastical jurisdiction in England. Wycliffe's point was that the proper situation was for every bishop to be under a king, as the Jewish priests were under David (with the proviso that only the English king could lay claim to Davidic lineage). He also applied his argument to other situations, primarily the contest between the emperor and the pope, arguing that "the pope ought, as he formerly was, to be subject to Caesar,"[9] as we find the Apostles subject to Roman rule in the New Testament—a duplication of Marsilius's argument.

That brings us to another important angle on Wycliffe's arguments. As Pope Gregory XI was heading back to Rome, thereby ending the Babylonian Captivity in Avignon, Wycliffe's views on disendowment came to his attention via an examination of his doctrines by a Benedictine monk, Adam Easton. What caught Easton's attention was the *profound similarity* between Wycliffe's writings and Marsilius's already condemned arguments from the *Defensor Pacis*. Pope Gregory thus condemned Wycliffe's

8 John Wycliffe, *On Civil Dominion*, I.382. Quoted in Edith C. Tatnall, "John Wyclif and *Ecclesia Anglicana*," *Journal of Ecclesiastical History* 20, no. 1 (April 1969): 21n1.

9 Our translation from A. W. Pollard's and C. Sayle's edition of John Wycliffe's *Tractatus de officio Regis* (London, 1887), 237.

ideas in 1377 and issued orders for his arrest, the result of which was not his incarceration but the creation of an even deeper animosity in Wycliffe toward the papacy.

All of this intricacy of complex intentions helps us understand more deeply another famous aspect of Wycliffe as a pre-Reformation figure, his efforts to translate the Bible into English (the translation actually being done by a small academic army of his followers and not by him). Here, we need to be careful not to confuse Wycliffe with typical Reformation views.

Unlike later Protestant reformers, Wycliffe did not hold to a priesthood of all believers or any notion that the truth of the biblical text was readily and perspicuously available to all who cast their eyes upon its pages. He had had too much experience of divisive readings of the Bible in his days as a university student and then professor, as well as in his battles against scripturally supported papal claims. In fact, for Wycliffe, "all human evil arises from a failure to venerate and understand Scripture correctly."[10]

Translating the Bible into English, in and of itself, wouldn't obviate this difficulty. To avoid the evil of misinterpretation, Wycliffe asserted that one who approaches Scripture must have definite prerequisites: a morally good character as evidenced in his actions, as well as *experience in studying philosophy*. For Wycliffe the latter meant not just the study of grammar, dialect, rhetoric, natural philosophy, and moral philosophy that he'd done at the university level, but *his own philosophy*, extreme realism, which was defined directly against Ockham's nominalism. (To be

[10] Wycliffe, *On the Truth of Holy Scripture*, I, ix.

all too short, while Ockham denied that names had any connection to any alleged universals in things, Wycliffe argued that universals in things are indeed real and related directly to God's mind. Therefore names are really connected to universals in things, and hence to God's mind. If this were not the case, Wycliffe asserted, then the names—that is, words—in Holy Scripture could not be vehicles of divine truth.)

The intricacies of this philosophical dispute are beyond the scope of the present study. Understanding nominalism is difficult enough, but Wycliffe's extreme realism is almost impenetrably complex. Our purpose in bringing it up here is twofold.

First, it makes evident that Wycliffe would not agree with the later Reformation notion that Scripture was easily understood. Instead, he asserted that only the highly educated could sort through it properly, philosophy being an essential part of this education. And not just any philosophy would do for this task, but only his extreme realism. Hence the need for an "academic army" to translate the Bible from Latin into English.

Second, it makes clear, politically, why the king needs academics at his side. Wycliffe asserted that the king should have his own academic court theologians, "doctors and worshipers of the divine law"[11] as he calls them, to ensure the proper interpretation of the text so that the king may "rule the men of his own kingdom according to

[11] From A. W. Pollard's and C. Sayle's edition of John Wycliffe's *Tractatus de officio Regis* (London, 1887), 48–49.

divine law."[12] These "doctors" certainly bear more than a passing resemblance to the court theologians of Marsilius and the experts of Ockham, however much Wycliffe might disagree with them on other points.

We might ask: If the Bible is in the hands of academic theological experts, then why not leave the Bible in Latin? Why have it translated into English? For Wycliffe, having the Bible in the vernacular was not an aberration but a continuation of God's plan, for "Moses heard God's law in his own tongue, so did Christ's Apostles. Latin is the mother tongue of Italy as Hebrew is for the Jews."[13] And if England truly was the New Israel, the nation chosen by God to carry forth his providential designs, then the Bible ought especially to be translated into the language of that holy nation as well.

That, as it turned out, was no easy task. In anticipation of the difficulties that would plague the later attempts by Protestant reformers to translate the Bible into the vernacular from the Hebrew and Greek, Wycliffe's small army of academics first had to sift through a number of Latin manuscripts to come up with what they judged was the best Latin version of the Bible. They then had to wrestle with getting the Latin into English, using all the available knowledge from the universities and what they deemed to be the best commentaries and glosses. All of this was guided by the proper philosophical and theological viewpoint, i.e., Wycliffe's. To ensure that preachers and

[12] John Wycliffe, *De civili dominio*, I, xxvi. Our translation.

[13] Quoted in Louis Hall, *The Perilous Vision of John Wyclif* (Chicago, IL: Nelson-Hall, 1983), 150.

theologians would not misuse the new English translation, the translators also published a three-thousand-page, Wycliffe-inspired guide called the *Floretum.*

As if Wycliffe's legacy was not complex and confusing enough, his writings against a corrupt clergy and the English translation of his Bible helped foment political revolt of the peasantry in England in 1381, thereby tainting Wycliffe as a political revolutionary, another black mark to go along with his being formally condemned as a follower of Marsilius. How could this be, given Wycliffe's adamant support of the king?

Inspired by Wycliffe, not just his writings but his preaching as well, the peasantry became ever more inflamed by the riches of the clergy, in particular the great and very rich monastic houses that owned land all over England and regularly mistreated the peasants as their tenants—for example, by charging them the equivalent of $300 each time a daughter was married, or confiscating their grinding stones and forcing them pay to use the monastery's instead, or having them work three-quarters of the year for the complete benefit of the monastery just to pay their rent.

But the peasant revolt against the monasteries was, at the same time, a revolt against the order of the realm and had to be addressed by the crown. Furthermore, the crown and nobles didn't want heavy taxation and economic oppression of the non-nobles to cease, we must understand; rather, they wanted to have the riches for themselves, and not allow them to be kept in the monasteries or to flow to Rome.

To muddy things up even more, lay followers of

Wycliffe and readers of his English Bible (known as Lollards) were soon coming to their own theological conclusions at odds with the Church's, and even with Wycliffe himself, thereby threatening the religious foundation of England's political order.

As a result, about fifteen years after Wycliffe's death in 1384, England's King Henry IV prohibited the production or ownership of a translated Bible. Another more famous King Henry, four Henrys hence, will have to deal with the translated Bible in his own way, and as we'll see, the political entanglements will be even more complicated.

For now, we can sum up our chapter on Wycliffe. Wycliffe's aim was not to provide support for Marsilius's arguments (which he hadn't read). Nor was it to side with Ockham (whose nominalism he detested). But the subordination of the Church to the state and the goal of disendowment of the Church and monastic houses duplicated their arguments even if not their intentions. Fitting the pattern, very strange bedfellows.

As with Ockham, Wycliffe's handing to the state full power over the Church, especially as set within the context of rising nationalism, fit all too well with the purely secular philosophy of Marsilius. When Marsilius's philosophy did in fact penetrate England during Henry VIII's great political-ecclesiastical revolution, Wycliffe's thought had certainly prepared the way. As Wycliffe's arguments spread, popularized by the Lollards, the revolution in Henry VIII's Church became nearly inevitable, even apart from the Protestant Reformation—hence, our assertion that Wycliffe is better understood as the morning star of the Church of England.

Of course, that doesn't mean that we can ignore the effects of the Reformation, either for England or the development of modern historical-critical scholarship, for they are considerable in both cases. To Luther we now turn.

Chapter Four

MARTIN LUTHER

In getting to the origins and development of the modern historical-critical method, it's tempting to brush away all the complexity of the German reformer Martin Luther and get to the main point.[1] If we might give in to that temptation momentarily, it would go something like the following.

In his attempt to reform the Church, Luther initiated a fundamental *theological* revolution, based upon twin doctrines: the Bible alone (*sola scriptura*) is the complete foundation of the faith, and in the Bible we find that we are justified by faith alone (*sola fide*) and not works. That revolution focused the entire attention of reformers on the biblical text itself, both to fend off Catholic counterattacks and to settle intractable disputes among themselves. Since the theological disputes proved unresolvable, and spilled over into political disputes, rulers had to settle both issues to keep the peace, thereby ensuring the politicization of

[1] Readers may wish to consult the extensive treatment of Luther in Hahn and Wiker, *Politicizing the Bible*, ch. 5, "Luther and the Reformation."

Scripture accordingly.

Moreover, the exclusive focus on the Bible as the sole authority caused a feverish scholarly search for the original Hebrew and Greek manuscripts, which in turn resulted in the discovery of a multitude of manuscripts with significant variations, none of which could be deemed original. Thus, the Great Divide between scholars, who could read the ancient languages and sort through the variants, and simple believers, who could only read the Bible in vernacular translation, began to open up. During the sixteenth century, both sides of the Great Divide were faithful believers. However, the long-term effect of the latter focus on the Bible would be the historical-critical divide between scholars (the academic experts), who regard the Bible as just another ancient text over which academic linguists and historians can engage their specialized crafts, and faithful believers still ignorant of these developments and therefore still holding the Bible to be the revealed, inerrant Word of God.

Having yielded to the temptation to simplify the developments in the Reformation, we now assure the reader that, while this synopsis is true as far as it goes, it fails to capture the actual complexity either of Luther and his situation or of the fallout of his attempt at reform. Filling in the needed details will allow us to see more clearly and deeply how both help bring about the assumptions and methods of modern historical-critical scholars.

As in our previous chapters, in order to understand the German reformer Martin Luther we must grasp his very complex political context, beginning with the important fact that there is no such thing as "Germany" at the time.

In the development of modern European nations, France, England, and now Spain were recognizably sovereign entities by the early sixteenth century, but the German people were as yet not unified into a nation (and would not be until the nineteenth century). As the historian S. H. Steinberg states,

> In reality, "the German section of the Holy Roman Empire," as was its official title, consisted of the patched-up relics of the medieval Empire, in which the age-old antagonism between the Emperor and the princes, the rivalry between the privileged group of electoral princes and the lesser princes, the quarrels between the princes and the representative Estates, and other feuds had, during the sixteenth century been overlaid and exacerbated by religious divisions.[2]

This patchwork political system long predated the Reformation, and, as Steinberg notes, the diffraction of Christianity brought about through Luther's attempts at reform would amplify existing political divisions, not create them.

That is no small point to make, for it means that the Reformation was born in an already volatile political context which couldn't help but to co-opt scripturally based doctrines and differences for already existing polit-

[2] S. H. Steinberg, *The 'Thirty Years War' and the Conflict for European Hegemony 1600–1660* (London: Edward Arnold Publishers, 1966), 19–22.

ical reasons. Of all the Germanic rulers, the seven most important were the Elector Princes, who, as we mentioned previously, had for centuries the privilege of choosing the Holy Roman Emperor (a German, not a Roman). That made these Electors (three of whom were archbishops, and four secular sovereigns) very powerful indeed. Although the Electors' prestige lay in their power over who got the imperial seat, they did not want an emperor to press his claims as head of the empire to reduce their own sovereign political power over their own territories.

Importantly, as we've noted previously, long before Luther, rulers in the West considered themselves to be the lords over the churches in their own territories—not just the various princes over the churches in their lesser realms but the emperor over Rome in his Empire. Those national or imperial claims over territorial churches could not help but conflict with the papacy's universal claims over the universal Church.

So, while at odds with each other, both Electors and emperors were united in their antagonism to the papacy. The Papal States in Italy were the source of rich revenues, much of which were siphoned off the Germanic territories. Moreover, it was evident to all at this time that the pope was almost entirely consumed by maintaining and even expanding his earthly estate (largely because in the fifteenth and early sixteenth centuries the papacy had been reduced to a political prize for warring Italian noble families, such as the Medici).

To make sure our own confusion matches the times, we add another layer of complexity, the messianic-nationalist aspirations of Germany. German princes were jealous of each other and the Germanic emperor, but all were jealous of the national unity of England and France and their consequent ability to rebuff papal claims, taxes, and tithes.

One response to this was the rise of a semi-mythical, semi-apocalyptic unifying vision of a Germanic messiah-emperor who would unite the German peoples against the corrupt Roman political papacy. (In two such accounts, *Reformatio Sigismundi* and *Book of One Hundred Chapters*, his name was Frederick; coincidentally, Luther's political protector would turn out to be Frederick III, Elector of Saxony.) In this popular messianic vision, once the corrupt papacy was defeated, the messianic-imperial deliverer would transfer the seat of Christendom to Germany, where it could be nestled in a reformed and hence simple, poor, holy, and apostolic-like Church. To this theological vision was added a much more political angle by others, where the unification of Germany was essential in throwing off the political interference of Rome, and in this effort both a Germanic emperor and a religious revolution would be most helpful.

All that messy political context will clarify our account of Luther's attempt at reforming the Church. Luther didn't start out as a religious reformer but as a rising member of the middle class sent to study law. One day—July 2, 1505, to be precise—he was traveling back from his parents' home to law school in Erfurt and, caught in a terrible thunderstorm, cried out, "Help me, St. Anne! I will become a monk!" A rash vow, but Luther took it seriously, entering the Order of the Hermits of St. Augustine about two weeks later. He was ordained a priest in a little less than two years.

Taking his vocation seriously had two entwined results. As Luther attempted sincerely to become a holy monk, the corruptions of the clergy seemed even more repulsive, and Luther himself became ever more agonized by his own struggles for holiness. The former resulted in him pounding his famous *Ninety-Five Theses* (more accurately, his *Disputation on the Power and Efficacy of Indulgences*) onto the door of the castle church at Wittenberg. The latter was resolved by his reading of St. Paul's Letter to the Romans, 1:17, "He who through faith is righteous shall live," which Luther, reading more broadly in St. Paul, took to mean that "a man is justified by faith apart from works of law" (Rom 3:28). Hence the end of his struggles as a monk and the beginning of this theological revolution via *sola fide*.

The theological revolution led to a new way of understanding the relationship of the Old to the New Testament. In Luther's understanding, the Old Testament embodied not just the Jewish Law, but the very notion that our works, our efforts, at becoming holy are related to divine reward. It was a book meant to frustrate us, showing us that we need a Redeemer who can do the work of redemption for us, making us holy by his merits—the very revelation of the New Testament. Realizing this, we can lay aside the struggle and angst of the Old Testament and embrace justification by faith alone as reported in the New.

As with Wycliffe, Luther soon came to believe that the Catholic Church would not reform itself. It had too much invested in its clergy and sacramental system being a fulfillment of the Old Testament priestly class and rites. The Church had to be forced to reform by political rulers.

And in parallel to Wycliffe, what cemented Luther's opposition to the papacy was the threat of excommunication. In defending himself against charges of heresy, Luther gave voice to the full expression of his views in a famous debate at Leipzig in the summer of 1519, where Luther declared that both popes and Church councils could err *so that* Scripture was the sole authority left. Hence, the birth of *sola scriptura*, which was a direct repudiation of papal authority (and an inadvertent duplication of Marsilius's strategy to root all authority in Scripture so as to undermine all extra-biblical papal claims).

In January of 1521, Luther was formally excommunicated. Like Wycliffe, he turned to shelter himself and his theological revolution under political protectors, and from there, he would launch theological reform using their political power as a shield and lance.

It was in this context—actually, in the year prior to his excommunication—that Luther published his *Appeal to the Ruling Class of the German Nationality as to the Amelioration of the State of Christendom*. In it, he made the case that the corruption of the Church could only be cured if the German princes and emperor would strip the "Romanists" of their power. This call fit snugly with Germany's long-standing messianic nationalism, but Luther gave it a theologically revolutionary biblical justification as well. Like Marsilius and Wycliffe, Luther asserted (using Romans 13:1–4 and 1 Peter 2:13–15) that everybody, including the pope, must be subject to the political rulers.

But Luther added (based upon 1 Peter 2:9) another doctrine, that "our baptism consecrates us all without exception, and makes us all priests," so that *all* laity, but especially emperors, kings, and princes, have "already been consecrated priest, bishop, or pope. . . . All have spiritual status, and [therefore] all are truly priests, bishops, and popes."[3]

With the "priesthood of all believers," as it came to be called, Luther elevated the secular power to the same status as the sacred, declaring them equal. Furthermore, if each ruler is a priest, bishop, and pope, then each may interpret the Bible for himself—the papacy has no monopoly on authoritative scriptural interpretation. The king's interpretation of Scripture counts as much as, if not more than, the corrupt papacy's (which Luther equated with the Antichrist).

Luther believed that these doctrinal assertions, which he took to be confirmed by Scripture, would break down the "walls" that the papacy had built to ward off reform. True enough, but they also had three very important, if unintended, ramifications.

The first one is obvious, and accords all too nicely with Marsilius's philosophy that had already significantly penetrated England and Europe: political rulers may now unite political power with scriptural authority, becoming both king and pope, a sure recipe for politicizing the Bible in the service of emperors, kings, and princes.

Second, almost immediately, other very earnest and equally learned reformers took Luther's revolutionary principles but (reading the same Bible) came to much different conclusions, thereby beginning the doctrinal

[3] Martin Luther, *An Appeal to the Ruling Class of German Nationality as to the Amelioration of the State of Christendom* in *Martin Luther: Selections from His Writings*, ed. John Dillenberger (New York: Doubleday, 1961), 408–409.

splintering of Protestantism which upset both Luther and the political order.

Third, given the flurry of Luther's works spinning off the printing presses, his message reached the ruled as well as the rulers, the peasants as well as the nobility. Since Luther had declared that the Bible is the sole authority, and it confirms the priesthood of all believers, the peasant class in German lands, *based upon their reading of holy Scripture*, initiated a rebellion in 1524 against both the ecclesial and political order—a parallel to the English peasant rebellion that shadowed Wycliffe's efforts.

Luther's response to the peasant rebellion magnified tremendously the Marsilian aspects of his argument. Before the rebellion, Luther's opponents declared that his new doctrines would lead to theological, then political chaos for precisely the reason that it did *in fact* lead to the peasant rebellion. If the Bible is the sole source of authority, and each of the baptized is equally a pope and equally capable of reading and interpreting Holy Writ, then soon enough the unwashed at the bottom of the political order will take Christ's words about the poor as license for rebellion.

The peasants offered a manifesto called the *Twelve Articles*, filled with a mixture of ecclesial and political demands. Following Luther's earlier words of defiance against papal pressure to recant, the peasants declared that they would not disavow any of their demands unless "it is proved to be against the word of God by a clear explanation of the Scripture."[4]

[4] The *Twelve Articles*, in *The Protestant Reformation*, ed. Hans Hillerbrand (New York: Harper & Row, 1968), 66.

To save his reforming principles from condemnation, Luther first offered a *Friendly Admonition to Peace Concerning the Twelve Articles of the Swabian Peasants* but doubled down on his call for absolute obedience of everyone to political authority as the carnage of the rebellion increased. Finally, in his *Against the Robbing and Murdering Gangs of Peasants*, he instructed the nobles to slaughter the rebellious peasants ruthlessly as a matter of their Christian duty to preserve the peace, without care as to who was guilty or innocent.

By September of 1525, the nobles had succeeded in smashing the rebellion, and the result for Luther was twofold. On the one hand, princes greatly appreciated his bestowal of absolute authority on the ruling class, and on the other, the peasantry now associated Luther with obeisance to the oppressive rulers. Lutheranism all too quickly became a theological instrument of political power, and (ironically) Luther's use of Scripture to demand absolute obedience to the rulers fit hand in glove with the secularizing thought of Marsilius that had been circulating widely for almost two centuries.

Returning to the second ramification of Luther's reform (i.e., the immediate splintering of the reform movement), Luther's twin principles of *sola fide* and *sola scriptura* were meant to break the spiritual and political power of Rome. To some extent, they were successful in doing so. But they also had the entirely unintended result, almost immediately, of creating rival interpretations of the Bible among those inspired by Luther's Reformation—Andreas von Karlstadt, the so-called Zwickau prophets (Nicholas Storch, Marcus Stübner, and Thomas Drechsel),

Huldrych Zwingli, and later on, John Calvin. His rivals in reform were, if anything, even more scholarly biblical exegetes but came up with positions entirely unacceptable to Luther.

One position was an obvious inference from one of Luther's principles: if we are saved by faith alone, and not works, then the sacraments are superfluous and, if superfluous, merely symbolic. Luther had reduced the Catholic sacraments from seven to two, Baptism and the Eucharist; his rivals removed the last two, using arguments from Scripture and *sola fide*. Thus were born the non-sacramental forms of Protestantism (such as the Anabaptists) and the quasi-sacramental (such as the Calvinists). For these reformers, Luther's keeping two sacraments smacked of popery, an incomplete reform.

But for Luther, their misinterpretation was demonic. In regard to the rejection of baptism as a sacrament, and hence the rejection of infant baptism, Luther remarked sadly, "I always expected Satan to touch this ulcer. But he did not wish to do it through the papists. It is among ourselves and among our own that this grave schism is set in motion, but Christ truly will quickly crush it under our feet."[5] Such was not the case, but Luther would later invite rulers to do the crushing as the rival views fanned out in all directions geographically.

In regard to Reformation disagreements about the Eucharist, Luther confessed, "I have often asserted that the ultimate goal of the devil is to do away with the entire sac-

[5] Quoted in Richard Marius, *Martin Luther: The Christian between God and Death* (Cambridge, MA: Belknap Press, 1999), 325.

rament and all outward ordinances of God. Then as these prophets teach, all that would count would be for the heart to stare inwardly at the spirit."[6] Luther himself was being prophetic, for that view would soon enough arise among the more radical Anabaptists and lead to a kind of mystical rationalism that prepared the way for the Enlightenment semi-deification of reason. While reformers like Karlstadt did not take this route, they did make the case that the Eucharist must be merely symbolic, and in fact, if it were mistakenly taken to actually be Jesus Christ himself, then worshipers would become idolaters, bowing down (like papists) before mere bread and wine. For Luther, Karlstadt was doing the work of the devil.

We must not forget the political implications of these theological disagreements. We've already seen the effects in the peasant rebellion, but another dangerous result came about through Luther's rival, Karlstadt. Against Luther, Karlstadt asserted that the Old Testament could not be set aside as irrelevant, but—in accordance with the principle of *sola scriptura*—remained authoritative along with the New. One result was that Karlstadt's followers took the Old Testament attacks on idolatry as mandates for action and thereby set off a zealous flurry of statue-smashing.

Luther was horrified and blamed Karlstadt for foolishly thinking that the "crude masses" are to be trusted with biblical interpretation. To do so created destructive

[6] Martin Luther, *Against the Heavenly Prophets in the Matter of Images and Sacraments*, in *Karlstadt's Battle with Luther: Documents in a Liberal-Radical Debate*, ed. Ronald Sider (Philadelphia, PA: Fortress Press, 1978), 119.

mobs that only the political rulers can quell. "Give a rogue an inch and he takes a mile. For why do we have sovereigns? Why do they carry the sword, if the masses are to rush in blindly and straighten things out themselves?"[7]

As with the peasant rebellion, in fighting against the excesses of other reformers, Luther had to contradict his notion of the priesthood of all believers for the sake of political peace. The common man—Luther called him "Mr. Everybody"—could not be trusted either to have the right interpretation of the Bible or to draw from it the prudent conclusions. The result of allowing each to be his own interpreter of the Bible was mob rule, and hence political chaos. As Luther chastised Karlstadt,

> Suppose Dr. Karlstadt won a large following . . . and the German Bible alone was read, and Mr. Everybody began to hold this commandment [from the Old Testament about the necessity of slaying idolaters] under his own nose, in what direction would Dr. Karlstadt go? How would he control the situation? Even if he had never intended to consent to something like that, he would have to follow through. The crowds would mutiny and cry and shout as obstinately, "God's Word, God's Word, God's Word is there. We must do it!" As he now cries against images, "God's Word, God's Word!" My dear lords, Mr. Everybody is not to be toyed with. Therefore God would have authorities so

[7] Luther, *Against the Heavenly Prophets in the Matter of Images and Sacraments*, 103.

that there might be order in the world.[8]

We can see here the fateful connection between Luther's reforming principles and his answer to the consequent political disorder they caused: political rulers must be called in to keep theological disagreements and confusions that arise from *sola scriptura* from becoming political revolutions.

For Luther, the use of political force was necessary not only because Mr. Everybodies came up with dangerous interpretations of the Bible. On the deepest level, the number of the truly redeemed who live by the Gospel was very small. The rest, the unredeemed sinners, were still under the Law, and hence must be kept under control by political laws.

The ironic result, as historian Richard Marius relates, was that "Luther preached more and more to emphasize the law"[9]—even in his own Wittenberg. In a sermon of late 1528, Luther fumed, "What shall I do with you, people of Wittenberg! I shall not preach to you the kingdom of Christ, because you don't take it up. You are thieves, robbers, merciless. To you I must preach the law!"[10]

For princes, this was a political boon, and it contributed in no small part to the decision by particular princes in the political patchwork of Germany to accept Lutheranism within their borders as the politically sanctioned form of Christianity. Others, of course, found alliances with

[8] Luther, *Against the Heavenly Prophets in the Matter of Images and Sacraments*, 103–104.

[9] Marius, *Martin Luther*, 476.

[10] Quoted in Marius, *Martin Luther*, 475.

the pope or Catholic kings to be more politically advantageous. In either case, the situation fit with the already existing notions that the ruler of each realm should decide what religion suits his political situation best, whether this notion had roots in the ancient or imagined nationalist prerogatives of Germanic princes, Marsilian doctrines that had permeated the upper classes, or some combination thereof.

Readers of history can't help but see the inevitability of the political principle of *cuius regio, eius religio*, "whose realm, his religion," that was invoked at the Peace of Augsburg (1555), the political truce that momentarily ended wars between Catholics and Lutherans—a principle repeated almost a hundred years later at the end of the Thirty Years' War (1648) between Catholics, Lutherans, and Calvinists. Needless to say, such a political solution, involving religious differences, could not help but contribute to the further politicization of the Bible (especially when we add the rise of messianic nationalism that, as we've seen, understood the nation as bearer of God's providence).

We will examine these wars and their implications for the development of the historical-critical method in later chapters, noting that they were fueled as much, if not more, by nationalist or otherwise political agendas as by religious differences. Here, we will sum up our account of Luther.

We've made clear that Luther's deference to political authority, as buttressed by Scripture, was a duplication of Ockham's arguments as well as Marsilius's. In Luther's more volatile political context, it meant that the Bible was being used as a political support, even a political instrument, for Germanic states against the papacy. But further politicization occurred because his Reformation principles yielded rival interpretations of Scripture that played into existing political conflicts, and even fed rebellious movements among the non-noble classes.

To this we may add another, less obvious point. When the frustrated Luther asserted that the "crude" masses needed to have the civil sword hanging over their heads, and Law and obedience continually dinned in their ears, he was inadvertently reaffirming the pagan philosophical view that religion is essentially an instrument to rule the unruly masses, thereby lending support to Averroists, followers of Marsilius, and others who will take up that pagan thread (most forcefully, Machiavelli, to whom we turn in the next chapter).

This focus on the Bible as an instrument of political peace will soon enough yield an essential feature of the historical-critical method, which we've seen in the first chapter, in which we surveyed a number of contemporary scholars: the real importance of the Bible, and hence biblical interpretation, is to provide *political* support for a particular agenda (Marxist revolution, feminism, etc.). In order to function as such a this-worldly instrument, however, the otherworldly, supernatural aspects of the Bible will have to be removed. Hence, the need for demythologizing. Luther did not contribute to this aspect—obviously, he would have considered it abhorrent—but others would (again, the importance of moving on to Machiavelli).

Chapter Five

THE PAGAN RENAISSANCE AND MACHIAVELLI

We now turn from the Reformation to the Renaissance, so that we may trace out important developments in the rise of the historical-critical method connected with the recovery of ancient Greek and Roman texts.[1] It's well known that the fifteenth and early sixteenth centuries, especially in Italy, are marked by the passionate search for ancient Greek and Roman manuscripts. This resulted in the recovery of ancient works that had been lost to the West for some time—most likely buried in monastery libraries.

Those engaging in the avid recovery of ancient works during this period generally go under the name Renaissance Humanists. For some of these Humanists, like Erasmus, ancient Greek and Roman works served Christianity, allowing for a kind of purification of faith, albeit

[1] We have added significant material to this chapter to flesh out what we provided in *Politicizing the Bible*, ch. 4, "Machiavelli."

one that focused largely on ethics and the education of politically virtuous citizens. But for others, this recovery of ancient thought went beyond appreciation to adulation, so there literally was, for them, a rebirth—a Renaissance—of paganism. The result was that these latter devotees began to see the world (including Christianity) through pagan eyes.

Considering both groups, then, the list of Renaissance Humanists contains not only Erasmus but Machiavelli, surely quite opposite in their approach to Christianity. It also contains those whose relationship to paganism and Christianity is ambiguous. For example, Lorenzo Valla (ca. 1407–1457) is certainly to be counted among the great Renaissance Humanists. He is famous for using philology to show that the Donation of Constantine was not authentic. He also inspired Erasmus's philological investigations of the Greek New Testament by his critical philological analysis of the Latin Vulgate Bible, an inspiration that led to Erasmus's publication of the Greek and Latin version of the New Testament in 1516. Finally, and perhaps most importantly in the long term, Valla was first to revive the arguments of the pagan materialist-hedonist Epicurus in his very ambiguous dialogue, *De Voluptate*, or *On Pleasure* (1431). In it, he takes the side of the Epicurean interlocutor over the Stoic, and then tries to affirm a positive connection of Epicurean materialism and hedonism with Christianity. Valla was thereby instrumental in the revival of materialism that will ultimately result in the rejection of the miraculous.

Sorting out the ambiguity of Renaissance Humanism is beyond the scope of this book. It is fair to say that scholarly attempts at characterizing all Renaissance Humanists as secret or open pagans, or the opposite, to paint them all as pious Christians, are both overplaying their hands and overlooking the obvious alternative—it was a mix.

For our purposes, we only need to understand that during this time period, pagan thought was reintroduced to the West. Some, like Machiavelli, took it on its own terms, not as a handmaid to Christian theology, but as a source of wisdom in its own right. Even if Machiavelli had been the single exception, it is clear from later developments that pagan ideas soon enough took on a life of their own, creating a source of cultural antagonism to Christianity that considerably predated the Enlightenment, the time period when the embrace of ancient paganism became widespread among the intelligentsia.

This had immense implications for the development of modern biblical scholarship, and for the intellectual and cultural reformulation of the West as a whole. The ideas of these pagan philosophers sound strikingly familiar. Much of modern thought is readily recognizable in them; so also are many of the assumptions of modern biblical scholars (as well as the methods that follow upon them).

An overview of a few key texts of this pagan Renaissance will allow us to understand more deeply Machiavelli's place in the history of modern Scripture scholarship as the next important repaganized philosopher after Marsilius, one who dared to treat the Bible as a demythologized and politicized text.

We may begin with the pagan notion already reintroduced by Marsilius, that religion is a fabrication of rulers, philosophers, or disingenuous priests used as an instrument to control the unruly masses. Marsilius named as his pagan sources Hesiod, Pythagoras, and others. Who the "others" may have been for Marsilius is a good question. We do know of the renewed interest in the Renaissance of the writings of the Greek historian Polybius, the Roman historian Livy, and the philosopher-historian Plutarch. In the time period between 1450–1700, Polybius's *Histories* went through thirty-six editions, Livy's *History of Rome* one hundred-sixty editions, and Plutarch's *Parallel Lives* sixty-two editions, at an average of about a thousand copies per edition (half in translations). In the short period from 1450 to 1550, the numbers are seventeen, twenty-seven, and eighteen respectively.[2] We know, then, that their works had wide circulation and hence influence, especially among the intellectual elite.

In his account of Rome, Polybius remarks that the Romans grasped the truth about the need for the political use of religion to control the ignorant populace—literally, putting the fear of the gods into them. If the state "could be composed of wise men," Polybius tells us, there would be no use for the "invisible terrors of religion." But such is not the case. As a consequence, wise rulers of the past dutifully maintain all the trappings of religion, and in this, they "did not act rashly and by chance in secretly introducing among the masses notions of the gods and Hades"; rather, "those who now cast out these things are most rash and irrational."[3]

[2] Peter Burke, "A Survey of the Popularity of Ancient Historians, 1450–1700," *History and Theory* 5, no. 2 (1966): 135–152.

[3] Polybius, *Histories*, VI, 56.6–13. Our translation.

Similarly, in Livy's treatment of Numa, he noted that the legendary founder and ruler of Rome—after Romulus—realized that he could not control those whom he ruled in peacetime without instilling in them the fear of the gods and his own special relationship to them. So Numa cleverly faked a miraculous meeting with the nymph Egeria, who (so he maintained) dictated to him the laws by which Rome should be ruled.[4] Numa's very human laws therefore appeared to have divine sanction.

Plutarch affirmed this story of Numa in his *Parallel Lives*, remarking that anyone who similarly had "to deal with hard-to-control and unappeasable multitudes and to impose great innovations in constitutions . . . should pretend to have a vision from the god."[5]

The ancient historians weren't the only source of these ideas. One of the clearest and most thorough statements of the political use of religion came from the fifth-century-BC Athenian Critias, in a fragment from one of his plays, *Sisyphus*. The fragment was preserved by the second-century-AD Greek philosopher and physician Sextus Empiricus, whose works also mediated philosophical skepticism to the Renaissance.[6]

In Critias's famous fragment we hear that in the very beginning the life of man was entirely unordered, and so men lived as beasts, by force and not by virtue, since there was no reward for being good. The invention of laws had

4 Livy, *History of Rome,* I, xix, 4–5.

5 Plutarch, *Parallel Lives*, Numa, iv.7–8. Our translation.

6 For the spread of Sextus Empiricus's works during this period see Luciano Floridi, "The Diffusion of Sextus Empiricus's Works in the Renaissance," *Journal of the History of Ideas* 56, no. 1 (Jan 1995): 63–85.

no effect because people would still do evil in secret. And then some "wise and clever man invented fear of the gods" so that the wicked might be frightened. He declared that the immortal gods see and hear everything that men do and deal with them accordingly. This wise and clever man "introduced the most cunning of teachings, covering up the truth with a falsehood," putting the gods up in the heavens, where mortals hear thunder and see lightning, there to mete out rewards and punishments to mortals on earth below. "With such fears did he surround mankind" and hence "quenched lawlessness by means of laws. . . . And so it was, I think, that some man first persuaded men to believe that the race of gods exists."[7]

Of course, as we've already seen with Marsilius, Averroism was well-known, especially in Italy, because of its continuing influence at the university at Padua. With the *Defensor Pacis* spreading out in influence, the subordination of the church to the state in imitation of the "wise and clever" founder of religion went with it.

As noted already with Lorenzo Valla, another very important strain of pagan thought was recovered in the 1400s and spread throughout the 1500s, that of the ancient materialist atomists, Epicurus (341–270 BC) and his Roman disciple, Lucretius (ca. 94–55 BC). The philosophical goal defining Epicureanism is not the pursuit of pleasure, as one might gather from the name of the school, but peace of mind, *ataraxia* in Greek.

7 Translation modified from Kathleen Freeman, *Ancilla to the Pre-Socratic Philosophers* (Cambridge, MA: Harvard University Press, 1970), 88.25, 157–158. See Sextus Empiricus, *Against the Physicists*, I.54.

What disturbs such peace? For Epicurus, *the* problem is religion, which arises from our fear of the gods that we feel every time thunder and lightning assail us from the heavens, or we are beset with diseases, or we find our hearts gnawed by anxiety about the state of our souls in the afterlife.

Before we go to Epicurus's "cure," we should mark the contrast between Epicureanism, on the one hand, and the work of Polybius, Livy, Plutarch, and Critias, on the other. While the latter claim that religion was a good philosophical invention necessary for creating political peace through fear of the gods, Epicurus asserted, to the contrary, that this fear is a bad thing because it disturbs our earthly peace. These two opposing strains will both be represented in modern appropriations of pagan thought—generally, the followers of Polybius and others are earlier and more moderate, the followers of Epicurus are later and more radical—and both will have very important effects on the development of modern political philosophy and modern biblical scholarship, as we shall see.

To return to Epicurus, his cure for our anxiety was his materialist atomism, which he borrowed from Democritus and used for purposes of removing the fear of the gods that disturbs our tranquility. His argument is very simple.

There are, he asserted, only two things in the universe: eternal material atoms and the void or space between them.[8] Since both the atoms and the void are eternal, there

[8] Epicurus, *Letter to Herodotus*, sections 38–44, in *The Epicurus Reader*, trans. Brad Inwood and L. P. Gerson (Indianapolis, IN: Hackett, 1994).

is no need to invoke eternal gods as creators. This is doubly the case because the chance banging and jostling of these eternal atoms that occurs throughout infinite time in an infinite universe creates an infinite number of worlds, with all kinds of randomly contrived creatures, earth being just one such world out of that infinite number.[9] And all that thunder and lightning? Not to worry! That's not the gods at all, but the effect of atoms banging against each other in the sky.[10]

Since all is material, then human beings have no immaterial, immortal souls. They do have souls, but they are material and mortal, made of finer atoms than their bodies. At death, they dissipate, disassociating just like the larger atoms of their bodies, and that is the end.[11] And so another source of anxiety caused by religion is gone: human beings are entirely mortal, so they are not subject to punishments from the gods in the afterlife.[12] "Get used to believing that death is nothing to us," for death is merely the dissipation of our atoms. Therefore, "when death is present, then we do not exist."[13]

Epicurus wasn't an atheist, or so he assured his readers. He maintained that the gods themselves were likewise made of atoms, the difference being that, unlike human beings, a "god is an indestructible and blessed animal"—that is,

[9] Epicurus, *Letter to Pythocles*, sections 88–89, in Inwood and Gerson, *The Epicurus Reader*.

[10] Epicurus, *Letter to Pythocles*, sections 101–104.

[11] Epicurus, *Letter to Herodotus*, section 67.

[12] Epicurus, *Letter to Herodotus*, sections 76–77, 81; *Letter to Pythocles*, sections 113–116.

[13] Epicurus, *Letter to Menoeceus*, sections 124–125, in Inwood and Gerson, *The Epicurus Reader*.

their atoms stay together forever. Happily, they are entirely unconcerned with human affairs, for if they weren't, they'd be anxious themselves about human goings-on rather than blessedly indifferent.[14] Many at the time, and thereafter, took Epicurus's strange affirmation of the gods to be a ruse to avoid the fate of Socrates, who was executed on charges of atheism.

Epicurus's Roman disciple Lucretius, also available from the 1400s on, was even more influential on the Renaissance (and the Enlightenment) than the master.[15] His beautifully written philosophical poem, *De Rerum Natura*, set out Epicurus's arguments even more thoroughly and persuasively, the explicit goal being to come to the aid of mankind suffering "under the oppressive weight of religion."[16] As with Epicurus, he used materialist atomism "to untie the knots of religion on the mind"[17] so that poor, suffering human beings could "cast down religion under foot" once and for all.[18]

Importantly, Lucretius added another aspect to the problems that religion caused, not just anxiety but "wicked-

[14] Epicurus, *Letter to Menoeceus*, sections 123–124.

[15] On the immense influence of Lucretius from the latter 1400s onward, see (along with the below-cited Peter Gay, *The Enlightenment*) Stuart Gillespie and Philip Hardie, eds., *The Cambridge Companion to Lucretius* (Cambridge: Cambridge University Press, 2007), chs. 8–9, 11–19; Alison Brown, *The Return of Lucretius to Renaissance Florence* (Cambridge, MA: Harvard, 2010); Gerard Passannante, *The Lucretian Renaissance: Philology and the Afterlife of Tradition* (Chicago, IL: University of Chicago Press, 2011).

[16] Lucretius, *De Rerum Natura*, I, 62–65. Our translation.

[17] Lucretius, *De Rerum Natura*, I, 931–932.

[18] Lucretius, *De Rerum Natura*, I, 78–79.

ness and impious deeds,"[19] such as Agamemnon offering his daughter Iphigenia as a human sacrifice to placate the goddess Artemis. "So great are the evil things religion is able to persuade men to do," *tantum religio potuit suadere malorum*, he repeatedly intoned, a Latin phrase that became the battle cry of multiple Enlightenment figures such as Voltaire.[20]

As with Epicurus, Lucretius removed the need for gods as creators of earthly creatures with his materialist atomism, offering an even more detailed account of the evolution of planets and stars, as well as living creatures (resembling in almost every respect Darwin's version, published over eighteen centuries after Lucretius).[21]

The wonders of nature do not, therefore, lead us to the existence of creator gods. Atoms and their chance concatenations do all the work of creating life. As with Epicurus, Lucretius removed the gods from death as well. We need not fear the afterlife because our material souls and bodies dissipate at death; therefore, "no one is handed over to the black abyss of Tartarus."[22]

The effect of Epicurus's and Lucretius's arguments on the development of modern materialism cannot be overestimated, especially as it comes to define in great part the philosophical foundations of the "scientific" worldview. Materialist science banishes all immaterial entities—God, angels, and immaterial souls, and with them, heaven and

[19] Lucretius, *De Rerum Natura*, I, 82–83.

[20] See especially Peter Gay, *The Enlightenment: An Interpretation: The Rise of Modern Paganism* (New York: Norton, 1966), 98–105.

[21] Lucretius, *De Rerum Natura*, V, especially 416–431, 771–877.

[22] Lucretius, *De Rerum Natura*, III, 966–1023.

hell. All are foolish fictions of prescientific religion. We need not be anxious. Christianity simply isn't true. Blind evolution explains how we got here, and where we are going is up to us. It is not an accident that these Epicurean ideas rose to full dominance in the nineteenth century, the very century that the historical-critical method was brought to its consummation in German scholarship.

Moving on to other influences, we've mentioned that modern skepticism owed much to the rediscovery of Sextus Empiricus but it also received a significant boost from Cicero as well. Cicero was arguably the single most influential classical author for the Renaissance and the Enlightenment. Unlike many other classical authors, his works had been embraced by Christians, and hence preserved and read during the Middle Ages, but these were Cicero's more popular, public, Stoic-friendly, and Christian-friendly, works praising piety and virtue, such as *De Re Publica* (*On the Republic*) and *De Officiis* (*On Duties*).

There was another side to Cicero that had lain dormant during the Middle Ages, his skeptical side rooted in his Academic philosophy (Academic philosophy being an ancient form of skeptical philosophy). This was, in fact, Cicero's real philosophical position, as evidenced in his *De Natura Deorum* (*On the Nature of the Gods*), *De Divinatione* (*On Divination*), and, most prominently, his *Academica,* and became immensely influential in spreading skepticism from the Renaissance onward.[23] Of course, as is well

[23] See Plínio Junqueira Smith and Sébastien Charles, *Academic Scepticism in the Development of Early Modern Philosophy* (Cham, Switzerland: Springer, 2017).

known, Cicero's *On the Nature of the Gods* was a model for David Hume's famous acidic criticisms of religion in the latter 1700s, which hit at Christianity directly.[24]

Although not a full-fledged proponent, Cicero was an authority on Stoicism, and so his works mediated the Stoic way of demythologizing Greek and Roman religion, as is evident in Book 2 of his *On the Nature of the Gods.* Here, the Stoic philosopher (Balbus) re-explains the fantastic elements of the fables of the poets on philosophical terms, thereby rendering them rational and palatable. He also restates the basics of Euhemerism, the deification of heroes, as the real source of popular deities. In both instances, the Stoic philosopher (much like the modern enlightened historical-critical scholar working with the Bible) stripped the ancient poetic texts of "false opinions, confused errors, and superstitions" to get to the real historical, natural origins, thereby separating *superstitio* from true and rational *religio* (the latter being entirely compatible with Stoicism).[25] The recovery of this Stoic approach to religious mythology will also inform the development of modern historical-critical methods in the eighteenth century. Of course, we've seen it at work in our first chapter where late twentieth-century scholars like Robert Funk and Dominic Crossan claimed that Jesus Christ is one more hero whose divinization must be rationally reversed so as to recover the real Jesus, the man.

Again, our point in going over all of this is to show how

[24] Peter S. Fosl, "Doubt and Divinity: Cicero's Influence on Hume's Religious Skepticism," *Hume Studies* XX, no. 1 (April, 1994): 103–120.

[25] Cicero, *De Natura Deorum*, II, xxiii–xxviii, 62–72.

many strains of thought that would later define the assumptions and outcomes of the work of modern historical-critical scholars from the Enlightenment onward are readily recognizable in ancient pagan philosophers that were recovered and received renewed appreciation in the Renaissance. Since the ancient pagans and their Renaissance devotees precede the rise of modern science by centuries, it's evident that the victories of modern science in the 1700s cannot be the source of the historical-critical scholars' assumptions, or the methods based upon these assumptions.

To make our case, we need to show that these assumptions were at work much earlier than the Enlightenment, and that brings us to Machiavelli. Machiavelli was one of the great figures of the pagan Renaissance, most famous for his infamous advice in *The Prince*, that an effective prince must not be hindered by notions of good and evil but should use whatever means he can contrive to get and maintain his power. He is less well known as a great-great-grandfather of the historical-critical method, but once we see how he treated the Bible, we'll understand that such an honor is appropriately bestowed.

There is no doubt of the influence of Livy, Polybius, and Plutarch in both Machiavelli's *The Prince* and his *Discourses on Livy*, which we shall take up in a moment. But mention should first be made of the influence of Lucretius, whose *De rerum natura* he "not only read but diligently copied, perhaps to improve his Latin but, more likely, to have a copy to read and reread when he liked."[26] While he

[26] Maurizio Viroli, *Niccolò's Smile: A Biography of Machiavelli*, trans. Antony Shugaar (New York: Hill and Wang, 2000), 9, and Chauncey

didn't dwell on Lucretius in his writings, it's clear upon closer inspection how influential he was for Machiavelli as a political philosopher, as Paul Rahe and others have cogently argued.[27] From Lucretius, Machiavelli received an entirely materialistic account of the cosmos, one that didn't need a Christian God—or any gods—to explain it. Chance, or fortune, is sufficient (hence the importance of *fortuna* in Machiavelli's argument, as that which the prince must both use and conquer, changing accidents into opportunities).

Although Machiavelli didn't advertise his indebtedness to Lucretius, his advice to princes clearly indicates that (like Lucretius) heaven and hell had been banished from his universe. We have every reason to believe that Machiavelli deserved his reputation as an atheist, not just because of his advice but also because there were already strong currents of atheism in the 1400s and early 1500s which had elicited equally strong reactions.

During this period, Italy was, in fact, considered a hotbed of atheism. Those alarmed by the spread of atheism at the time referred to such unbelievers as Epicureans, a-Christists, Lucianists (Lucian was a second-century-AD Epicurean critic of Christians), libertines, materialists,

E. Finch, "Machiavelli's Copy of Lucretius," *The Classical Journal* 56, no. 1 (October 1960): 29–32.

[27] Paul Rahe, "In the Shadow of Lucretius: The Epicurean Foundations *of* Machiavelli's Political Thought," *The History of Political Thought* 1 (2007):30–66. See also Filippo Del Luccese, et al, eds., *The Radical Machiavelli: Politics, Philosophy and Language* (Leiden and Boston: Brill, 2015); and Ada Palmer, *Reading Lucretius in the Renaissance* (Cambridge, MA: Harvard University Press, 2014).

free-thinkers, skeptics, and even pantheists,[28] and Italy was considered the source, precisely because of its recovery of pagan texts. As Nicholas Davidson makes clear, "The conviction that Italy was a breeding-ground for atheists was . . . commonplace in the early modern period, especially among foreign visitors to the Peninsula."[29] To cite an example, in the middle of the 1500s the English scholar Roger Ascham reported that in Italy "a man may freelie discourse against what he will, against whom he lust: against any Prince, against any gouernement, yea against God him selfe, and his whole Religion."[30]

Our concern is not to trace the history of atheism in Machiavelli's Italy—although it is important to realize that modern atheism did not arise as a result of the victories of modern science, but centuries prior. It does make us aware, however, that the common attribution of atheism to Machiavelli makes sense given the presence of unbelief even before his time and, more importantly for our purposes, his irreverent treatment of the Bible.

On Machiavelli's behalf, the sad state of the Church in the late 1400s and early 1500s easily led to cynicism about religion. The corruption of the papacy and the cardinalate

[28] See David Wootton, "New Histories of Atheism," in Michael Hunter and David Wootton, eds., *Atheism from the Reformation to the Enlightenment* (Oxford: Clarendon Press, 1992), 13–53, names cited on 25. For additional background see also George Buckley, *Atheism in the English Renaissance* (Chicago: University of Chicago Press, 1932).

[29] Nicholas Davidson, "Unbelief and Atheism in Italy, 1500–1700," in Hunter and Wootton, *Atheism from the Reformation to the Enlightenment*, 55–85. Quote from 55.

[30] Quoted in Davidson, "Unbelief and Atheism in Italy, 1500–1700," 55–56.

was evident to everyone, but especially to Machiavelli, who was surrounded by it from his youth and immersed in it later on in his dealings, as a government official in Florence, with the Borgia and Medici popes.

So, in parallel to Marsilius, the corruption of the papacy provided a lamentable background that made cynicism about religion in general and Christianity in particular very attractive. Duplicating Marsilius's reaction, Machiavelli also turned to this material world as our only real concern, rejecting "imagined republics and principalities that have never been seen or known to exist in truth," for the "effectual truth" in this material world.[31]

Obviously, Machiavelli was referring to Plato directly in these words, in whose *Republic* Socrates builds a "city in speech" in an effort to vindicate the claims of justice on our souls. This city, Socrates concedes near the end of the dialogue, doesn't exist on earth but, perhaps, in a pattern in heaven. Machiavelli casts aside such imagined republics as having no relevance for politics in the real world.

But Machiavelli was also implicitly rejecting the Christian kingdom of God in heaven as only imaginary, as he made clear elsewhere. The deepest problem with Christianity, Machiavelli (somewhat circumspectly) argued, is that it deflects us from effective politics in this world. In contrast to the ancient pagan political religion, Christianity makes citizens effeminate and hence incapable of true political freedom. "For our religion . . . makes us esteem less the honor of the world, whereas the Gentiles, esteem-

[31] Niccolò Machiavelli, *The Prince*, trans. Harvey Mansfield (Chicago: University of Chicago Press, 1985), XV, 61.

ing it very much and having placed the highest good in it, were more ferocious in their actions." Following Christ, who declared that his kingdom was not of this world and humbly accepted humiliation and death, Christians glorify "humble and contemplative men more than active men," the result being that Christianity "has then placed the highest good in humility, abjectness, and contempt of things human." By contrast, the ancients placed the highest good in political and military glory, and therefore in "greatness of spirit, strength of body, and all other things capable of making men very strong." Christianity's "mode of life thus seems to have rendered the world weak," creating men trying "to go to paradise," who therefore "think more of enduring beatings than of avenging them." Such "effeminate" men do not make good soldiers and therefore leave the world "disarmed" and without the this-worldly glory evident in the ancient pagan Roman Republic and then Empire.[32]

Machiavelli didn't suggest that we should do away with religion but, rather, return to the ancient wisdom of the pagan rulers and subordinate religion to this-worldly political glory. Nor does he opt for creating a new de-Christianized civil religion based on the model of pagan religion. That task would be taken up in the 1700s by Jean-Jacques Rousseau. Instead, Machiavelli attempted a kind of pagan reforming of Christianity, effected through a new method of approaching Scripture.

[32] Niccolò Machiavelli, *Discourses on Livy*, trans. Harvey Mansfield and Nathan Tarcov (Chicago: University of Chicago Press, 1996), II.2.2, 131–132.

To put it concisely, Machiavelli treated the Bible as a pagan philosopher or historian would treat any religious text, as a set of mythological stories one had to sort through to get to the actual facts. Machiavelli therefore initiated the treatment of the Bible that much later becomes the acknowledged essential pillar of the historical-critical method. As our contemporary scholar Edgar Krentz asserts in his *The Historical-Critical Method*, the "revolution" embodied in the historical-critical method is that the "biblical books" are treated not as holy texts but as "historical documents to be studied and questioned like any other ancient sources." By this method, admits Krentz proudly, the "Scriptures were . . . secularized."[33] Krentz places the revolution in nineteenth-century Germany, thereby showing (along with almost all such scholars) a significant, critical lack of historical knowledge of his own presuppositions.

Returning to Machiavelli, his particular method of biblical analysis was to place biblical figures beside semi-mythical and historical figures from ancient Greece and Rome, the goal being to compare them (using his own philosophy and the aid of pagan historians) as equivalent figures. The biblical figure that he works with the most (in *The Prince* and, in more detail, his *Discourses on Livy*) is Moses, whom he considers, with Theseus, Lycurgus, Romulus, Numa, Solon, and Cyrus, as a great *political* founder.

Setting aside Solon and Cyrus, by placing Moses in a list with the semi-mythical founders of Rome (Romulus and Numa), Athens (Theseus), and Sparta (Lycurgus),

[33] Edgar Krentz, *The Historical-Critical Method* (Philadelphia: Fortress Press, 1975), 30.

Machiavelli was cleverly implying that Moses, too, was semi-mythical (and by doing so, also implied that reading accounts of the other legendary founders in pagan historians would illuminate our understanding of Moses). Like the stories of these other founders, the biblical account of Moses is a mixture of legend and fact.

But, sorting through fiction and fact, Machiavelli wanted the "real" Moses to illustrate his arguments in *The Prince.* Moses thereby became an example of Machiavelli's political philosophy, illustrating that brutal, allegedly immoral acts are necessary in founding a regime. He began his analysis with the legendary founder of Rome, Romulus, who killed his brother Remus. For Machiavelli, this deed was entirely excusable because the end (founding a republic) justified any means necessary. So while "the deed accuses him, the effect excuses him; and when the effect is good, as was that of Romulus, it will always excuse the deed."[34]

What is shocking, at least to readers of the time, was that Machiavelli immediately goes on to declare that "one could give infinite examples to sustain the things written above, such as Moses, Lycurgus, Solon, and other founders of kingdoms and republics who were able to form laws for the purpose of the common good."[35] Machiavelli thereby turned the attention of readers away from Moses's call by God and all the miracles of the Exodus, and focused it instead on Moses's murder of the Egyptian and, even more, on the slaughter of the idolaters at Mount Sinai. As

[34] Machiavelli, *Discourses on Livy*, I.9.2.

[35] Machiavelli, *Discourses on Livy*, I.9.3.

he later states, "Whoever reads the Bible judiciously will see that since he [Moses] wished his laws and his orders to go forward, Moses was forced to kill infinite men who, moved by nothing other than envy, were opposed to his plans."[36] Moses the Machiavellian.

But brute force isn't enough, Machiavelli reminded his readers. Wise leaders realize that they need religion to control those whom they rule. Romulus murdered his rival, and such deeds are often necessary to establish rule, but his successor Numa "turned to religion as a thing altogether necessary . . . to maintain a civilization" once it had begun. In order to ensure that Romans remained obedient, Numa feigned a secret meeting with a nymph who (he alleged) dictated Rome's sacred laws to him. The lesson for Machiavelli was timeless. While subjects cannot always be persuaded to obey on rational grounds alone, "wise men who wish to take away this difficulty have recourse to God. So did Lycurgus; so did Solon; so did many others who have had the same end as they."[37] Since Moses has been in the list of rulers for the entire discussion, the reader rightly infers that Moses feigned divine sanction for his laws as well.

Thus, the real way to understand Moses, if we follow Machiavelli's exegetical lead, is as the semi-mythical founder of Judaism who embodied both the brutality of Romulus and the cleverness of Numa. That doesn't mean that religion can ever take the place of brutality. Both brutal force and religion are necessary, so the effective

[36] Machiavelli, *Discourses on Livy*, III.30.1.
[37] Machiavelli, *Discourses on Livy*, I.11.1–3.

prince is simultaneously (in Machiavelli's words) a warrior *and* "a prophet"—that is, a religious leader who pretends a connection with the gods. Both are necessary.

This assertion led Machiavelli to one of his most direct attacks on Christianity, for those who follow out his inference. He asserted that "all the armed prophets conquered and the unarmed ones were ruined." Contriving a miracle—be it a secret meeting with a nymph or a secret meeting with God on Mount Sinai—is essential to controlling the unruly masses. But "things must be ordered in such a mode that when they no longer believe, one can make them believe by force. Moses, Cyrus, Theseus, and Romulus would not have been able to make their peoples observe their constitutions for long if they had been unarmed."[38]

And unarmed prophets? They are crucified. Machiavelli does not dare say this directly, even though the reader can hardly avoid drawing that blasphemous conclusion—blasphemous in the context of the still-Christian sixteenth century but quite ordinary as an assumption of today's historical-critical scholars, as we've seen in the first chapter.

Through the eyes of a pagan Roman, Jesus Christ's mission was a failure, and Christianity was a religion that sapped the strength of soldiers who should be fighting for the safety and glory of the fatherland. That is how Machiavelli saw the founder of Christianity, and he meant for his audience—the princes of Italy, but also any savvy rulers—to understand this lesson. That would enable them to use Christianity as an instrument without letting

[38] Machiavelli, *The Prince*, VI, 24.

it ruin the citizenry. In order to shake loose the shackles of Christianity, Machiavelli engaged in a new and quite blasphemous approach to the Bible.

The pagan assumption that Christianity isn't true but is instead a particularly bothersome religion to the state (the very assumption of the Roman Caesars who persecuted the Church) became, through Machiavelli, a new way of analyzing the biblical text, one that was overtly political and secular and supported his philosophy of *realpolitik*. Again, like Polybius, Livy, Plutarch, and Critias, he believed that religion was a necessary instrument for political control; therefore, public atheism would completely undermine the use of religion as an instrument of the state. His analysis of Moses teaches that lesson to princes.

That lesson is the source of his famous advice in *The Prince*, that a ruler must learn to be "a great pretender and dissembler" so that "he should appear all mercy, all faith, all honesty, all humanity, all religion"—and, Machiavelli emphasized, "nothing is more necessary to appear to have than this last quality." While a prince must appear to be religious, he will find that "he is often under a necessity, to maintain his state, of acting against faith, against charity, against humanity, against religion." Therefore, he must "know how to enter into evil, when forced by necessity," even while appearing pious.[39] The reconstructed Moses provides that lesson exegetically.

This is a very important aspect of Machiavelli's revolution: the direct rejection of Christian morality for the sake of this-worldly political glory. It is the ultimate source

[39] Machiavelli, *The Prince*, XVIII, 70.

of the deep moral antagonism Christians experience so vividly today between Christian morality and the morality of secularized society. This is an essential thing for us to see very clearly, and to keep in our minds as we cover developments after Machiavelli. Later figures integral to the development of the modern historical-critical method (such as Spinoza and John Locke) will assert that we can exegetically remove Christian theological doctrines from the Bible (as divisive) and retain the essentials of morality from Scripture (upon which we all agree, even atheists) so that we can achieve earthly political peace untroubled by doctrinal disputes (and Christianity can thereby prove to be useful as a moral support for political peace). But as we see with Machiavelli, pure secularism produces a view of morality radically at odds with the Bible (and so it has done, historically, by the mid-twentieth century and on into the twenty-first). For this reason, we should be skeptical of the frequent assertion that there is no real connection between doctrine and morality. More on this point as it unfolds in the following chapters.

It is also important to note that other philosophers whom we'll soon meet, and who are integral to the ongoing development of the historical-critical method, will substitute other political programs for Machiavelli's but will follow the same exegetical pattern of secularizing the biblical text, removing the miraculous, so that the Bible is suitable for their own political agenda. These figures—primarily the seventeenth-century philosophers Thomas Hobbes, John Locke, and Benedict Spinoza—are generally considered by modern biblical scholars to be some of the earliest founders, the great-grandfathers of the historical-critical method just before the dawn of the Enlightenment. What our contemporary scholars characteristically don't realize is that these three are in a direct line from Machiavelli.

We'll analyze their thought in later chapters. Before doing that, we need to finish Part I of our analysis with Henry VIII's England, because it is in that notorious tyrant that we see all the developments we've surveyed so far come together.

Chapter Six

HENRY VIII AND HIS CHURCH

As JUST NOTED, in Henry VIII's England, nearly everything we've seen so far—Marsilius, Wycliffe, the Reformation, and Machiavelli—coalesces and produces the Henrician state church, completely subordinated to the king.[1] Given Henry's complete control over his church, Scripture became a politicized instrument of the personal and political aims of the crown.

The result of this subordination will cause even greater politicization in the future as new kings, new queens, and rival political factions vie for the power over the church that Henry bestowed upon the state. The long-term effects for the development of the historical-critical method will be immense, so much so that we are justified (as biblical scholars James Barr and Henning Graf Reventlow also argue) in regarding sixteenth- and seventeenth-century England, rather than nineteenth-century Germany, to be

1 For a deeper analysis see Hahn and Wiker, *Politicizing the Bible*, ch. 6, "England and Henry VIII."

the real "cradle of biblical criticism."[2] The crucial events in the sixteenth century will be the Henrician revolution, covered in this chapter, and in the seventeenth century, the English Civil Wars, covered in a later chapter.

Let's stand back and look at Henry's revolution in light of what we've covered so far. If we think back over Wycliffe's immensely influential arguments about the crying need to reform the Church in England, and his solution (the forced disendowment of churches and monasteries by the king and the subordination of the church to the crown in a national church), then Henry VIII's creation of the Church of England over which he is the Supreme Head and his ruthless suppression of England's monastic houses and confiscation of their wealth are almost entirely predictable outcomes of following Wycliffe's call for reform.

If we add to that the direct influence of both Marsilius and Machiavelli through Henry's closest political advisors, then Henry's evidently political motives for reform and his ruthlessness in going about it are fully intelligible as well.

If, moreover, we realize that messianic nationalism, which had formed England's self-understanding since (at least) the fourteenth century, would seek a national church that naturally conflicted with the papacy's universal claims, Henry's break with the papacy in the early sixteenth century is an entirely unsurprising result.

And finally, if we bring to mind the politically disruptive effects of Wycliffe's and Luther's reforms on the

2 The words are from Barr's introduction to Henning Graf Reventlow, *The Authority of the Bible and the Rise of the Modern World*, trans. John Bowden (Philadelphia, PA: Fortress Press, 1985), xii.

peasant classes of England and Germany, we can fully understand why Henry VIII's theological reforms, and hence his use of Scripture, were politically conservative, keeping the Protestant Reformation at bay. Not to overplay this point too much, but we might say that the Church of England was a national church designed (through much turmoil and over many decades) to fend off both Catholicism and Protestantism.

Oh, and we ought to mention the little matter of Henry's desire to get an annulment of his marriage to his first wife, Catherine of Aragon. Leaving this for last allows us to see this event not as the cause of Henry's creation of the Church of England but as the match that finally lit the great heap of preconditions that had been piling up for two centuries. To be more exact, it was an unrequited match: Anne of Boleyn refused Henry's plea (set out in a torrid love letter) "to do the duty of a true and loyal mistress, and to give up yourself, body and heart, to me," in return for his solemn promise to give up all his *other* mistresses (but not his wife).[3] For the ambitious Boleyn, it was queen or nothing. Henry would begin seeking an annulment from Catherine in 1527, although she would remain England's queen for six more years.

As with our previous chapters, we've got to grasp the big-picture complexity of the political situation in which all this occurs, and that will help make sense of some of the peculiarities. (Prepare to be confused!)

To begin with, Catherine of Aragon's marriage to

[3] Ladbroke Black, *The Love Letters of Henry the Eighth* (London: Blandford Press, Ltd., 1933), 29.

Henry's brother, Henry VII, was a political union of Spain and England, Catherine being the daughter of Ferdinand and Isabella. When Henry VII died, Henry VIII married Catherine, receiving an unremarkable papal dispensation from Pope Julius II (1503–1513), the nephew of Pope Sixtus IV (1471–1484).

These were typical Renaissance popes, entirely bent on using the papacy for this-worldly gain. Sixtus IV (Francesco della Rovere) acquired the papacy through massive bribes and immediately began turning "the Papal State[s] into an Italian principality by recourse to all means, lawful and unlawful," and then set about "the unseemly promoting of the Pope's relatives,"[4] endowing them with rich bishoprics and abbeys through his shameless nepotism. His nephew, Pope Julius II (Giuliano della Rovere), was "the most ferocious pope of the period," in historian Eamon Duffy's words. "Known to his contemporaries as *il terrible*, an untranslatable word that suggests a violent force of nature rather than a personality, Julius stormed up and down the Italian peninsula in his suit of silver armor at the head of his own troops."[5] Duffy continues, "There is no escaping the utterly secular character of such a pope. It was said of him that there was nothing of the priest about him but the cassock, and he did not always wear that."[6] All this just to remind us of the politicization

4 Hans-Georg Beck, Karl Fink, Josef Glazik, Erwin Iserloh, and Hans Wolter, *From the High Middle Ages to the Eve of the Reformation*, vol. IV of *History of the Church*, ed. Hubert Jedin and John Nolan (New York: Seabury, 1980), 543–544.

5 Eamon Duffy, *Saints and Sinners: A History of the Popes*, 3rd ed. (New Haven, CT: Yale University Press, 2006), 190.

6 Duffy, *Saints and Sinners*, 190.

of the papacy at this time and the corruption that helped to cause the Reformation.

We need to bring in the Holy Roman Empire as well. Interestingly enough, Henry VIII fancied himself a contender to be the emperor when Maximilian I died in 1519. After a great battle of bribery, it was actually Charles V who gained the imperial crown and reigned for forty years, outliving Henry VIII by almost a decade. Charles happened to be the nephew of Catherine of Aragon, and (understandably) ill-inclined to smile upon Henry VIII's soon-to-arise campaign for annulment from his aunt. Moreover, as the chief political defender of Catholicism against the Protestants, he would become an enemy of Henry's eventual break with Rome.

Ironically, Henry originally sided with the papacy when Luther's revolution first broke out in Germany, receiving the title of Defender of the Faith in 1521 from Pope Leo X (Giovanni di Lorenzo de' Medici) for his treatise, *Defense of the Seven Sacraments*. Henry's efforts here were more likely rooted in his political aspirations than any genuine religious conviction. One can hardly read his chapter defending the sacrament of marriage as heartfelt, given his string of mistresses—at the time of the writing he was bedding Mary Boleyn, a married woman and sister of Anne Boleyn, his future paramour. Pope Leo's character was not above reproach either. He had gained the papacy through the political maneuvering of his powerful father, Lorenzo de' Medici.

It was another Medici, Giulio di Giuliano de' Medici, who, as Pope Clement VII (1523–1534), clashed with Henry VIII's plans to annul his marriage to Catherine.

Clement was the illegitimate son of Lorenzo Medici's brother, Giuliano de' Medici. Giuliano was killed in the famous Pazzi Conspiracy, with full consent of Pope Sixtus IV, the Rovere family being the bitter political enemies of the Medicis. Pope Clement would formally deny Henry VIII's request for an annulment in 1527 (not unreasonably since there was no real theological or moral reason to grant it, and every reason to deny it politically, because, after the sack of Rome by Emperor Charles V, Clement was loathe to cross the imperial nephew of Catherine of Aragon).

A great tangled mess! We have every sympathy with the reader's struggle to keep this jumbled mass of politics, corruption, and ambition straight. If England is indeed the "cradle of biblical criticism," it was a cat's cradle, with multiple, intertwining strands creating knots of confusion for anyone attempting to straighten out the connections. With this tangle in mind, we may look at some of the important particularities of the Henrician revolution.

Our concern is with the politicizing effect of his revolution on the Bible, and nowhere is this more clear than in the great battle Henry initiated in 1527 over holy Scripture. Henry passionately believed that two passages from Leviticus would provide biblical warrant for his annulment from Catherine: "You shall not uncover the nakedness of your brother's wife; she is your brother's nakedness" (18:16) and "If a man takes his brother's wife, it is impurity; he has uncovered his brother's nakedness, they shall be childless" (20:21). Therefore, Henry reasoned, Pope Julius II's dispensation allowing him to marry his dead brother's wife was null and void. The Bible trumps the pope.

Not content with mere royal assertion, Henry decided

to enlist support from scholars. And so, as historian J. J. Scarisbrick reports, "a galaxy of Greek and Hebrew scholars, Christian and Jew, of theologians and canonists, of religious houses and universities, first in England and then on the Continent, were to be called upon to provide evidence for the king." This army of scholars was met by rival armies of those moved, for theological or political reasons, to support Catherine of Aragon's case against Henry. "By 1529–30 the king's divorce had occasioned an international debate as violent and swift-moving, though on a much smaller scale, as the contemporary conflict between Catholic and Protestant polemicists,"[7] where combatants wrestled over rival interpretations of Holy Writ.

In 1531, Henry had the results gathered into a "laborious pamphlet," to use the words of historian G. R. Elton, "which at length rehearsed the scriptural, patristic, early conciliar and medieval authorities on the King's side."[8] It was labor enough just to get through the title, which, like many works of the time, attempted to reveal the entire contents for those disinclined to go beyond the title page: *The Determination of the most famous and excellent Universities of Italy and France, that it is unlawful for a man to marry his brother's wife and that the pope hath no power to dispense therewith.*

By this time the unscrupulous Thomas Cromwell had risen in the political ranks to become the chief royal

[7] J. J. Scarisbrick, *Henry VIII* (Berkeley and Los Angeles: University of California Press, 1968), 164.

[8] G. R. Elton, *Policy and Police: The Enforcement of the Reformation in the Age of Thomas Cromwell* (Cambridge: Cambridge University Press, 1972), 174–175.

apologist and architect of Henry's revolution. At his command, the newly installed Archbishop of Canterbury, the pliable Thomas Cranmer, proclaimed Henry's marriage to Catherine annulled in May of 1533. In the fall of 1534, Henry's Parliament passed the Act of Supremacy, declaring "that the King our Sovereign Lord, his heirs and successors, kings of this realm, shall be taken, accepted, and reputed the only Supreme Head on earth of the Church of England, called *Anglicana Ecclesia*."[9]

Henry thereby became the head of the now nationalized church, a perfect example of a Marsilian king. As we recall, Wycliffe had not read Marsilius but came up with a similar reform scheme that subordinated the national church to the king, a case of resemblance without direct influence. Certainly, Wycliffe's scheme, through Lollard popularization, helped prepare the way for Henry to become "the only Supreme Head on earth of the Church of England." But with the Henrician court, the influence of Marsilius was quite direct. As historian Paul O'Grady points out, "In articulating the arguments for a national church directed by Henry, there was a wide search by Henrician polemicists for earlier works that developed a theory of national sovereignty. Chief among these was the *Defensor Pacis* of Marsilius." Marsilius was admired not only by Thomas Cromwell himself but also by a small phalanx of disciples of the *Defensor Pacis* whose common task it was to provide propaganda for Henry's new politi-

[9] Gerald Bray, ed., *Documents of the English Reformation* (Minneapolis, MN: Fortress Press, 1994), 113–114.

cal order.[10] Cromwell himself saw to the translation of an English edition of Marsilius's *Defensor Pacis*, completed in 1535. So it was that the Marsilian and Wycliffian strains of political subordination of the church to the state fused in Henry's revolution.

Marsilius was not the only influence in Henry's court. Machiavelli's arguments also made their way to England through a group of scholars that had been studying in Padua, Italy, where manuscripts of Machiavelli's works were circulating. Chief among these scholars were Richard Morison and Thomas Starkey, who entered the service of the king, under the guidance of Cromwell, in the 1530s. It is unlikely that Henry VIII read Machiavelli directly, but according to Reginald Pole, one of England's great intellectual lights who refused to go over to Henry's cause, Cromwell was deeply influenced by Machiavelli. While some scholars debate this, there is no doubt about Machiavelli's influence on the royal advisors and propagandists Morison and Starkey. Certainly, the brutality of Henry's actions in gaining control of Parliament and bending the church to his aims made him one of the greatest and earliest exemplars of Machiavelli's *The Prince.*

Given that Henry was now in complete control of the English church, bishops, theologians, and priests were under his direct political control as servants of the state. Thus Henry ended up creating the court theologians, the Scripture experts, "doctors and worshipers of the divine law" serving the crown advocated by Ockham, Marsilius,

[10] Paul O'Grady, *Henry VIII and the Conforming Catholics* (Collegeville, MN: The Liturgical Press, 1990), ch. 3.

and Wycliffe. Doubtless, Ockham and Wycliffe conceived of these theologians advising the king to have the aim of forming him properly in regard to God's Word. Just as certain, Marsilius intended them to be political servants using Scripture to buttress political power. While many such divines in the Church of England may have conceived of themselves along the lines of Ockham and Wycliffe, there can be no doubt that Henry and many of his chief advisors viewed them as Marsilius had envisioned.

We also need to say something about the Bible itself, given that Wycliffe had initiated the translation into English from the Latin. Henry soon enough came up with his own royal edition of the English Bible. By the time of Henry, Greek and Hebrew manuscripts were available, and so the drive to bypass the Latin Vulgate and get to the original languages had begun in earnest. In England, the result was William Tyndale's English translation, which surpassed Wycliffe's as the standard.

We'll take up Tyndale's story in a moment. But we first need to correct some common misconceptions about scriptural developments leading up to Tyndale. The drive to the original languages in biblical studies is popularly presented as entirely a Protestant effort, fueled by Luther's doctrine of *sola scriptura*. According to this account, the reform-minded humanist Erasmus produced his 1516 edition of the New Testament, with a Greek and a Latin translation on facing pages, and then Luther and other reformers set about translating the Bible into their own vernacular—all to the dismay of the Catholic hierarchy. This seemingly fulfilled the goal of Erasmus, who stated in the forward of the third edition of 1522 that he "would like to see it [the

New Testament] turned into all the languages there are."[11]

Erasmus's New Testament was not, however, the first scholarly attempt to recover the original languages. That honor goes to the *Complutensian Polyglot Bible*, the result of efforts begun in 1502 under the direction of Francisco Ximenes de Cisneros, a Spanish Catholic cardinal. This was an enormous scholarly work of six volumes, with the Bible laid out, column by column, in the original languages of the Old and New Testaments (Hebrew, Greek, and Aramaic), as well as the Septuagint Greek and Latin. The sixth volume included dictionaries of all these languages. It was not printed in full until 1520.

Cardinal Ximenes dedicated the *Polyglot* to Pope Leo X, laying out both the importance of having the original languages and the difficulties inherent in trying to translate texts from them. "There are many reasons, Holy Father, that impel us to print the languages of the original text of Holy Scripture," he began. "Words have their own unique character, and no translation of them, however complete, can entirely express their full meaning. This is especially the case in that language [Aramaic] which the Lord Himself spoke." Translatability from one language to another always runs up against this very difficulty, and the Bible was no exception. But the labors of translating from the original languages must be done because of the "diversity in the Latin manuscripts" with variant readings due, in part, to the "ignorance and negligence of copyists." So, like "St. Jerome and St. Augustine and other ecclesiastical

[11] See Desiderius Erasmus, *The Praise of Folly and Other Writings*, ed. and trans. Robert Adams (New York, NY: Norton, 1989), 134.

writers advise us to do," we must "examine the authenticity of the books of the Old Testament in the light of the correctness of the Hebrew text and of the New Testament in the light of the Greek copies."[12]

We see, then, that the popular version of the story is incorrect. The Catholic attempt to recover the original languages of the Bible preceded the Protestant Reformation, and (of course) the Reformation only added to the desire for more and earlier manuscripts. As we shall see, very soon the search for manuscripts in the original languages turned up even more copied manuscripts with more and more textual variations—the very problem that, as we saw in Chapter 1, brought the one-time Bible-believing evangelical Bart Ehrman to lose his faith.

We'll hold off on further discussion of translations and multiple manuscripts until the next chapter. Enough has been said to provide the proper background for our story of William Tyndale. Tyndale used Erasmus's Greek New Testament for his own English translation, of which over eighteen thousand were printed between 1526–1528. One might think that King Henry VIII would be pleased, but instead he gave orders to have him hunted down on the Continent—he'd left England in 1524.

Why? Two very real political reasons: the English peasant revolt of 1381 that was inspired by Wycliffe's English translation of the Bible, and the German peasant rebellion of 1524–1525 inspired by Luther's German trans-

[12] Quoted in John Olin, *Catholic Reform: From Cardinal Ximenes to the Council of Trent, 1495–1563* (New York: Fordham University Press, 1990), "Cardinal Ximenes' Dedicatory Prologue to the Complutensian Polyglot Bible, 1517," 61–64.

lation of the New Testament. At the command of Henry, English agents captured Tyndale in Antwerp in May of 1535, and he was strangled to death, his body burned at Vilvoorde in early October of 1536.

What no doubt worried Henry just as much as the Bible being translated into the vernacular was that Tyndale's translations came with marginalia that made his more radical Protestant leanings very clear, and the king did not want a Protestant reform that could inspire rebellion. He wanted a state church firmly under his control.

Tyndale, following Wycliffe, had tried to give him just that. In an effort to have the king treat his translating efforts favorably, Tyndale published *The Obedience of a Christian Man* (1528) explicitly to deny the belief that vernacular Bibles "causeth insurrection and teacheth the people to disobey their heads and governors, and moveth them to rise against their princes and to make all common and to make havoc of other men's goods."[13] On the contrary, Tyndale wrote, "Christ himself taught all obedience,"[14] and this was reaffirmed by St. Paul in Romans, Chapter 13, both being a continuation of the absolute rule of kings in the Old Testament. "For God hath made the king in every realm judge over all, and over him is there no judge. He that judgeth the king judgeth God, and he that resisteth the king resisteth God and damneth God's law and ordinance." Absolute obedience to the king is commanded by God, declared Tyndale, "though he be the

[13] William Tyndale, *The Obedience of a Christian Man*, ed. David Daniell (London: Penguin Books, 2000), "Prologue," 26.

[14] Tyndale, *The Obedience of a Christian Man*, "Prologue," 30.

greatest tyrant in the world."[15]

Henry VIII actually read Tyndale's *Obedience of a Christian Man*, a copy being given to him by Anne Boleyn after she'd read it approvingly. "This is a book for me and for all kings to read," he exclaimed enthusiastically.[16] Tyndale's theory, ironically, served to justify completely Henry's orders to have him rounded up and executed—and Anne beheaded, for that matter.

To add to the irony, Henry ultimately objected not to a translation of the Bible into English but to a translation that was not authorized *by him*. And so we have the *Great Bible* of 1539, sanctioned by Henry and his advisors, commissioned by Thomas Cromwell to be prepared by Myles Coverdale (who relied on Tyndale's translation, minus the parts that offended Henry). The frontispiece features Henry on his throne as Supreme Head of church and state, handing a copy of the Bible to Cromwell and Archbishop Cranmer. God floats approvingly overhead, much smaller than the king. A more concise picture of the politicization of the Bible couldn't be imagined.

The problem was, of course, that when new kings or queens of England entered the picture, a revolution in the Church of England and its interpretation of Scripture had to occur to conform to the ever-changing political conditions, as well as to the theological convictions of the rulers. The next king, Edward VI, Henry's son through his third wife, was a young man controlled by the more radical Protestant faction vying for control of England. Queen Mary

15 Tyndale, *The Obedience of a Christian Man*, 39–41.

16 Quoted in Scarisbrick, *Henry VIII*, 247.

I, the daughter of Henry and his first wife, tried to bring England back to Catholicism, an effort which was reversed by Elizabeth I, the daughter of Henry and his second wife, who brought England back to a very moderate version of the Anglican state church firmly under control of the crown. So ended the sixteenth century in England in a more settled version of Henry's church.

Things would not remain settled for long, as in the seventeenth century the crown began to lose its absolute control of Parliament, leading ultimately to the English Civil Wars of mid-century, where both the king and the people lose their heads, the first quite literally and the second metaphorically, in their frenzied embrace of radical political and biblical views. As we'll see, these wars give birth to a new emphasis on the political control of the interpretation of the Bible, which we'll examine in our chapters on Thomas Hobbes and John Locke.

To sum up this chapter, as stated at the beginning, Henry VIII represents well the various streams of influence we covered in Part I, from Marsilius's and Machiavelli's repaganized assertion of the state control of religion in general and the Bible in particular, to the Ockhamist and Wycliffian push for reform of the church through the state—all of which helped to politicize the Bible in England from the time of Henry forward.

In Part II, we will look in more detail at the philosophical revolution in the early seventeenth century that follows upon Machiavelli, one that redefines the whole cosmos according to the tenets of materialism that we've seen had arisen during the fifteenth and sixteenth centuries. Before going on to this philosophical revolution, we'll set out the confusions that followed from the renewed focus on the Bible from the Protestant doctrine of *sola scriptura* that helped set the stage.

PART II

Chapter Seven

THE FALLOUT FROM *SOLA SCRIPTURA*

WE MUST NOW EXAMINE in some more detail the fallout from the Protestant attempt to ground its reformation of Christianity entirely in the Bible alone—that is, in Luther's doctrine of *sola scriptura*. Since this is rather complex, we'll first set out an overview and then fill in some of the details.

We recall Luther rejected the Catholic Church's declared authority to be the interpreter of Scripture for two reasons. First, in his eyes, the evident corruption of the Church, especially the papacy, entirely undermined the Church's claim to be the divinely ordained, magisterial caretaker of orthodoxy through its tradition (*traditio*) of interpretation. Second, Luther's doctrine of justification by faith alone, *sola fide*, rendered the Church itself, as a sacerdotal institution, unnecessary: all that was needed, as other reformers urged against Luther's desire to keep two sacraments, was for the individual to accept the saving knowledge of Christ's sacrifice, which was readily available in the Bible.

Removing the Catholic Church's *traditio* as a locus of

authority guaranteed that almost the entire battle between Catholics and Protestants would therefore be fought on scriptural grounds. Since Luther claimed that the Catholic Church was an unscriptural aberration, Catholic apologists were very often led to argue the opposite, that the Church's institutional structure and doctrines were in fact grounded in Scripture and that it was the Protestants whose views were unbiblical.

As if this Catholic-Protestant battle over the holy text were not divisive enough, Protestants fought even more fervently over biblical interpretation amongst each other. As we recall, Luther almost immediately found that his fellow Protestants, using the same founding principle of *sola scriptura*, came up with quite different, irreconcilable views of the Christian faith. Precisely because all the reformers agreed that the Bible alone must be the authority to settle these deep disagreements, the textual, exegetical battles were even more heated between rival Protestants.

The interesting effect among Protestants was twofold. First, the doctrine of *sola scriptura* collapsed in less than a century, as disagreements about what the Bible actually said caused seemingly irreparable splintering, which had political ramifications. "By the middle of the sixteenth century," notes Michael Legaspi, "the Reformation had remade societies and governments: churches and territories across Europe lay in a patchwork of state-sponsored confessions, with the division between Lutheran and Reformed [Calvinist] often as rigid as the one between Catholic and Protestants."[1]

1 Michael Legaspi, *The Death of Scripture and the Rise of Biblical Studies*

In hindsight, the divisions seem inevitable. Moreover, the attempt of each theological party to vindicate its cause in the Bible necessitated a turn to the original languages, not just Hebrew and Greek but Aramaic as well. That, however, meant a search for, and confrontation with, multiple manuscripts in the original languages that brought to light variant readings, which themselves became part of the battle over what the Bible actually says. A key result was that no one could hope to participate in this increasingly divisive conflict unless he was very well versed in the ancient languages and the science of philology. The simple believers among the priesthood of all believers were soon left far behind.

And so, within Luther's century, the first cracks in what would later become the Great Divide were already opening between the simple believers and the academically trained biblical scholars, although at this point the latter were still believers. These scholars were, in fact, necessary to produce new translations in the vernacular, the Bible that was meant to serve as the authoritative text for believers unable to read the original languages. The predictable problem was that there were soon multiple vernacular translations in multiple languages, in significant part, following theological divisions. As Jonathan Sheehan observes, in both Germany and England, "Protestants developed the vernacular Bibles that symbolized their confessional commitments and their distinction from the authority of Rome," but these vernacular translations had to be redone as new manuscripts were discovered, a

(Oxford: Oxford University Press, 2010), 17.

process that seemed to call into question the solidity of the Bible.[2]

The result was that by the early 1600s a kind of exhaustion set in. Those in charge of each distinct Protestant confession realized that it was publicly unsettling to the faith that was supposed to be grounded in the absolutely true and unalterable Word of God if the printing presses kept churning out altered translations as scholars wrestled with variant readings that arose from the availability of more original language manuscripts. Since these theological divisions were also politically very unsettling, a solution fell together during the latter part of the sixteenth and early seventeenth centuries. Put a stop to new vernacular translations so that the common people may have a stable Bible; construct explicit theological confessions that allow the adherents of each position to define, as its own *traditio*, how their position understands the faith and consequently how it must understand the approved version of its vernacular Bible; and finally, let the scholars continue their work *without* disturbing the faithful.

And so arose the initial version of the Great Divide, with the lay faithful and those who minister to them on one side, and the academic biblical scholars on the other, although, as mentioned, it was not yet as great as the later divide, the Great Divide of today, that we've witnessed in the first chapter.

With this overview in place, we may now fill in some illuminating details. As we noted in our chapter on Henry

[2] Jonathan Sheehan, *The Enlightenment Bible: Translation, Scholarship, Culture* (Princeton and Oxford: Princeton University Press, 2005), xiii.

VIII, the return to the original languages predated Luther and his Reformation. The *Complutensian Polyglot Bible* was an enormous scholarly enterprise begun in 1502 under the direction of a Spanish Catholic cardinal, Francisco Ximenes de Cisneros.

Again, Cardinal Ximenes was clear that such an immense project was necessary because of the variety of readings in extant Latin manuscripts that called into question some of the translations in the Catholic Church's accepted and hallowed Latin Vulgate. The Vulgate was the Church's own version of the vernacular Bible. Latin was not some obscure language for the early Christians in the West. It was simultaneously the lingua franca of the Empire and the language of the common Roman citizen. Early Latin vernacular translations had existed, but somewhere around AD 380 Pope Damasus instructed Sophronius Eusebius Hieronymus, known to us as St. Jerome (347–420), to undertake revisions to the Latin, using the original languages for correction.

By the early 1500s, Latin had long ceased to be the vernacular, but the Vulgate functioned as the authoritative translation of the Bible as defined through centuries of the Catholic Church's *traditio* (understood not as "traditional" in the sense of something merely done for a long time, but as the deposit of faith originating in the Apostles and handed down, Latin *tradere*). Precisely *because* the Catholic Church's *traditio* was so long and deeply formed, it defined the framework of scriptural interpretation and retranslation as well. Cardinal Ximenes was undertaking the same kind of project as Jerome, setting up the scholarly apparatus to correct the Vulgate but doing so within the guardrails of centuries of *traditio*.

With long-established *traditio* as a framework, the difficulties posed by variants in ancient manuscripts did not cause the same kind of problem for Catholics as it would for Protestants. The Church, rooted in the Apostles, predated the writings of the New Testament and the settling of the New Testament canon itself, as well as any manuscripts that might still exist. Therefore (thought Catholics) the Church's *traditio* could sort through the variants in new manuscripts as they arose and decide which were authentic.

In turning away from *traditio* and grounding faith entirely in the biblical text, Luther created a problem for Protestants that the feverish search for ancient manuscripts was supposed to solve. Finding *the* original manuscript of the Bible became of the utmost importance so that the Latin Vulgate could be bypassed and the Bible could be rendered into new vernaculars directly from the original languages. Once this task was completed, these vernacular translations could function as the sole foundation of the faith. And so, as Sheehan aptly remarks, "Protestants praised translation as the cornerstone of their religious revolution," and thus "developed the vernacular Bibles that symbolized their confessional commitments and their distinction from the authority of Rome."[3]

The turn to the original languages was, therefore, the key to demonstrating that the Catholic Church's *traditio* was wrong and that (against other Protestants) one's particular confessional interpretation was right. Conse-

[3] Sheehan, *The Enlightenment Bible*, xiii.

quently, "translations were tools for consolidating biblical authority and wresting it from opponents," Catholic or Protestant.[4]

Interestingly, Erasmus, often credited with initiating this great push to the vernacular, was Catholic. Scholars have not quite figured out what manuscripts formed the foundation of the *Complutensian Polyglot*, but Erasmus gathered his Greek manuscripts (for the most part) from a collection of manuscripts in a Dominican monastery at Basle, and very hastily produced his Greek-Latin New Testament.[5] His second edition became the scholarly source for Luther's translation, and many others as well.

The problem was in the haste. As Bruce Metzger notes, Erasmus relied almost completely upon "two rather inferior manuscripts . . . dating from about the twelfth century." Even more questionable, when the one manuscript he had for the Book of Revelation lacked the last six verses, Erasmus simply "depended upon the Latin Vulgate, translating this text into Greek,"[6] thereby supplying the reader with an entirely fabricated version of the "original" Greek.

Even as others snatched up Erasmus's text and began their own translation efforts, Erasmus himself was revising his own, the fourth and final edition being issued in 1527. Interestingly, Erasmus "had seen Ximenes' Polyglot Bible shortly after the publication of his own third edition in 1522, and wisely decided to avail himself of its

[4] Sheehan, *The Enlightenment Bible*, xiii.

[5] See Bruce Metzger, *The Text of the New Testament: Its Transmission, Corruption, and Restoration*, 2nd ed. (New York and Oxford: Oxford University Press, 1968), 97–99, 269 (fn. for 99, line 9).

[6] Metzger, *The Text of the New Testament*, 99–100.

generally superior text in the improvement of his own." Metzger continues, "Erasmus' text is inferior in critical value to the Complutensian, yet because it was the first on the market and was available in a cheaper and more convenient form, it attained a much wider circulation and exercised a far greater influence than its rival," the *Complutensian*.[7]

Because Erasmus's Greek editions became authoritative, the scholarly shortcomings became the foundation of vernacular translations for the various Protestant efforts, and Erasmus's Greek itself took on almost holy status as a kind of *Textus Receptus*, especially as reproduced in the Stephanus editions of the mid-1500s (which also used the *Complutensian*).

The number of vernacular translations and retranslations produced in Luther's century is worth noting. In Germany, Luther's Bible went through multiple editions with at least seven significant revisions between 1534 and 1546. In England, there were five significant revisions between 1535 and 1571. Similar state-sponsored translations were made and revised in Switzerland, the Netherlands, and France during the 1500s.[8] "During the sixteenth century," Sheehan sums up, "the Protestant Bible across Europe was under pressure, unstable, and changeable."[9]

As already noted, the unfortunate result of the attempt to ground faith in the Bible alone was that, as new manu-

[7] Metzger, *The Text of the New Testament*, 102–103.

[8] Sheehan, *The Enlightenment Bible*, 15.

[9] Sheehan, *The Enlightenment Bible*, 14.

scripts were found and more scholarly efforts showed the inferiority of Erasmus's manuscripts and his scholarship, the divide between the accepted vernacular translations and the latest scholarship became increasingly greater. The continual revision itself was undermining *sola scriptura*. In Sheehan's words, "The principle of *sola scriptura* only functions if we know what the *scriptura* actually says: if there is no consensus about the *scriptura*, the principle has little weight."[10]

Again, the response was to stop the production of new translations and treat the favored vernacular version as authoritative—that is, as itself being the Word of God. Given the fusion of political and theological aims during this time, the need for political stability was just as deeply felt, and consequently, ceasing the production of new translations was a political act as well. This can be seen most clearly in Germany and England.

In Germany, for instance, "Lutherans invested Luther's Bible with the same divine attributes that they gave to Luther himself"; that is, Luther was pictured as directly and divinely inspired by God—just like the writers of the Bible themselves—in getting the original languages into the German vernacular. Ergo, so were the translations he produced. But Luther did not work alone as a singly inspired translator; he had to assemble "a court of scholarly assistants, in particular for the translation of the Old Testament, whose challenges," Luther himself confessed, he "could not face without [their] presence . . . and assis-

[10] Sheehan, *The Enlightenment Bible*, 16.

tance."[11] A host of scholars mediated between the Hebrew and Greek, and the final decisions in German.

We cannot forget the political dimension of his translation. As we've seen, Luther wanted his translation to stand as a bulwark against both Roman Catholics and reformers who disagreed with him, and both threatened the political order of the German principalities that accepted Lutheranism. He was especially concerned about the radicals—the Mr. Everybodies—who, like the peasants that caused the uprising, would pick up the vernacular translation and draw from it politically destructive conclusions. Luther's conservative reaction to the radicals made Lutheranism politically attractive. As historian Richard Marius remarks, "Princes found advantages to going over to the Lutheran side" given "his demand for obedience among the people."[12]

That meant, ultimately, state oversight of the Lutheran confession. In Luther's own Wittenberg, the Prince Elector of Saxony controlled the Lutheran churches, as overseen by his civil servants. This was not peculiar to Saxony, as historians R. W. Scribner and C. Scott Dixon show. "From the very beginning" of the Reformation in Germany, "*the institutionalization of reform was an erastian phenomenon*: that is, the church was subjected to the control of secular authority."[13] This did not arise with the Reformation but, as we've seen, was part of a long-standing desire of kings and princes in Europe to subordinate religious institutions

[11] Sheehan, *The Enlightenment Bible*, 8.

[12] Marius, *Martin Luther*, 434–435.

[13] R. W. Scribner and C. Scott Dixon, *The German Reformation*, 2nd ed. (New York: Palgrave Macmillan, 2003), 154.

to the state. The Protestant state needed a stable vernacular Bible to buttress its claims against Roman interference and more radical Protestant political unrest; Luther needed the state to protect his reforms from the same quarters.

We can see a variation of the same kind of political entanglements in England. The King James Bible was, as its name indicates, a translation done by a multitude of court scholars under the orders of King James I in the early 1600s. All English speakers recognize the hallowed status of this translation. Looking back at the actual situation in which it was produced, it's difficult to believe that the translating work of a small army of scholars was done with the Holy Spirit as Dove at each of their ears, especially if we add to the picture the impatient king hovering overhead, ensuring that the translation supported royal absolutism.

This translation was undertaken because King James I (1603–1625) believed the previously accepted English translation, the Geneva Bible, was politically seditious. It had been translated by more radical Protestant exiles during the rule of the very Catholic Queen Mary (1553–1558). Since they'd done it in the Republic of Geneva, the home base of John Calvin, it smacked of a more radical Reformed branch of Protestantism (in England, called the Puritans) than could appeal to the restored Anglican monarchy after Mary's execution. Queen Elizabeth I (1558–1603) put up with it—the Geneva translation having gained cultural ascendancy because it was inexpensively printed and, therefore, readily available—but King James would not.

The problem was even more in the notes than the translation, for they were, in King James's words, "very partial, untrue, seditious and savouring too much of dangerous and traitorous conceits."[14] Under the influence of Calvin, who lived in a republic and was therefore free to impugn tyrant kings, the Geneva Bible's notes boldly declared the opposite of Luther's call for absolute obedience: God wishes tyrant-kings to be overthrown. As Calvin said in one of his commentaries, "Earthly princes deprive themselves of all authority when they rise up against God, yea, they are unworthy to be counted amongst the company of men. We ought rather to spit in their faces than to obey them when they . . . spoil God of his right."[15]

The King James version was first printed in 1611 and became the only authorized version of the vernacular under James, the Supreme Head of both church and state. Soon enough, the only Geneva Bibles one could get had to be smuggled in from the Netherlands.[16] In a few short decades, there would be a revolution of those in England who were sympathetic to Calvin's Reformed theology, his commentaries, and the Geneva Bible: they would have their revenge in the English Civil Wars at mid-century.

Before tracing out wars and any further political developments in regard to vernacular translations, we need to return to the scholars. As noted above, even though particular vernacular versions of the Bible could be politically and theologically "frozen" for the sake of stability, the scholars

[14] Quoted in Christopher Hill, *The English Bible and the Seventeenth-Century Revolution* (London and New York: Penguin, 1994), 64.

[15] Quoted in Hill, *The English Bible and the Seventeenth-Century Revolution*, 59.

[16] Hill, *The English Bible and the Seventeenth-Century Revolution*, 58.

continued their labors. At first they stuck to reprinting the now-standard Greek of Erasmus, which formed the basis of the vernacular translations, but as more ancient manuscripts were collected, editions also included variant readings in the footnotes or margins, such as in Brian Walton's London Polyglot (1655–1657) and in John Mill's New Testament (1707). Mill's scholarship was attacked by some as unsettling to the faith because he included about thirty thousand textual variations. In 1734, Johann Albrecht Bengel, who was upset by Mill's variations, decided that he would include, in his footnotes, a ranking of the variants, designating which were, in his judgment, superior to the so-called Textus Receptus, for which he was roundly condemned as attacking the faith (even though his intention was to build it up).

We have noted these developments into the early eighteenth century to make clear that the trajectory of academic biblical scholarship climbed further and further away from the faithful's daily use of their vernacular translations. In other words, the Great Divide between the academic Bible and the vernacular that opened up in the sixteenth century just kept getting greater in the seventeenth.

Unfortunately, the seventeenth-century political scene in German and England became more, rather than less, tumultuous. We've already mentioned the English Civil Wars (1642–1651) but must add the more famous war of religion on the Continent, the Thirty Years' War (1618–1648). According to the insightful analyses of Sheehan and Michael Legaspi, these wars simultaneously made more clear the need for state-sanctioned vernacular translations of the Bible to buttress political order, and demonstrated the futility (at least to some) of trying to create stable politics with multiple, incompatible revealed texts.

Since the religious adherents of the different creeds could not settle their differences in the sixteenth century, the political rulers took matters even more into their own hands in the seventeenth. So it was, as Sheehan argues, that "in the end, the history of the seventeenth-century Bible followed that of seventeenth-century politics: *cuius regio, eius religio*," whose realm, his religion. The settlement that ended the Thirty Years' War "was matched by the tacit acceptance of *cuius religio, eius scriptura*," whose realm, his Scripture. "Stable Protestant theologies and stable Protestant theocracies needed stable vernacular Bibles" for the nonacademic laity who made up the vast majority of the political population.[17] (Nor must we forget that by this time, the Catholic Church had relented and produced its own vernacular translations from the Vulgate: in English, the Douay–Rheims Bible, published in parts between 1582–1610, the New Testament first, and then the Old Testament. But the Vulgate continued to function as the Church's Bible.)

Standing back and looking at these two centuries, we see that by the early 1600s both Catholics and all the main Protestant branches had their own translations of the Bible that functioned for the daily life of the priests, ministers, and laypersons, and each had its own *traditio* or confession that produced, used, and protected its translation. But the wars of the first half of the seventeenth century seemed to demonstrate the futility of trying to

[17] Sheehan, *The Enlightenment Bible*, 24.

bring political order through the emphasis on religious differences.

And here, oddly enough, is where the academic biblical scholars come back in. According to both Sheehan and Legaspi, the academics of the late seventeenth and eighteenth centuries came to the aid of the political and religious confusion, an effort that culminated in the historical-critical method as brought to its perfection in nineteenth-century Germany. They produced what Sheehan calls the Enlightenment Bible, a version of the Bible "created by scholars who saw that the scriptural Bible"—that is, the vernacular, confessional Bible—"embedded as it was in confessional particularities, was inimical to the socio-political project from which [the Enlightenment project and hence] Enlightenment universities drew their purpose and support."[18]

On this account, the eighteenth-century Enlightenment itself was a reaction to politically and socially destructive religious conflict among Christians in the previous two centuries, and sought to bring peace through a kind of academic deconstruction and reconstruction of the Bible, a project which hit full speed in nineteenth-century Germany. For Legaspi (following Sheehan), German academics of the nineteenth century were, therefore, "conservative progressives"—that is, they weren't radical secularizers who rejected the Bible but cautious Enlightenment progressives who retooled it for political use. They "took the cultural obsolescence of confessional Christianity for granted and aimed at the creation of an irenic social order based on reason,

[18] Legaspi, *The Death of Scripture and the Rise of Biblical Studies*, viii.

morality, and the growing power of the state."[19]

There is much merit in this argument, as we shall see. It explains, in part, how it is that academic Scripture scholarship became politicized as the result of scholars who sincerely wished to carry forward what they understood to be the core teachings of Christianity (almost invariably moral as opposed to doctrinal) and did so, in many instances, against increasingly hostile enemies of the faith.

Looking back over the previous chapters, this account connects nicely to what we deemed to be the origins of the modern historical-critical method. If Sheehan's and Legaspi's argument is accurate—and we think that it is, in the main—then in emphasizing the *irenic* political solution as defining the new approach to Scripture, historical-critical scholarship proved itself to be the heir of Marsilius of Padua's *Defensor Pacis*, where state-sponsored scholars use the Bible as a kind of political instrument that must be preserved culturally in order to stabilize and expand secular rule. A not unimportant task in nineteenth-century Germany, which finally saw its national unification and threw itself into the fateful pursuit of its imperial ambitions!

At the same time, their thesis needs significant amendment. To begin with, it seems to follow the self-understanding of historical-critical scholars themselves, the self-understanding that our *Politicizing the Bible* and the present work are calling into question. As we noted in the first chapter, historical-critical scholars almost invariably regard their origins as the eighteenth-century

[19] Legaspi, *The Death of Scripture and the Rise of Biblical Studies*, ix–x.

Enlightenment, which itself was defined by the new materialist scientific worldview that denied the possibility of the miraculous. The eighteenth-century Enlightenment also severely criticized revealed, biblically based religion as a source of irrational practices and bloody political conflict (looking back at the religious wars of the previous century as vindication of their views). Many Enlightenment luminaries, especially Voltaire, endlessly quipped from Lucretius, *tantum religio potuit suadere malorum*, "so great are the evil things religion is able to persuade men to do." It would seem, in many ways, that Sheehan and Legaspi are following this Enlightenment self-understanding that historical-critical scholars themselves generally embrace: the historical-critical method began in the eighteenth-century Enlightenment as a reaction to religious warfare.

Noting the influence of Lucretius helps us recall our thesis. As we've seen, the roots of modern historical-critical scholarship predate the Enlightenment by almost five centuries, the Thirty Years' War and English Civil War by three centuries, and the Reformation itself by two centuries. It cannot, then, be entirely characterized as a reaction to religious warfare in the 1600s.

Moreover, the philosophical roots of modern materialism stretch back even further, to pre-Christian ancient Greece (Epicurus) and Rome (Lucretius). The rediscovered manuscripts of these ancient materialist atomists had been circulating in Europe since the latter 1400s, gaining a growing number of adherents among the intelligentsia in the 1500s and 1600s, and defined the scientific revolution. This materialism helped define the entirely this-worldly aim of the new secular political philosophies (a point that will become even more clear in the following chapters) and was essential in the historical-critical desire to remove miracles from the text.

And so to see the development of the historical-critical method solely or principally as the result of the religious wars of the 1600s overlooks both the fact that the method's origins significantly predate these wars, as well as the immensely important influence on the intellectual transformation of European intellectual culture brought about by the recovery of pagan authors such as Epicurus and Lucretius, as well as the seminal contributions of thinkers like Marsilius and Machiavelli.

It also overlooks something of the utmost significance. The belief that the Thirty Years' War—the paradigmatic war that seemingly illustrates the Lucretian thesis that religion is *the* cause of political and social conflict—has been powerfully called into question by more recent scholarly research. As William Cavanaugh and others have cogently argued, the so-called wars of religion were *not* primarily concerned with doctrinal disputes; they were, rather, the final stages of the birth of modern centralized European states.[20] In other words, the source was *nationalism*, which, as we've seen, had its origin three centuries prior to the Thirty Years' War and, as we'll see in the next chapter, determined the way that existing religious differences would be politicized in the war.

[20] William T. Cavanaugh, *The Myth of Religious Violence: Secular Ideology and the Roots of Modern Conflict* (Oxford: Oxford University Press, 2009), 123–180; and Cavanaugh, "'A Fire Strong Enough to Consume the House': The Wars of Religion and the Rise of the State," *Modern Theology* 11 (1995): 397–420.

That is not to discount the ill effects of religious quarrels among Christians, but to put them in a deeper, more accurate historical perspective. It's clear that, in the Enlightenment *self*-understanding as it looked back on the previous two centuries, Lucretius seemed to be right: religion was *the* cause of war. If that were indeed the case, a reasonable response would be to transform the Bible from a weapon of slaughter wielded by sectarians into a peaceful political instrument benevolently employed by the state. This self-understanding would make sense of how certain key historical-critical scholars in the eighteenth and nineteenth centuries might understand their own efforts.

But if the Thirty Years' War was, in fact, far more political than religious, then the Enlightenment (historical-critical scholars included) misunderstood the deeper causes of the conflict. Or to put it another way, it just might be that the Enlightenment misunderstood the conflicts of the seventeenth century because it viewed the wars through the eyes of Lucretius, thereby mistaking religious division as the sole or primary cause of the war and a state-sponsored politicizing of the Bible as the cure.

A key consequence of this mistake would be that the Enlightenment solution of politicizing the Bible would not have, historically, the desired curative, irenic effects. That would seem to be the case: the nineteenth-century culmination of the historical-critical method in Germany's state-sponsored universities was also the century of the Franco-Prussian War (1870–1871), which solidified the unification of Germany and its attempt at empire. This, in turn, led to the nationalist wars of the twentieth century, World War I and II, the most destructive wars in history, wars which were not caused by religion.

But we are getting far ahead of ourselves. To return to the first half of the seventeenth century, we need to examine the Thirty Years' War in some detail to determine if it was actually more political than religious. That will allow us to assess the accuracy of the Enlightenment self-understanding. This will be even more rewarding if we could also reveal the origins of the Enlightenment view of the Thirty Years' War during the war itself.

As it turns out, all of this can be done by examining the writings of René Descartes, who not only lived during the war but also participated in it. Focusing on Descartes's philosophical revolution, hatched in the midst of the war (as he tells it), triples our reward since he is one of the great advocates of the new materialism, which ultimately denies that miracles can occur. It is of no small importance that Descartes considered his philosophical materialism to be *the* solution to the wars caused by religious quarrels. This will help us to sort out, in later chapters, the relationship between Descartes's solution and the later solutions of historical-critical scholars. To the Thirty Years' War and Descartes we now turn.

Chapter Eight

DESCARTES AND THE THIRTY YEARS' WAR

IF THE DIVISIONS between Christians were in fact *the* cause of the Thirty Years' War (1618–1648), then we would expect to find that it was a conflict in which Catholics fought Protestants over essentially theological disagreements. On this assumption, we should find the Catholic king of France, the Catholic Holy Roman Emperor, the Catholic rulers of the various German principalities, and of course the Catholic popes all lined up against the various German Protestant princes, kings, and dukes who were likewise uniting against their common Catholic foes.

But that is exactly what we don't find when we examine the actual complexities of the Thirty Years' War; instead, we find dynastic and nationalist claims at the heart of the conflict, claims that long predated this war and almost assuredly would have been sufficient to cause the Thirty Years' War *even if the Reformation had never happened.*

This becomes clear if we consider the inevitable clashes between the Holy Roman Emperor, whose theoretical imperial reach would cover all of Europe but whose practical attempts at making good his imperium conflicted directly with German princes (Catholic or Protestant), Catholic France, and the Papal States. If we add that by the early 1600s the Protestants themselves were deeply at odds, especially Lutherans versus Calvinists, we can understand that we are far from a simple Catholic-Protestant divide. To fully grasp this, we must step back into the sixteenth century and take a closer look at the conflicts leading up to the Thirty Years' War in the first half of the seventeenth.

The Holy Roman Emperor during the first half of the sixteenth century was Charles V (emperor, 1519–1556), a Spanish king of the Habsburg dynasty—his mother was Joanna the Mad, daughter of Ferdinand and Isabella, rulers of Spain, and his father was Philip the Handsome of the House of Habsburg, the son of Holy Roman Emperor Maximilian I. Thus, Spanish and imperial power were united in the very Catholic Charles, who thereby represented all three of these claims at once.

From the viewpoint of the Catholic king of France, the popes, and the Catholic and Lutheran Germanic princes, Charles was a common threat, and a very big one at that. Dynastically, he controlled Spain, the Netherlands, Austria, part of France, large parts of Italy, Bohemia, and Hungary. It looked as if he would swallow Europe and make good his claims to empire, thereby becoming a kind of second Charlemagne. To those under his shadow in the first half of the 1500s, it looked as if a *Spanish* king was about to impose *Spanish* Catholicism on everyone else, including the pope.

Understanding this, we can see what was really at issue

with the first so-called religious war, the Schmalkaldic War (1546–1547). The Lutherans had indeed created the Schmalkaldic League to thwart Charles's ambitions, but the reason Charles failed in his attempt to crush Protestant opposition was that the Catholic Valois monarchy in France threw its resources in with the Lutherans. We also note that German Catholic princes were equally opportunistic in this war: the Lutheran Duke Moritz of Saxony fought on the Catholic emperor's side against the other Lutheran princes, although when the political winds shifted, the Duke switched his alliance to the French Catholic king against the Spanish Catholic emperor.

The Peace of Augsburg (1555), which ended this phase of conflicts and enshrined the principle *cuius regio, euis religio*, was signed by Emperor Charles V precisely because Catholic opposition thwarted his imperial ambitions to impose one imperium, one faith on Europe. Furthermore, this principle of "whose realm, his religion" excluded all non-Lutheran Protestants, whom the Lutherans hated as much as, if not more than, Catholics. Charles's great Habsburgian holdings fell apart at this point as well and were thenceforth divided between the Spanish and Austrian branches of the dynasty. As a result, by the beginning of the 1600s, the imperial power diminished greatly, thereby enhancing the nationalist powers that conflicted with it (especially that of Catholic France).

The Thirty Years' War was therefore a continuation of the dynastic ambitions of the Austrian Habsburgs, as conflicting with the increased power of national kings (especially French) and local princes in still-divided Germany. We recall that Germany was not a united nation but a patchwork of principalities. As historian Richard Dunn well describes it, what we now call Germany was "divided into three hundred autonomous political units, of which at least three dozen had some importance. The real rulers of Germany were the local princes."[1] They ruled according to their own political advantage, with religion being considered as secondary and instrumental to their political aspirations.

This was, in the early 1600s, nothing new. In the previous century, the "German princes, Catholic and Lutheran, had in effect ganged up against the Habsburgs. They had observed, correctly enough, that Charles V had been trying not only to crush Protestantism but to increase Habsburg power and check the centrifugal tendencies within the empire." Essential to this effort had been the deft political use of religious differences. Dunn continues, "The princes, both Lutheran and Catholic, had . . . been trying to turn the Reformation crisis to their own personal advantage, by asserting new authority over the local churches, tightening ecclesiastical patronage, and squeezing more profit from church revenues."[2]

By the dawn of the 1600s, Calvinism had become, if anything, even more widespread and powerful than Lutheranism. A sign of this was that, of the seven Prince Electors of Germany who decided who would become the next Catholic Holy Roman Emperor, only one was Lutheran but two were Calvinist. As if that weren't enough, as we've

1 Richard Dunn, *The Age of Religious Wars, 1559–1715*, 2nd ed. (New York: W. W. Norton & Company, 1979), 60.

2 Dunn, *The Age of Religious Wars, 1559–1715*, 60.

mentioned already, Lutherans and Calvinists detested each other.

These very political intricacies intertwined with religious differences help explain the odd alliances, both before and during the Thirty Years' War. In the years just preceding the war, the Catholic League was formed in 1609 against the Protestant Union, but the Catholic League excluded the Austrian Habsburgs (since being swallowed by the Catholic emperor was as abhorrent as allowing Protestantism to spread and exert more power), and the Protestant Union received an immense boost from the French Catholic King Henry IV, who benefitted from everyone else's political weakness.

As is well known, the great military leader Gustavus Adolphus greatly helped the Protestant cause in the war, but even here, there is significant ambiguity. Adolphus was the Lutheran king of Sweden who, in the years just before the Thirty Years' War, was fighting with the equally Lutheran king of Denmark, Christian IV, over Baltic trade. Adolphus was an excellent military leader, but his cause was considerably helped along through subsidies from none other than France's Cardinal Richelieu, who believed that using the Lutherans against the Holy Roman Emperor would help France against the Habsburgs. It seems likely that the Catholic king and his cardinal were not the only ones to hold this opinion. Pope Urban VIII did as well. As historian S. H. Steinberg remarks, "Whether Urban actively subsidized Gustavus Adolphus is a matter of dispute; he certainly welcomed the successes of the Swedish and French armies."[3] Anything to keep the Catholic Habsburgs from gaining political control of the Papal States.

Clearly, then, religious beliefs were not primary for these figures. By contrast, they seemed to take a rather Machiavellian approach, using religion to support their political aims. We do not throw out this nefarious adjective casually. We've already seen the influence of Machiavelli in England. Since the early 1500s Machiavellianism had spread out through Europe as well, under the name of the doctrine of *raison d'état* ("reason of state"). According to this principle, rulers are justified in doing whatever contributes to the well-being of their state, all questions of morality and religion aside.[4]

As R. H. Steinberg explains, this was especially evident in Catholic France. "The emergence of France as the political and cultural leader of Europe" in the 1600s "was due largely to the fact that the French statesmen of the period," especially Cardinals Richelieu and Mazarin, "deliberately severed the traditional bond of religion and politics and made the novel concept of *raison d'état* their guiding principle." This Machiavellian "exclusion of religious standards enabled France to destroy Protestantism in France and to secure religious and political uniformity at home," the reli-

[3] Steinberg, *The 'Thirty Years War' and the Conflict for European Hegemony 1600–1660*, 13–14.

[4] On the spread of Machiavelli's ideas in regard to reason of state, see Friedrich Meinecke, *Machiavellianism: The Doctrine of* Raison d'Etat *and Its Place in Modern History*, trans. Douglas Scott (New York: Frederick A. Praeger, Publishers, 1965) and Peter Donaldson, *Machiavelli and Mystery of State* (Cambridge: Cambridge University Press, 1988).

gious serving the political, "and to perpetuate the split of western Christendom" elsewhere (so little did these cardinals regard Catholic unity as a desirable goal). For them, "public affairs were directed by a *raison d'état* which no longer needed and used supernatural arguments for the pursuit of worldly ends."[5]

And so divergent political aims dragged the war out, and in great part, it lasted so long because of the intractable conflict between the Catholic emperors and Catholic kings. However intricate its origins, "the war had become a Habsburg-Bourbon dynastic struggle, with the original religious, ethnic, and constitutional issues laid aside,"[6] notes Richard Dunn.

That wasn't the only reason the war lasted thirty years and caused so much damage. Just as significant was the large-scale use of private mercenary armies, who were mercenary in every sense. They were armies consisting *not* of zealous religious partisans but of professional soldiers driven by gain. Entirely unconcerned with the religious issues, they saw war as a way to earn a living, often a very lucrative one, especially for the successful leaders. Finishing the war quickly meant putting oneself out of a profitable job. And so mercenary armies kept their soldiers in the field, especially when the leaders were negotiating with various bidders, dragging out the war as a kind of strategy to increase the desperation of the bidding parties.

As a result, we see the same disregard for religious prin-

5 Steinberg, *The 'Thirty Years War' and the Conflict for European Hegemony 1600–1660*, 99.

6 Dunn, *The Age of Religious Wars, 1559–1715*, 89.

ciples found among army commanders as we do among the political rulers. Ernst von Mansfield, one of the key mercenary leaders, was himself a Catholic but was originally hired by Protestants. He later became a Calvinist, as Dunn remarks, switching "sides several times, always working for the highest bidder."[7] Von Mansfield's equal in the mercenary field was Albrecht von Wallenstein, a Protestant hired by the Catholic Emperor Ferdinand II.

That brings us to the soldiers themselves. They were not, as we just noted, religious partisans but professional soldiers for hire. "The raising, training and employment of armies in the first half of the seventeenth century was in essence a large-scale, private enterprise industry," S. H. Steinberg explains. In the Thirty Years' War, as elsewhere, "both the officers and the men regarded military service as a means of making money and furthering their private interests." Against the notion that combatants were enflamed by sectarian rivalries, we find that "love of adventure, hope of advancement, dissatisfaction or distress [with their previous situations] were the motives which induced men to flock to the standards raised by solvent entrepreneurs and to sell themselves to the highest bidder."[8]

Another reason that the war was so devastating for Germany was not the fierceness of the fighting itself but the fact that food and pay for the troops were largely gotten by booty and pillage, the burden of which fell on local populations. As armies depleted resources in one area, they

[7] Dunn, *The Age of Religious Wars, 1559–1715*, 84.

[8] Steinberg, *The 'Thirty Years War' and the Conflict for European Hegemony 1600–1660*, 99–100.

moved on to the next, bringing misery upon one location after another, even when they weren't fighting.[9]

Indeed, letting their soldiers loose on the local populations was actually a way for mercenary commanders to reward them and increase their loyalty. As one participant in the war explained, truly good leaders allowed their soldiers "some liberty of booty: to the end that they might prove the more resolute another time, for Souldiers will not refuse to undergoe any hazard, when they see their Officers willing to reward them with honour and profit."[10] Hence the wide-scale carnage of the German lands and civilians.

In the body count of the soldiers themselves, a large percentage of deaths was due to dysentery, caused by unsanitary conditions and insufficient food (and too much alcohol). When pay was too low and conditions poor, which was much of the time, mercenary soldiers would turn to pillaging for money and food, thereby taking an additional toll on the civilian populations.[11] None of this destruction had anything to do with religion but was, rather, inherent in the nature of mercenary warfare of the time.

One very important mercenary soldier, a young man about twenty-one years old, had signed up right at the start of the Thirty Years' War in 1618 as a volunteer in the army of Prince Maurice of Nassau, and hence was stationed in Holland. In this capacity, he was defending Protestantism against the Spanish-Austrian monarchy. A year later, that

[9] Richard Bonney, *The Thirty Years' War, 1618–1648* (Oxford: Osprey, 2002), 26.

[10] Bonney, *The Thirty Years' War, 1618–1648*, 71.

[11] Bonney, *The Thirty Years' War, 1618–1648*, 33–34.

same soldier found himself in Germany, having joined up with the army of the Catholic Duke of Bavaria, Maximilian I, taking up on the Catholic side. A typical mercenary.

The soldier's name? René Descartes.[12] In 1619, as he reports in his autobiographical *Discourse on Method*, "I was in Germany . . . where the wars—which are still continuing there—called me; and . . . the onset of winter held me up in quarters where . . . I remained for a whole day by myself in a small stove-heated room."[13] It was here in this *poêle* (a heated room he'd rented outside the city of Ulm to give himself some needed time away from his fellow soldiers) that Descartes allegedly conceived of a new mode of philosophizing, and thereby became the father of modern philosophy.

Readers of Descartes's *Discourse on Method* all too often overlook this important political-theological context of the birth of Cartesian philosophy, but Descartes himself indicates the importance. As he informs the reader, *he alone* is going to refound philosophy so that skepticism and confusion can once and for all be overthrown. This solitary work is necessary because "there is less perfection in works made of several pieces and in works made by the hands of several masters than in those works on which but one master has worked."[14] Seasoning his account with contrived humility,

[12] For a more thorough analysis of Descartes see Hahn and Wiker, *Politicizing the Bible*, ch. 7, "Descartes and the Secular Cosmos."

[13] Descartes, *Discourse on Method*, III.31. We use Donald Cress's translation from the original French edition, contained in Renè Descartes, *Discourse on Method* and *Meditations on First Philosophy* (Indianapolis, IN: Hackett Publishing Company, 1980).

[14] Descartes, *Discourse on Method*, II.11.

he asserts that *he* is that master, the master of knowledge who has contrived *the* philosophical method.

And then, as if in a kind of aside, he remarks that "it is quite certain that the state of the true religion, whose ordinances were fixed by God alone, ought to be incomparably better governed than all the others."[15] *Ought to be*. But the implication one draws is that Descartes wouldn't be sitting in the middle of a war between Catholics, Lutherans, and Calvinists *if* there were real religious certainty "fixed by God alone." Disunity in philosophy is the result of "several masters" working at odds and in fits and starts over time; unity is brought about by one master rebuilding amidst that disunity. The implication is that the disunity of Christianity is the result of many masters rather than one at work, and that disunity has serious and devastating political implications, as the Thirty Years' War seems to demonstrate.

As we have just seen, however, the Thirty Years' War was not actually primarily religious, although religious disagreements certainly played a considerable part. But whatever the reality, it certainly *seemed* that way to Descartes, and somehow his famous method, put forth in the context of that war, is offered as a cure for the ills of disunity and confusion in theology as well as in philosophy—and, we might wonder, in politics as well.

It will help us to assess Descartes's method if we first look at the effects of its widespread, almost immediate influence. His method of producing certainty was built upon a kind of scorched-earth skepticism: radical

[15] Descartes, *Discourse on Method*, II.12.

doubt cleared the ground upon which his philosophy was constructed. The historical effect of accepting Cartesianism, as the distinguished historian of skepticism Richard Popkin argues, was twofold: (1) "the launching of 'the new philosophy' with Descartes's presentation of his method for overcoming skepticism and his construction of the new metaphysical basis for science," and (2) "the unfolding of the theological consequences of a historical and critical approach to the Bible."

On this account, the historical-critical method is, in a very deep sense, Cartesianism applied to the Bible. In Popkin's words, "Modern philosophy issuing from Cartesianism and modern irreligion issuing from Bible criticism became two of the central ingredients in the making of the modern mind, the 'enlightened' scientific and rational outlook." These are not two separate developments but "parts of a common intellectual drama," wherein "the development of modern irreligion" is the effect of "the application of the Cartesian methodology and the Cartesian standard of true philosophical and scientific knowledge, to the evaluation of religious knowledge."[16]

If Popkin's assessment is correct, then the eighteenth-century Enlightenment view of reason, science, and religion and its assiduous application to the Bible in nineteenth-century Germany are both the result of a carefully crafted revolution birthed in early sixteenth-century Germany by a Frenchman amidst the ravages of the Thirty Years' War. For Descartes, the Thirty Years' War proved once

[16] Richard Popkin, "Cartesianism and Biblical Criticism," in *Problems of Cartesianism*, ed. Thomas Lennon, John Nicholas, and John Davis (Kingston and Montreal: McGill-Queen's University Press, 1982), 61–81; quotes from 61.

again the Lucretian assertion, "So great are the evil things religion is able to persuade men to do," *tantum religio potuit suadere malorum*, and Descartes's method, at its critical core, was designed to remove this evil once and for all.

Bringing in Lucretius awakens us to the possibility that Descartes was not as revolutionary as he himself declared, but fits snugly into the developments we've been tracing from the early 1300s. To understand all of this more clearly, we turn to an analysis of Descartes and his method.

The difficulty for this thesis would seem to be that rather than dwell on the true religion (Christianity in his *Discourse on Method*), Descartes humbly sets it aside from consideration so that he can concentrate on the philosophical task at hand. The important thing to note is the *way* he sets it aside.

Following Marsilius and Averroes before him, Descartes assumes a pose of humble fideism, informing the reader condescendingly that he "revered our theology, and I desired as much as the next man to go to heaven; but having learned as something very certain that the road is no less open to the most ignorant than to the most learned, and that the revealed truths leading to it are beyond our understanding, I would not have dared to subject them to my feeble reasonings."[17] For Descartes, then, reason is of no help in regard to revelation; faith is pure fideism, an act of the believing will.

Attentive readers may wonder if that might be, for Descartes, the cause of so much religious confusion, and hence conflict. He himself points out a problem with

[17] Descartes, *Discourse on Method*, I.6–8.

scriptural authority that increases the reader's suspicion, asserting that for the faithful "God's existence is to be believed in because it is taught in the Holy Scriptures, and, on the other hand . . . the Holy Scriptures are to be believed because they have God as their source." The reason for this circularity, he argues, is that "faith is a gift of God." [18]

A skeptic might then counter—bringing in Descartes's previous point—that if God is the master architect of the Bible, then the gift of faith should result in unity, not disagreement, over textual interpretation. The fact that reason is incapable of demonstrating anything in regard to faith—the assumption of fideism—would seem to be the cause of that disunity in biblical interpretation.

However, things are not that simple for Descartes, because philosophy itself is splintered into different sects, and has been for its entire history. That is why Descartes also professedly brushes aside the various claims of all previous philosophers: it would seem that reason itself suffers from the same kind of disunity as faith.

His proposed cure—ensconced in his method—is to discard everything that is in any way doubtable, on the assumption that only "the things we conceive very clearly and distinctly are all true." [19] Dubious things must not be clear and distinct or we wouldn't doubt them or disagree about them.

Descartes then goes about his famous exercise in finding ultimate certainty by subjecting everything to acidic skepticism, doubting anything and everything,

[18] Descartes, *Meditations on First Philosophy*, Dedication, 2.
[19] Descartes, *Discourse on Method*, IV.33.

including his own senses, and even whether he can know for certain that he is awake or dreaming. He ends this exercise with the alleged cure for all skepticism: that it is at least certain and clear to him that he must exist because he is engaged in the mental activity of doubting. In his words, "this truth—*I think, therefore I am*—was so firm and certain that the most extravagant suppositions of the skeptics were unable to shake it." He draws the conclusion that "I could accept it without scruple as the first principle of the philosophy I was seeking."[20]

There are several odd things about his method and conclusion. First of all, to declare one to be the first principle of philosophy is rather a high honor, given that God was considered to be the first principle by previous philosophers like Aristotle and St. Thomas. That would make Descartes himself a substitute for the creator.

Second, anyone familiar with Descartes's other writings knows he asserted that the only sciences that satisfied the twin criteria of truth, clarity and certainty, were mathematics and geometry, which he himself unified in a new creation of his, what we sometimes refer to as Cartesian geometry. The brilliance of this creation was that it allowed the precision of numbers to be united with geometric extension. What made this creation even more profound, for Descartes, was that he conceived of nature itself being *entirely reducible* to geometric (i.e., physical) extension. The result was that his new Cartesian geometry mapped directly onto nature itself and entirely described it: Descartes's nature *was itself* essentially geometric exten-

[20] Descartes, *Discourse on Method*, IV.32.

sion, and so his thoroughly materialist science of nature was completely clear and certain.

In Descartes's philosophical system intellectual skepticism is thereby overcome through a science of mathematized-geometrized nature. In this science alone, there is clarity and certainty, and hence truth. What makes it so clear and certain, however, is that both the science and nature itself are entirely determined, devoid of all contingency, where the laws of nature, as laws of mathematical-geometry, are necessary and unbreakable, allowing no variation, interruption, exception, or violation.

It would be more accurate to say that the skepticism still remains—in reason, in science, in the method—because all that is *not* amenable to the mathematical-geometric analysis of nature is dubious (or, as we have come to say, "subjective").

With the victory of Cartesian philosophy, it's quite easy to see what would happen to the Bible if scholars came to believe that to have a biblical *science* one must adopt a *method* that removed everything from holy Scripture that violated the mathematical-geometric laws of nature. They would of necessity produce a demythologized text, devoid of miracles, one that (since the miraculous foundations of revelation were removed) could not be a source of doctrinal disagreements.

As Popkin noted, that was indeed the result of applying Cartesian philosophy to the Bible, thereby making Descartes the creator of a method that defined how the Bible would thereafter be interpreted. It is as if Descartes himself had taken the place of the Holy Spirit, determining what interpretation of the Bible is allowed (which makes some sense of him putting himself in the divine position of the first principle of philosophy).

But he put himself in the place of the creator God in another, even deeper way at the end of the *Discourse on Method*. If nature is reducible to material geometric extension, then, like wax, we can remold it according to our will. We may let Descartes speak for himself about the possibilities.

> For these general notions [of my science] show me that it is possible to arrive at knowledge that is very useful in life and that in place of the speculative philosophy taught in the Schools, one can find a practical one, by which, knowing the force and the actions of fire, water, air, stars, the heavens, and all the other bodies that surround us . . . we could . . . make ourselves, as it were, masters and possessors of nature. This is desirable not only for the invention of an infinity of devices that would enable us to enjoy without pain the fruits of the earth and all the goods one finds in it, but also principally for the maintenance of health, which unquestionably is the first good and the foundation of all the other goods in this life; for even the mind depends so greatly upon the temperament and on the disposition of the organs of the body that, were it possible to find some means to make men generally more wise and competent than they have been up until now, I believe that one should look to medicine to find this means . . . [so that] we might rid ourselves of an infinity of maladies, both of body and mind,

> and even perhaps also the enfeeblement brought on by old age.[21]

The ultimate goal of his new science of nature is quite Promethean—his philosophical vision was, after all, conceived in front of a fire. Descartes here promises a kind of technological Eden, a new creation wrought by human power for human material ends. This is, of course, another key aspect of the Enlightenment vision; the miracles of applied materialist science would deliver a much different kind of salvation than that promised by the Bible. We might say that Descartes's method removes the miracles from the Bible to make room for the miracles in the laboratory.

This utopian technocratic vision fits very well with Marsilius's stunted understanding of politics, which leaves behind consideration of the soul and concentrates political life on the goods of the body. Those familiar with Descartes's arguments might wonder what has become of the soul, in these final words of the *Discourse*, especially since Descartes's famous proof of the existence of the soul declares that the soul doesn't depend on the body at all. In his earlier words, "I was a substance the whole essence or nature of which was merely to think, and which, in order to exist, needed no place and depended on no material thing. Thus this 'I,' that is, the soul through which I am what I am, is entirely distinct from the body."[22] Here, at the finale of the *Discourse*, the mind seems to depend entirely

21 Descartes, *Discourse on Method*, VI.61–62.
22 Descartes, *Discourse on Method*, IV.32–33.

on the body. Which is it?

That ambiguity is difficult to sort out, and it well represents the Cartesian dualism of soul and body wherein the soul, rather than being the form of the body, was instead a kind of ghost in the machine, unconnected to the body and at least implicitly redundant to its mechanical workings.

Whatever Descartes may have intended about the soul, we will find that two of the acknowledged "fathers" of modern Scripture scholarship, Thomas Hobbes and Benedict Spinoza, dropped the dualism and opted for pure materialism. Since they are also the intellectual fathers of the modern materialist view of nature and hence science, they are essential in our understanding why miracles were anathema to modern historical-critical scholarship.

In the next chapter we turn to Hobbes, who, like Descartes, set his intellectual efforts in the context of a war—in his case, the English Civil Wars. Whereas Descartes set aside faith to focus the reader's attention on the splendors of his new method, and let others sort out the implications for the analysis of the Bible, Hobbes embraced both materialism and biblical exegesis.

Since we end this chapter with mention of war, we might revisit our consideration of the Thirty Years' War that began this chapter. We have shown that scholars have successfully called into question the notion that this war was essentially religious. If its causes were actually political, then where did the notion that it was essentially religious come from?

In historian S. H. Steinberg's assessment, "The label of a 'war of religion' between Roman Catholics and Protestants has been attached to the 'Thirty Years War' by

German writers whose philosophy of history was determined successively by the rationalism of the eighteenth, the liberalism of the nineteenth and the agnosticism of the twentieth century."[23] In other words, it was an Enlightenment notion that was retroactively applied to the Thirty Years' War so as to confirm the Enlightenment assumption that (following Lucretius) if religion was subtracted, peace would be the result. If our arguments are correct, this Enlightenment notion can be traced back, in no small part, to Descartes, whose philosophical method did so much to form the understanding of method in the historical-critical method.

Seeing this now deepens our understanding of Sheehan and Legaspi's thesis that the historical-critical method, as it culminates in nineteenth-century Germany, had as its goal the perfection of a scholarly method of approaching the Bible that would produce the result of bringing peace where once there was religious discord. It is correct insofar as we understand how influential Cartesianism was in defining modern philosophy, and hence the self-understanding of the Enlightenment (and, consequently, of the historical-critical scholars). The German historians who recast the Thirty Years' War as primarily a war of religion and the German Scripture scholars who were busily removing all that was doubtful and miraculous from the biblical text were engaging in two sides of the same Cartesian project—and probably doing it in the very same universities, albeit in different departments.

[23] Steinberg, *The 'Thirty Years War' and the Conflict for European Hegemony 1600–1660*, 96.

Chapter Nine

THE ENGLISH CIVIL WARS AND THOMAS HOBBES

As with the Thirty Years' War, we must understand the political dimension of the English Civil Wars as well as the religious, and in England they were very tightly intertwined. If we boil it down to the essentials, the basics are as follows.

There were three political-religious factions in England: the king and the noble class, who were beneficiaries and proponents of the state Anglican Church; the non-noble rising commercial class, which was generally related to the Calvinist-based Presbyterian Church; and finally, the lower class, which consisted of the more radical Protestants, usually classed as religious Independents.

The king (in this instance, Charles I) ruled over Parliament, the state, and the Anglican Church. The nobles and bishops ruled England at the behest of the king through Parliament's House of Lords. The rising commercial class expressed their rule through Parliament's House of Commons, which, as they gained more economic and political power, came into greater conflict with the king and the noble class. The lower classes expressed their frustration at being ruled by everyone else.

The English Civil Wars, which began in 1642, were the result of commercial class rebellion against the monarchy and nobles. They were ultimately won by the commercial class because it brought on board the lower classes, thereby creating an immensely powerful army with their combined numbers. This was the famous New Model Army as headed by Oliver Cromwell.

Once Charles I was executed (on January 30, 1649) and the nobles routed, a Commonwealth was set up in mid-May of the same year. A Commonwealth was considered by its proponents to be the equivalent of the ancient Roman Republic (which likewise disposed of a king, Lucius Tarquinius Superbus, who was exiled rather than decapitated), an anti-monarchial, republican government ruled through a political assembly.

In this instance, however, the Parliament that declared England to be a Commonwealth was what remained after the more politically and theologically radical lower classes in Parliament had abolished the House of Lords and purged the House of Commons of its more moderate elements. The moderates were the commercial-class Presbyterians who had expressed both the desire to negotiate with Charles I and their horror at the lower class "rabble" in Parliament who had been politically empowered by military service in the New Model Army.

During the Commonwealth period, England was therefore ruled by the lower classes through a much-reduced Parliament (called the Rump Parliament), and a kind of democratic anarchy ensued, politically and religiously. The spread of the most radical political, theological, and social ideas was helped immensely by the complete breakdown of state censorship in the early 1640s, and the willingness of printers to print anything that would turn a profit.

To cite some important examples of the breakdown of order, the radical Diggers, Levellers, and Ranters used biblical authority, and in some cases entirely undermined it, in their attempts to overturn the established political-religious order. In 1649, the Diggers came into existence when six soldiers entered a church, declared the end of the Sabbath, church tithes, ministers, church magistrates, and the Bible itself—all of which had been used by those in power to keep the peasants from owning land that they could work and feed their families. They then marched outside to dig up the soil which they now claimed to be their own.[1]

Gerrard Winstanley, originally a Digger who became a True Leveller, reported that he had a religious vision that "the earth should be made a common treasury of livelihood to whole mankind, without respect of persons."[2] His politically leveling vision had its root in Scripture, asserted Winstanley, for "in the beginning of time the great creator, Reason, made the earth to be a common treasury," so "the poorest man hath as true a title and just right to the land as the richest man." The revolutionary result: "All laws that are not grounded upon equity and reason, not giving a uni-

1 See Christopher Hill, *The World Turned Upside Down: Radical Ideas during the English Revolution*, reprint ed. (London: Penguin Books, 1991), 110.

2 Hill, *The World Turned Upside Down*, 112.

versal freedom to all . . . ought . . . to be cut off with the King's head."[3]

This proclamation was equally alarming to the propertied classes that had been cut off from Parliament. Winstanley's interpretation of the Bible was as radical as his politics. For him, the Bible was, at best, an allegory of truths known by natural reason, and so he happily rejected the reality of the Garden of Eden, the Virgin Birth, and Jesus Christ's Resurrection.[4] Clearly, such ideas did not originate with twentieth- and twenty-first-century historical-critical scholars.

Ranter Jacob Bauthumley was even more radical, affirming outright pantheism, claiming that God "does not exist outside his creatures," so that God is in "this dog, this tobacco pipe, he is me and I am him"; he is "dog, cat, chair, [and] stool."[5] Since we are all God, then our actions must be holy; therefore (so some Ranters reasoned), we do not actually commit sins, no matter what we do.[6] And since we're God, then we obviously don't need any other alleged inspiration, so the Bible itself may be jettisoned. Not only was the Bible superfluous to Gods, but (sounding a Lucretian note) it "hath been the cause of all our misery and divisions . . . of all the blood that hath been shed in the world," and consequently, there would never be peace until all Bibles were burned![7]

[3] Quoted in Hill, *The World Turned Upside Down*, 132–133.

[4] Hill, *The World Turned Upside Down*, 144–145.

[5] See Hill's chapter on the Seekers and the Ranters, ch. 9. Quotes from 206.

[6] Hill, *The World Turned Upside Down*, 207–208.

[7] Hill, *The World Turned Upside Down*, 262–263.

Since this very Lucretian idea was mouthed by a politically radical Ranter in the midst of upending society, one can imagine that even (and perhaps especially) religious skeptics among the nobles and the commercial propertied classes in England were seeing the political need to reaffirm both political power and the Bible to shore it up. That would entail state-sponsored university churchmen to set the proper interpretation of Scripture, a kind of Divide where the academic elite would help the state control the masses.

In that regard, many religious radicals, who used the Bible rather than burning it, rejected the need for academic scholarship to mediate their access to the Bible. As Cobbler How explained, in his *The Sufficiency of the Spirits Teaching without Humane-Learning* (1640), the Spirit speaks directly to the reader of the text, and each reader must decide for himself what that Spirit is saying to him without any academic or political mediator.[8] The notion that, somehow, academic scholars could or should act as subordinates to political power was here, by Cobbler How, soundly rejected—all the more reason why some later philosophers and scholars might believe that their exegetical goal is to establish political peace, through scholarship and against political radicalism. As if to anticipate such retrenchment, many radicals like Cobbler How called for the abolition of universities precisely because, so they believed, biblical scholars worked to place layers of intellectual boundaries between the ordinary reader and the

8 Christopher Hill, *The English Bible and the Seventeenth-Century Revolution* (New York: Penguin, 1994), 198.

text *so that* the poor couldn't discover the Bible's fundamental revolutionary message.[9] (We are not far from the Marxist, and even feminist, biblical scholars we viewed in the first chapter, although they claim to be scholars taking the side of the oppressed masses.)

That politically revolutionary scriptural message, so declared Abiezer Coppe in *A Fiery Flying Roll* (1650), is that the Bible and political history make clear that "honour, nobility, gentility, property" have been "the cause of all the blood that ever hath been shed from the blood of the righteous Abel to the blood of the last Levellers that were shot to death."[10] Sounding a common exegetical theme of the radicals, Coppe was connecting Cain to the noble and propertied class, and Abel to the poor and politically powerless, and there was no doubt on whose side God was.

To fulfill the providential rule of the poor, the uneducated had to wrest the Bible from the hands of the politically powerful. As Arise Evans asserted, the Bible has been too long a political instrument of the oppressors, held "in great men's hands, so that they might do as they pleased with the people that knew little or no Scripture." For Evans, this justified the civil war itself: "Here is the Good Old Cause that God raised our Army to stand for," meaning, of course, the New Model Army.[11] The radical soldiers of

[9] Hill, *The English Bible and the Seventeenth-Century Revolution*, 198–200.

[10] Quoted in Hill, *The English Bible and the Seventeenth-Century Revolution*, 214.

[11] Quoted in Hill, *The English Bible and the Seventeenth-Century Revolution*, 229.

the New Model Army and their supporters believed that the generals, and especially Cromwell himself, had been chosen as the "rod of God" who have "a commission from the Lord to scourge England's oppressors" (as one Joseph Salmon proclaimed).[12]

Thus, in this time of political and intellectual turmoil, the Bible became politicized, and weaponized, from below. But, we must repeat, some radicals simply rejected Scripture entirely. As it was reported in 1656, a great many of them picked up on themes from Polybius, Livy, Critias, and Machiavelli, and so counted "the Scriptures mere inventions of wise men, to keep the simple in awe under their rulers," some asserting even that "Moses concocted the whole story of creation" as a means of political control.[13] Others, like William Erbery and William Walwyn, claimed that the number of contradictions found in the Bible undermined its alleged inspiration, thereby increasing the suspicion among the radicals that it was a merely human-made political instrument.[14]

If we understand this phase of the English Civil Wars and aftermath to be yet another instance of lower-class revolt connected to the peasant laity reading the Bible—that is, a variation of the Peasant Revolt in England of 1381 blamed on Wycliffe and the German Peasant revolt of 1524 blamed on Luther—then we can appreciate why

12 Quoted in Hill, *The English Bible and the Seventeenth-Century Revolution*, 216–217.

13 Hill, *The English Bible and the Seventeenth-Century Revolution*, 231, 234.

14 Hill, *The English Bible and the Seventeenth-Century Revolution*, 231–232.

royalists and parliamentarians would both want to regain political control of Scripture to avoid social chaos.

Beginning in December of 1653, the immediate political cure for such chaos was a military dictatorship headed by Cromwell, who was given the velvety-sounding title that gloved his iron hand, Lord Protector of the Commonwealth. Cromwell's own assessment of the Civil Wars was that "religion was not the thing at first contested for, but God brought it to that issue at last . . . and at last it proved that which was most dear to us."[15] This is, perhaps, a fair assessment, given that political and economic divisions were so closely connected to theological divisions.

After Oliver Cromwell died, and his son Richard showed he was not made of the same stuff as his father, the monarchy was restored in 1660, with the king's powers much reduced by Parliament. England was thereby returned to its original position, but it was now Parliament that dominated the nation politically. The Anglican Church was reestablished as the state church, where those in power wanted to ensure that religious and political radicals were firmly suppressed.

It was here, in these wars, that key English architects of the historical-critical method believed they saw with the utmost clarity the deep necessity of the political sovereign controlling the interpretation of the Bible for the sake of civil peace. Two of the most important of these architects were Thomas Hobbes and John Locke, who are, not coincidentally, also two of the most influential modern

[15] Quoted in Maurice Ashley, *The Greatness of Oliver Cromwell* (New York: Collier Books, 1962), 65.

political philosophers (along with Machiavelli). Given the political and religious anarchy brought about by the underclass revolt, both reaffirmed the absolute importance of the state regaining and keeping control of religion. In regard to the political use of the Bible, these two thinkers carried forward what came before them (i.e., all that we've witnessed in the previous chapters) and defined what came after them. In what remains of this chapter we will focus on Thomas Hobbes.

To summarize, in Hobbes's thought we find all of the following: Marsilius's complete reduction of politics to the goods of the body, the complete Marsilian subordination of the church and Scripture to the state (via a declaration of *sola scriptura*), and the ancient pagan belief revived by Averroes and Marsilius that religion is a purely political instrument invented by the wise to rule the masses; Ockham's nominalism united to Epicurean materialist atomism that incorporates a Cartesian-like mathematical-materialist account of nature which denies the existence of any and all spiritual entities and excludes the miraculous; Wycliffe's subordination of the English national church to the English state, as affirmed by the actual practices of Henry VIII; Machiavelli's complete denial of good and evil as the foundation for political reasoning, and his atheism as well.

All of these streams come together in Hobbes's most famous work, the *Leviathan*, which is, again, one of the most influential books of modern political philosophy. It is all too often overlooked that the *Leviathan* contains extensive exegeses of Scripture; indeed, his treatment of Christianity and the Bible takes up the entire second half of the book. His exegesis is marked by the union of all of these just-mentioned elements brought together for the sake of constructing a lasting civil peace—a very Marsilian goal indeed. As we shall see, Hobbes's *method* of approaching the Bible is defined by the union of the above-mentioned elements, all bent to his very secular political aim.

Hobbes was born in 1588 during the reign of Queen Elizabeth I. While James I ruled England (1603–1625), young Hobbes was a secretary to Francis Bacon. As a tutor to nobles, he spent much of his time in Europe during the Thirty Years' War and returned to England in the midst of the reign of Charles I (1625–1649). On his various forays in Europe, he met both Galileo and Descartes (with whom he had a kind of intellectual sibling rivalry in regard to his advocacy of the new materialism) and became friends with the chief advocate of Epicurean atomism, Fr. Pierre Gassendi.

As an advocate of royal supremacy, Hobbes realized his pro-royalist writings would bring him into conflict with the increasingly rebellious House of Commons in Parliament, so in late 1640 he escaped to Europe just before the outbreak of the First Civil War, and would not return until 1651 (the year his *Leviathan* was published). England was still in the midst of the democratic anarchy of the Commonwealth, which the dictatorship of Cromwell would cure.

The publication of the *Leviathan* in 1651 put Hobbes's entirely materialistic account of nature and human nature in full public view, thereby solidifying Hobbes's reputation as England's chief atheist. The deliciously lengthy title of one of Bishop John Bramhall's writings against Hobbes, *The Catching of Leviathan* (1658), well represents the preponderant reaction at the time: *The Catching of Leviathan, or the Great Whale. Demonstrating, out of Mr. Hobs his own Works, That no man who is thoroughly an Hobbist, can be a good Christian, or a good Common-wealths man, or reconcile himself to himself because his Principles are not only destructive to all Religion, but to all Societies; extinguishing the Relation between Prince and Subject, Parent and Child, Master and Servant, Husband and Wife: and abound with palpable contradictions.*

As the *Leviathan*'s arguments became better and better known, Hobbes's reputation as the Godless wrecker of all things good only grew. After the Great Fire of 1666 burned four-fifths of London, a committee within the House of Commons was given the task to "receive Informacion toucheing such bookes as tend to Atheisme Blasphemy or Prophanenesse or against the Essence or Attributes of God. And in particular . . . the booke of Mr Hobbs called the Leuiathan."[16] The fire in the ominous year could only have been God's punishment for allowing such a scoundrel to live in England.

Hobbes earned his reputation, and so it's hard to choose the most alarming aspects of his arguments. Certainly his complete denial of good and evil rank, and rankled, highly. As he argued, "Good, Evill, and Contemptible, are ever used with relation to the person that useth them: There being nothing simply and absolutely so; nor any common Rule of Good and Evill, to be taken from the nature of the

[16] Quoted in Noel Malcolm, "A Summary Biography of Hobbes," in *The Cambridge Companion to Hobbes*, ed. Tom Sorell (Cambridge: Cambridge University Press, 1996), 35–36.

objects themselves."[17] There was also his famous declaration that our natural state was one of war, which since there was no rule of good and evil in nature, "to this warre of every man against every man, this also is consequent; that nothing can be Unjust. The notions of Right and Wrong, Justice and Injustice have there no place. Where there is no common Power, there is no Law: where no Law, no Injustice. Force, and Fraud, are in warre the two Cardinall virtues."[18] All of this led to the conclusion that, in order to save ourselves from mutual self-destruction in war, we must submit to the absolutely arbitrary will of the civil sovereign, another repugnant concept. Of course, when the chaotic Civil Wars produced governmental anarchy that was finally remedied by the dictatorship of Cromwell, Hobbes no doubt felt that history had illustrated the central political thesis of the *Leviathan.*

At the heart of all of these alarming statements was Hobbes's most shocking argument of all, his straightforward, uncompromising materialism. "The World, (I mean . . . the *Universe*, that is, the whole masse of all things that are) is Corporeall, that is to say, Body; . . . and that which is not Body, is no part of the Universe: And because the Universe is All, that which is no part of it, is *Nothing*; and consequently *no where*."[19] What was real, ultimately,

[17] Thomas Hobbes, *Hobbes's Leviathan*, reprint of the 1651 edition of *Leviathan, or The Matter, Forme, & Power of a Common-wealth Ecclesiasticall and Civill* (Oxford: Clarendon Press, 1965), I.6, pp. 39–41 [23–24]. See also I.15, 122–123 [79–80]. From here onward pagination will be from the Clarendon Press reprint of 1965, but the page numbers of the original edition will be put in brackets.

[18] Hobbes, *Leviathan*, I.13, 98 [63].

[19] Hobbes, *Leviathan*, IV.46, 524.

were material atoms, and so everything could be reduced to the motion and position of these atoms. What appears to be real to us in our everyday experience—cows, pigs, oak trees—is reducible to the invisible material substrate. Hence, "cow" or "pig" or "oak tree" are merely convenient and conventional *names* we use on the level of experience; there are no universal species or forms, as Aristotle had argued. (Hobbes thereby united Ockham's nominalism with Epicurean atomism, a union that yielded the conclusion we've mentioned above, that the names "good" and "evil" have no substance but are merely names we attach to whatever happens to affect our own particular atomic constitution causing us, respectively, pleasure and pain.)

The direct implication of this materialism—already clearly seen in Epicureanism—was that there was no such thing as an immaterial soul. For Hobbes, this was important because the belief in the immaterial soul that could leave the body after death was the source of the belief in ghosts, and this belief kept "in credit the use of Exorcisme, of Crosses, of holy Water, and other such inventions of Ghostly men."[20]

By "Ghostly men," Hobbes was mainly referring to Catholic priests, who, in their fundamental allegiance to Rome, represented a source of political rebellion within the English realm. But if (in accordance with materialism) there are no souls and hence no disembodied spirits walking the Earth striking fear into the uneducated, the power of the priests would be significantly reduced. In Hobbes's very political and pointed words, "If this super-

[20] Hobbes, *Leviathan*, I.2, 17 [7].

stitious fear of Spirits were taken away, . . . and many other things depending thereon, by which, crafty ambitious persons abuse the simple people, men would be much more fitted than they are for civill Obedience."[21]

If disembodied spirits are impossible, then they can be removed from the Bible. One can now see quite clearly why Hobbes informed the reader in his Epistle Dedicatory to the *Leviathan*, "That which perhaps may most offend [readers], are certain Texts of Holy Scripture, alledged by me to other purpose than ordinarily they use to be by others. But I have done it with due submission, and also (in order to my Subject) necessarily; for they [i.e., certain passages of Scripture] are the Outworks of the Enemy, from whence they impugne the Civill Power."[22] Removing immaterial spirits from the text—a task routinely done by later proponents of the historical-critical method—was defined by Hobbes in terms of an overtly political goal. This does not remain, for Hobbes, an abstract premise. It becomes an essential aspect of Hobbes's *method* of biblical exegesis. Since there cannot really be immaterial entities, then all references to "spirit" in the Old and New Testaments, even the Spirit of God, are merely *metaphorical.*

To give just a few examples of Hobbes's extensive, politicized exegesis, the Spirit of God moving upon the waters in Genesis 1:2 actually meant "Wind," which as a material cause was doing "God's work."[23] In Genesis 41:38, Spirit of God was a metaphor for wisdom in Joseph, and in Exodus

21 Hobbes, *Leviathan*, I.2, 17–18 [7–8].

22 Hobbes, *Leviathan*, Epistle Dedicatory. The dedication is to "Mr Francis Godophin."

23 Hobbes, *Leviathan*, III.34, 304 [208].

28:3, where God instructed Moses "to speak to the wise of heart, whom I have filled with a spirit of wisdom" to make Aaron's garments, it only meant a certain kind of skill displayed in a particular type of artisanship.[24] When the Bible referred to the spirit of wisdom, understanding, counsel, fortitude, or fear, what was "manifestly . . . meant, [was] not so many Ghosts, but so many eminent *graces* that God would give him [i.e., the recipient]."[25] The word spirit might also merely refer to "extraordinary Zeal, and Courage," as in Judges and Samuel.[26] Hobbes at his most thoroughly Epicurean even asserted that in Genesis 2:7, where it states that God breathed into man the breath of life, it actually meant that God gave him life, "not that any Ghost, or incorporeall substance entred into; and possessed his body."[27] Turning to the New Testament, Hobbes informed the reader that when St. Paul (in Romans 8:9) used the term "*Spirit of Christ*," he did not mean "thereby the *Ghost* of Christ, but a *submission* to his doctrine."[28] And finally, when the text referred to Jesus himself as full of the Holy Ghost or Holy Spirit, these "may be understood, for *Zeal* to doe the work for which hee was sent by God the Father."[29]

What is so interesting about Hobbes's materialist exegetical efforts in these instances is both how novel they

[24] Hobbes, *Leviathan*, I.8, 60 [38] and III.34, 304–305 [209].

[25] Hobbes, *Leviathan*, III.34, 305 [209]. Hobbes cites Exodus 31:3–6, 35:31, and Isaiah 11:2–3.

[26] Hobbes, *Leviathan*, III.34, 305 [209]. Hobbes cites Judges 3:10, 6:34, 11:29, 13:25, 14:16–19, and I Samuel 11:6 and 19:20.

[27] Hobbes, *Leviathan*, III.34, 306 [209]. Hobbes cites Job 27:3 and Ezekiel 2:30.

[28] Hobbes, *Leviathan*, III.34, 306 [210].

[29] Hobbes, *Leviathan*, III.34, 306 [210].

were then (hence, the reason for so many accusations of his atheism) and how very ordinary such arguments have become among historical-critical scholars of the nineteenth, twentieth, and now twenty-first century.

We must not forget the political context of the applied materialism of his method of exegesis. Again, for Hobbes the existence of spirits led, politically, to rebellion—that is, to a house (or kingdom) divided—and "*a Kingdome divided in it selfe cannot stand*." The king must therefore have complete control over religion, as Henry VIII himself declared in his Act of Supremacy, and the existence of immaterial entities would always threaten his sovereignty, for "men will be frighted into rebellion with the feare of Spirits."[30] By this Hobbes meant not only at the behest of Catholic priests, but also in regard to the radical Protestant Independents who claimed immediate inspiration by the Spirit to upend England and throw it into civil war and democratic chaos.

There must be one sovereign, and one religion completely under his control. That is why the sovereign political authority *should* adopt Hobbes's materialist mode of exegesis—at least according to Hobbes. In displaying his absolutist state-affirming exegesis, Hobbes set out a much clearer account both of *why* the political sovereign needs court theologians and the *method* they should employ in their interpretation of the Bible.

Based on his materialist foundation, it might seem that Hobbes would have eliminated all miracles. He does, but not quite. The point of any actual miracles is not to reveal

[30] Hobbes, *Leviathan*, II.18, 139 [92–93].

God's power, Hobbes declared, but to confirm the authority of the political sovereign whose rule comes directly from God (Moses being a key example for Hobbes, who, like Machiavelli, turns Moses into a political ruler). Such few miracles as have happened were, then, only "*for the making manifest to his elect, the mission of an extraordinary Minister for their salvation*,"[31] the minister being the political sovereign. The goal of any miracle, consequently, is entirely for the sake of buttressing the power of political sovereigns, so as to render "men . . . the better inclined to obey them."[32] Miracles disrupt civil peace; therefore, the sovereign, as Defender of the Peace (to recall Marsilius), must control them—but that was, of course, the counsel of the wise pagans and Machiavelli as well.

And so, in the present day, "Gods Supreme Lieutenant," the "Soveraign power," is the judge of all miracles, both past and present, including whether there is the miracle of the transformation of the Eucharist, so that "if a man pretend, that after certain words spoken over a peece of bread, that presently God hath made it not bread, but a God, or a man, or both, and neverthelesse it looketh still as like bread as ever it did; there is no reason for any man to think it really done; nor consequently to fear him, till he enquire of God, by his Vicar, or Lieutenant [i.e., the political sovereign], whether it be done or not."[33]

The political sovereign must exercise this same absolute power over the Bible itself, for "Soveraigns in their

[31] Hobbes, *Leviathan*, III.37, 341 [235].

[32] Hobbes, *Leviathan*, III.37, 339 [234].

[33] Hobbes, *Leviathan*, III.37, 344 [237].

own Dominions are the sole Legislators; [so that] those Books only are Canonicall . . . which are established for such by the Soveraign Authority."[34] His political authority even reaches up to God, for only those "Attributes [of God] which the Soveraign ordaineth" are to be permitted.[35]

Never one to shrink from making startling claims through scriptural exegesis, Hobbes even asserted that the absolute political authority over the Bible comes from the Bible. "Moses, and Aaron, and the succeeding High Priests were Civill Soveraigns," Hobbes argued, and since they were in charge of the Law, therefore, "the Canonizing, or making of the Scripture Law, belonged to the Civill Soveraigne."[36] In fact, all laws were "made Canonicall by Moses the Civill Soveraign," a surprise, perhaps, to those who thought God gave the Law.[37]

In an exegetical move to reinforce this point, one that foreshadowed many a historical-critical scholar two and three centuries later, Hobbes declared that the entire Old Testament including the Prophets was "lost in the [Babylonian] Captivity and sack of the City of Jerusalem," but found and re-canonized under Ezra after captivity. In short, the Old Testament canon as we largely know it was not the work of the Holy Spirit or the Church but of a single political sovereign in whom religious and political power were fused: Ezra was the "High Priest" and hence also "their Civill Soveraigne"; therefore "it is manifest, that

[34] Hobbes, *Leviathan*, III.33, 291 [199].

[35] Hobbes, *Leviathan*, II.31, 283 [193].

[36] Hobbes, *Leviathan*, III.42, 403–404 [282].

[37] Hobbes, *Leviathan*, III.42, 404 [283].

the Scriptures were never made Laws, but by the Soveraign Civill Power."[38]

Hobbes took his own advice about absolute obedience to the will of the sovereign in these matters, proclaiming, "I can acknowledge no other Books of the Old Testament, to be Holy Scripture, but those which have been commanded to be acknowledged for such, by the Authority of the Church of *England*."[39]

It might seem that the New Testament canon would have been the result of the early Church, through the Holy Spirit, defining what books were truly inspired, but this Hobbes would not allow, for it might give power of the church over the state. So Hobbes argued that, prior to the early fourth-century emperor Constantine, there "were not obligatory Canons, that is, Laws, but onely good, and safe advice," found in a variety of writings, "for the direction of sinners in the way of salvation, which every man might take, and refuse at his owne peril, without injustice."[40] The New Testament canon only came about because it was "authorized by Constantine the Emperour," thereby proving that "the Books of the New Testament, though most perfect Rules of Christian Doctrine, could not be made Laws by any other authority then [sic] that of Kings, or Soveraign Assemblies."[41]

And so there is no other aspect to Scripture than the political, both in constitution and aim. "In summe, the

[38] Hobbes, *Leviathan*, III.42, 405 [283–284].

[39] Hobbes, *Leviathan*, III.33, 291–292 [199].

[40] Hobbes, *Leviathan*, III.42, 406–407 [284–285].

[41] Hobbes, *Leviathan*, III.42, 410 [287].

Histories and the Prophecies of the old Testament, and the Gospels and Epistles of the New Testament, have had one and the same scope, to convert men to the obedience of God," or more exactly, to those who "did represent the person of God."[42]

In Hobbes, we therefore have the first (but not the last) exhaustive attempt at politicizing the Bible, one that carries forth the seeds sown from the early fourteenth century onward and brings them all into full bloom.

Taking all this together, one can certainly say that Marsilius (or Machiavelli, for that matter) could not hope for a more radical subordination of Scripture to the state. But that raises a question: If Hobbes goes so far in politically redefining the Bible, and his philosophical foundation is so obviously indebted to Epicurean materialism, why doesn't he simply eliminate religion entirely?

The answer is that he agreed with Marsilius, Machiavelli, and the ancient pagans about the necessity of religion as an instrument of political rule. The natural "seeds" of religion, he informed readers, are ineradicable, and wise men use them for political purposes. In his account, which could have been lifted directly out of Book Five of Lucretius's *De Rerum Natura*, Hobbes argued that we poor human beings are continually troubled by "Anxiety." Every man "in the care of future time, hath his heart all the day long, gnawed on by feare of death, poverty, or other calamity." This would be bad enough, but it is coupled with belief in invisible, immaterial powers that control our lives, and hence multiply our anxiety. Thus arises the belief that "good, or

[42] Hobbes, *Leviathan*, III.33, 299 [204].

evill fortune" is caused by "some *Power*, or Agent *Invisible*." The "old Poets" were right, Hobbes concluded: "The Gods were at first created by humane Feare," coupled with ignorance (unaware that in a material universe immaterial beings cannot exist).[43]

These "seeds" of religion, fear and ignorance, Hobbes maintained, "have received culture from two sorts of men." The first are the wise pagans, praised by Critias, Polybius, Livy, Plutarch, Marsilius, and Machiavelli—those who "have nourished, and ordered them [the seeds], according to their own invention." The second are those who "have done it, by Gods commandement, and direction." But whether pagan or Judeo-Christian, the political aim is identical: "Both sorts have done it, with a purpose to make those men that relyed on them, the more apt to Obedience, Lawes, Peace, Charity, and civill Society."[44]

Almost certainly Hobbes considered himself among the line running from Critias up through Machiavelli, a sign of which is that he reduced the Judeo-Christian God's purposes to the same political level as those of the pagan gods. But *that* should make us very, very hermeneutically suspicious of Hobbes's extended, detailed exegetical efforts that define the second half of the *Leviathan*, especially as Hobbes is regarded even by contemporary Scripture scholars as a kind of distant father of the modern historical-critical method.

The usual reason for this attribution is that Hobbes was one of the first to deny the Mosaic authorship of the

[43] Hobbes, *Leviathan*, I.12, 82–83 [52–53].

[44] Hobbes, *Leviathan*, I.12, 85 [54].

Pentateuch. Even that attribution is highly inaccurate, showing only a passing acquaintance by historical-critical scholars and historians with the *Leviathan*'s extended treatment of the Bible. Hobbes did somewhat qualify Moses's authorship, arguing that (for example) since Deuteronomy 34:5–12 spoke of Moses's death, "it is therefore sufficiently evident, that the five Books of *Moses* were written after his time, though how long after it be not so manifest."[45] But Hobbes wasn't completely denying Mosaic authorship: "Though *Moses* did not compile those Books entirely, and in the form we have them; yet he wrote all that which hee is there said to have written."[46]

The real importance of Hobbes's treatment of Moses for understanding the history of modern biblical scholarship is not that he mildly qualified Mosaic authorship, but as we have seen above, that he made Moses into a prototype of Hobbes's political sovereign who controls every aspect of religion for the sake of civil peace. It is this *political* goal that defines his entire *method* of scriptural interpretation, one that in so many ways adumbrates the later developments among historical-critical scholars.

As noted above, Hobbes returned to England and published his *Leviathan* in the same year, 1651, during the time that the increasingly anarchic democratic Rump Parliament tried to rule over an increasingly anarchic democratic Commonwealth. One notes, in reading the *Leviathan*, that Hobbes referred to England being a Commonwealth but spoke more often of the locus of political power being in

[45] Hobbes, *Leviathan*, III.33, 293 [200].

[46] Hobbes, *Leviathan*, III.33, 293 [200].

the Sovereign—a wide enough term for Rump Parliamentarians to infer that he was speaking of the sovereign power residing in the people through its representative government. Of course, he was already well-known as a royalist, and so it is doubtful that anyone was fooled by Hobbes's deference to England's quavering democracy: the *Leviathan* clearly affirmed absolute monarchy in theory of the kind that even Henry VIII hadn't achieved in practice.

That made Hobbes's *Leviathan* unacceptable to the intellectual, political, and religious radicals *and* moderates. When moderates joined with royalists in reinstating England's monarchy with Charles II in 1660, the king's power was significantly qualified by Parliament, in particular, the commercial class dominating the House of Commons. After almost three decades of royalist scuffling, oligarchic rule through Parliament was reaffirmed in the Glorious Revolution of 1688.

The further development of the modern historical-critical method shifted its efforts accordingly, and this in two directions. The moderates, who rejected both royal absolutism and radical democratic rule, politicized the Bible in support of a commerce-based oligarchical regime. The main philosophical-political architect of the moderates was John Locke, who took Hobbes's materialist foundations and reformed his entire theory to affirm parliamentary oligarchy (politicizing the Bible accordingly). The political goal of Locke's reformulation was to keep both royalists and radicals at bay.

Locke's influence was immense. He is considered to be, along with Machiavelli and Hobbes, one of the great founders of modern political philosophy, of the eighteenth-century Enlightenment, and of the historical-critical method. To link all of this to the centrality of England's political turmoil in the development of the historical-critical method, Locke was also, theoretically and practically, the architect and chief apologist for the Glorious Revolution.

The radicals, who rejected both royal absolutism and oligarchic rule, politicized the Bible in support of democracy. The most influential figure here was Benedict Spinoza, another acknowledged father of the modern historical-critical method but also the greatest apologist of the Radical Enlightenment. He, too, took Hobbes's philosophical foundation and re-formed it for radical philosophical and political ends, and likewise politicized the Bible accordingly. Spinoza had a significant following, chief among them Richard Simon and John Toland.

Rather than focusing on the great moderate John Locke next, we turn first to Spinoza, Simon, and Toland, the radicals. We do this not only because their efforts predated Locke's (at least in regard to publication) but also because Locke's moderation is best understood as a reaction to radicalism.

Chapter Ten

THE RADICALS: SPINOZA, SIMON, AND TOLAND

As noted in the previous chapter, Hobbes is often counted as a pre-Enlightenment, distant father of the modern historical-critical method. With Benedict Spinoza, the acknowledged patrimony is even stronger, given the explicit aims of his exegetical method of interpreting the Bible in his *Tractatus Theologico-Politicus* (published anonymously in 1670). Spinoza, a radical himself, set off a radical reaction that deeply defined the trajectory of modern biblical scholarship's developments. Two of the most influential figures in this regard, whom we will also treat in this chapter, are the Catholic priest Richard Simon and the Protestant (of sorts) John Toland.[1]

To begin with the fount of radicalism, in the *Tractatus* Spinoza entirely removed all possibility of miracles

[1] For a more in-depth analysis of these figures, see Hahn and Wiker, *Politicizing the Bible*, ch. 9 ("Spinoza and the Beginning of the Radical Enlightenment"), ch. 10 ("The Ambiguous Richard Simon"), and ch. 12 ("Revolution, Radicals, Republicans, and John Toland").

from the text, stripped the prophets of any claim to truth by reducing their utterances to purely subjective psychological causes, made of the Bible a mere book of moral platitudes rather than a revelation of God, and multiplied the seeming confusions and contradictions in the text so as to neutralize it as a source of authority for anything other than morality. It would be quite easy for anyone familiar with the more radical assertions of historical-critical scholars from the nineteenth century onward to find the same ideas all set out quite bluntly long beforehand in Spinoza's *Tractatus Theologico-Politicus*. Hence, his recognized status as a precursor of the historical-critical method.

But Spinoza's arguments were themselves not his own inventions. He was directly indebted to Descartes and Hobbes (and Averroes and Machiavelli, for that matter), carrying forth the full-blown materialism and setting out with great thoroughness the implications in his method of interpreting the Bible. As with Hobbes, he was branded an atheist for his efforts, and taken to be a warning of what happened when one followed in the footsteps of Descartes and then Hobbes. Indeed, his thought was so radical that even other suspected atheists (like Pierre Bayle) and avowed atheists (like David Hume) expressed concern about the corrosiveness of Spinoza's thought.

Spinoza therefore earned his reputation as the chief figure of the Radical Enlightenment. In scholar Jonathan Israel's apt words, he was "the supreme philosophical bogeyman of Early Enlightenment Europe. . . . In fact, no one else during the century 1650–1750 remotely rivaled Spinoza's notoriety as the chief challenger of the fundamentals of revealed religion, received ideas, tradition, morality, and . . . divinely constituted political authority."[2] One might think Spinoza's reputation would serve as a warning to later historical-critical scholars of his intellectual patrimony.

Such questions aside for the moment, it is clear that Spinoza served as a vivid warning to both the orthodox and moderates alike that the burgeoning radical thought simmering underneath the surface of respectability that had boiled over in the English Civil Wars was now sweeping through Europe and coming to a head in the Netherlands with Spinoza. Atheism was a danger to faith and political order, in the latter case undermining even the ability to use religion as an instrument of the state.

Benedict Spinoza was born in Amsterdam in 1632, in the very center of the Cartesian revolution that would soon spread out from the Netherlands all over Europe. He was a Marrano, a descendant of Jews who had been forcibly converted to Christianity in Portugal. His family had moved to the Netherlands to escape such persecution and practice their Judaism openly. Young Spinoza came into contact with Cartesian thought, embraced it, and as a consequence was excommunicated by the local Jewish community in 1656 because of the "horrible heresies" he taught and practiced, and so was "banished from the nation of Israel."[3]

His notorious reputation would only increase. The publication of his *Tractatus Theologico-Politicus*, which even

[2] Jonathan Israel, *Radical Enlightenment: Philosophy and the Making of Modernity 1650–1750* (Oxford: Oxford University Press, 2001), 159.

[3] Quoted in Yirmiyahu Yovel, *Spinoza and Other Heretics: The Marrano of Reason* (Princeton, NJ: Princeton University Press, 1989), 3.

though anonymous was rightly suspected to have come from Spinoza, was formally condemned by the States of Holland in 1673, along with "other atheistical and heretical writings," such as Hobbes's *Leviathan*.[4]

Condemnation brought official confiscation, but also even more notoriety and hence influence. Spinoza would die in 1677. By that time the banned *Tractatus* was selling all across Europe, repeated condemnations only increasing its success. This was not due solely to the effect of curiosity following upon notoriety. Spinoza's followers had prepared "a complex operation designed to mask the launching of successive new editions" to avoid the censors and "facilitate international distribution."[5]

So it was that, in Jonathan Israel's words, "by the mid-1670s Spinoza stood at the head of an underground radical philosophical movement rooted in the Netherlands but decidedly European in scope. His books were illegal but yet, paradoxically, excepting only Descartes, no other contemporary thinker enjoyed, over the previous quarter century so wide a European reception, even if in his case that reception was overwhelmingly (even if far from exclusively) hostile."[6]

Before descending into the *Tractatus* to observe the unfolding of Spinoza's method of biblical interpretation, we must understand his pantheistic philosophy as set out

[4] See Jonathan Israel, "The Banning of Spinoza's Works in the Dutch Republic (1670–1678)," in *Disguised and Overt Spinozism around 1700*, ed. Wiep Van Bunge and Wim Klever (Leiden: E. J. Brill, 1996), 3–14.

[5] Israel, *Radical Enlightenment*, 281.

[6] Israel, *Radical Enlightenment*, 285.

in his *Ethics* because it is the source of his denial of the miraculous.

Descartes offered a problematic dualism of matter and spirit, but one which at least seemed to allow for a spiritual God. Hobbes jettisoned immaterial spirits and embraced complete materialism, skirting the difficulty of fitting God into the picture by declaring him entirely incomprehensible. Spinoza collapsed God into nature, making God himself material and nature so many endless manifestations of the divine. Of course, many suspected that Spinoza's pantheism was a ruse, and he was merely an atheist asserting that nature is the only thing that's eternal.

Spinoza's pantheistic reasoning set out in his *Ethics* was as follows. "Existence belongs to the nature of substance" precisely because "God, or substance . . . necessarily exists," so we may conclude that "there can be, or be conceived, no other substance but God."[7] Tersely put, God is nature (substance) and nature is God, and everything we see in nature (including ourselves) is merely a material modification of God. The result was the complete divinization of everything, or, to come at it from the other end, a complete profanation of God. Further, Spinoza's pantheism entailed complete determinism: "Nothing in nature is contingent, but all things are from the necessity of the divine nature determined to exist and act in a definite way."[8] God and nature are identical; therefore, the laws of nature are iden-

[7] Baruch Spinoza, *Ethics*, I, Props. 7, 11, 14, in Baruch Spinoza, *Ethics; Treatise on the Emendation of the Intellect; and Selected Letters*, trans. Samuel Shirley (Indianapolis, IN: Hackett Publishing, 1992).

[8] Spinoza, *Ethics*, I, Prop. 29.

tical to God; God cannot contradict himself; consequently, miracles are impossible.

Given this foundation in pantheism, Spinoza declared in the *Tractatus*, "If something were to come about in nature which did not follow on the basis of its laws," then "it would necessarily conflict with the order that God has set in nature for eternity through the universal laws of nature; and so it would be contrary to nature and its laws." Since God is nature and nature is God, "a miracle, whether [it is considered to be] contrary to nature or above nature, is a mere absurdity."[9] Therefore, the existence of any miracle reported in the Bible "signifies nothing else but a work whose natural cause we cannot explain on the mode of some other, usual thing; or, at least, that the one who writes or narrates the miracle cannot so explain it."[10]

While his pantheism, and consequent denial of the miraculous, may seem far-fetched, Spinoza fully realized that there was only one way to affirm the existence of God *and* at the same time deny the miraculous. If God is other than nature, then as creator, he is not bound by any "laws" of creation or nature itself, and miracles are therefore possible. If, on the other hand, nature is an entirely self-driven, determined, eternal machine running according to its own laws, then no God is necessary. It is only if one collapses God into the self-driven, determined, eternal machine of nature that God cannot act against his laws because he *is*

[9] All quotations from Benedict Spinoza, *Theologico-Political Treatise*, trans. Martin Yaffe (Newburyport, MA: R. Pullins & Company, 2004), 6.1.33–34. The numbers refer to the chapter, paragraph, and sentence number rather than the page number of the translation.

[10] Spinoza, *Theologico-Political Treatise*, 6.1.17.

the materially determined nature-machine and, as God, cannot contradict himself.

We point this out because many later biblical scholars will assert both that God exists and that miracles are impossible because they would violate the laws of nature. They will then set themselves to the task of cleaning up miracles from the biblical text, not realizing the incoherence of their assumptions. This Deistic approach, where God the creator does his initial work but is somehow prohibited from any further interference by alleged inviolable laws, is contradictory: an intelligent and powerful being sufficient to bring the universe into existence would have ample intelligence and power to manipulate what he created.

Realizing this helps us understand more clearly *why* Spinoza introduced his pantheism as the only way that one can keep God but jettison the miraculous. One might then ask the obvious question: Why does Spinoza want to keep God? Another question follows upon this: Why does Spinoza want to keep the Bible at all? In other words, why doesn't he just declare it an irrational, mythical text that we ought to dispose of, rather than engage in exegetical acrobatics to reconstruct it?

Spinoza himself supplied the answers in his *Ethics*. Following the ancient pagan philosophers and historians Averroes, Marsilius, Machiavelli, and Hobbes, Spinoza asserted that human beings are divided into three classes, according to their intellectual capacities. As we've come to expect, the highest type are the philosophical—in Spinoza's case, those who understand that nature is divine because it is eternal, and (following Descartes) that both our intellect and nature are mathematically defined. Only a very few are capable of intuiting the fundamental identity of mathematics and matter, let alone working through the mathematics. At the other end of the spectrum, we have the great mass of human beings, the lowest type, who are entirely incapable of this kind of abstract thinking. In contrast to the philosophers, they are only capable of "opinion, or imagination," the most defective form of "knowledge," wherein they perceive "individual objects presented . . . through the senses in a fragmentary and confused manner without any intellectual order." Spinoza adds a middle layer consisting of those who aren't up to the level of the philosophers but can follow their arguments, and so stand above the great ignorant mass of mankind.[11]

Unsurprisingly, being ruled by opinion and imagination "is the only cause of falsity," whereas those on the top two levels hold to what is "necessarily true."[12] Spinoza thereby sets up his own version of Averroes's double truth, where there is a Great Divide between those few philosophers who truly know and the great mass of mankind who are ignorant—and the latter must be ruled by religion.

Spinoza's arguments from the *Ethics* are brought into his *Tractatus* as fundamental assumptions in his approach to the Bible. As we've seen, the philosophical few know that miracles are impossible; therefore, they realize that "when Scripture says that this or that was done by God or God's will," it means "nothing else but that it was done in accordance with the laws and order of nature, and not, as

[11] Spinoza, *Ethics*, II, Prop. 40, Scholium 2.

[12] Spinoza, *Ethics*, II, Prop. 41.

the vulgar opine, that nature meanwhile stopped acting or that its order was temporarily interrupted."[13]

The Bible speaks this way *precisely because* it is a book meant for the vulgar, the unscientific or prescientific multitude. Spinoza declared: "It is not part of Scripture to teach matters through natural causes, but only to narrate those matters that broadly occupy the imagination." This is precisely the "method and style which better serve . . . for impressing devotion in the psyches of the vulgar."[14]

The mass of mankind is simply not capable of philosophical knowledge and so would be unmoved by philosophical arguments, either intellectually or morally. They need a storybook that "narrates matters in the order and phrases by which it can move human beings—and mainly the plebs—to devotion in the greatest degree; and because of this, it speaks of God and of matters quite improperly, no doubt since it is not eager to convince reason, but to affect and occupy human beings' fancy and imagination."[15] Rather than the Bible being inspired by the Holy Spirit, it was, Spinoza asserted, written in accordance with the "spirit of the plebs," appealing to their unscientific imagination," focusing on "only very simple matters, which can be perceived even by the slowest."[16]

As with Marsilius and Hobbes, Spinoza reminded readers of the ancient pagan philosophical use of religion for political purposes. The plebs of any age have never

[13] Spinoza, *Theologico-Political Treatise*, 6.1.47.
[14] Spinoza, *Theologico-Political Treatise*, 6.1.54.
[15] Spinoza, *Theologico-Political Treatise*, 6.1.64.
[16] Spinoza, *Theologico-Political Treatise*, 13.1.2–4.

been able to follow moral reasoning any more than philosophical reasoning, and therefore, being irrational, they are morally unruly (quite literally). The ancient wise lawmakers therefore invent heaven and hell, "promising upholders of the laws what the vulgar love most [i.e., the pleasures of heaven], and on the other hand threatening those who violate them with what the vulgar fear most [i.e., eternal punishments]. And so they have endeavored to curb the vulgar as a horse by the rein, so far as it can be done," thereby making them morally obedient.[17]

Spinoza adopted the "wisdom" of the ancient philosophers in his method. His method produces an interpretation of Scripture that can rein in the vulgar and ensure political and moral obedience. To do this, everything but the morality must be removed—that is, anything that could bring the vulgar to rebellion or make them believe that God could reveal to them truths above those provided by the new philosophical materialism.

The aim, and hence the result, of his method is, again, the erection of Spinoza's version of Averroes's double truth, a version very familiar to us today wherein "reason is the realm of truth and wisdom, whereas Theology is that of piety and obedience."[18] To be precise, piety is reduced to obedience, and "obedience toward God consists only in love of neighbor."[19]

Spinoza assiduously applied his method to the text to ensure that his principles would be amply illustrated.

[17] Spinoza, *Theologico-Political Treatise,* 4.2.2.

[18] Spinoza, *Theologico-Political Treatise,* 15.1.36.

[19] Spinoza, *Theologico-Political Treatise,* 13.1.9–10.

First and foremost, natural explanations had to replace alleged miracles. So, he informed readers, the plague of locusts vexing the Egyptians was caused by a strong wind that blew them in. Elisha seemed to raise a boy from the dead, but the boy was not actually dead; he was revived by the prophet placing his body on him and warming him up. The sun didn't stand still while Joshua fought; rather, the toil of the battle made the soldiers think the day was longer than usual. Christ's spittle and dust were actually medicinal in curing a blind man.[20] (We recall these same kinds of natural explanations for miraculous events by our contemporary biblical scholars canvassed in the first chapters—truly Spinoza's great-grandchildren.)

Spinoza also removed miracles by explaining them as mere Jewish hyperbole, a cultural-linguistic exaggeration for imaginative effect. According to Spinoza, himself a Jew, Jews have a habit of referring natural events directly to God, without really intending them to be considered as miraculous. So, for example, in Isaiah 48:21, the prophet speaks hyperbolically in saying that God provided water in the desert during the Jews' return from Babylonian exile, but he really meant "to signify nothing else but that the Jews, as it happened, discovered fountains in the desert by which they eased their thirst."[21]

If there are incidents of miracles that cannot be reduced to natural or cultural-linguistic causes, then Spinoza assured readers that they were "inserted in Sacred Writ by sacrilegious human beings. For whatever is contrary to

[20] Spinoza, *Theologico-Political Treatise,* 6.1.56, 6.1.58–59, 6.1.73.

[21] Spinoza, *Theologico-Political Treatise,* 6.1.80–85.

nature is contrary to reason; and what is contrary to reason is absurd, and therefore refutable as well."[22] The exegete may safely excise them all from the text.

As for the prophets, since they lived centuries before the mathematical-materialist revolution, they cannot have had any special knowledge of God. They could only have been ruled by imagination like the vulgar, especially vivid imaginations, in fact—that is, they were poets, not philosophers. Rather than look for truth from prophets, the scientific biblical exegete must discover the peculiar, subjective character of each prophet that defines his imagination. As Spinoza informed readers, "The revelation itself varied with each Prophet with respect to the disposition of the temperament of the body, with respect to that of the imagination, and with respect to the pattern of the opinions he had embraced beforehand." If the prophet was naturally cheerful, his prophecies were optimistic; if he was sad or angry, he prophesied doom; if an elegant and educated courtier, he uttered his prophecies eloquently and spoke of crowns and thrones; and if rustic, he prophesied in "a cruder style," using images of shepherds, vines, cows, and sheep; and if a soldier, his prophecies were martial.[23] The goal of the exegete has therefore shifted from the discovery of divine truth of prophecy to the historical and psychological conditions of the prophet himself.

What about Jesus? Since it would be quite dangerous for Spinoza to submit Jesus Christ to such psychological analysis, he instead asserted that Jesus, knowing the

[22] Spinoza, *Theologico-Political Treatise,* 6.1.67.

[23] Spinoza, *Theologico-Political Treatise,* 2.5.1–2.6.8.

sub-rational capacities of his audience, "accommodated himself to the mental cast of the populace"—that is, "to the mental cast of the plebs."[24] He may have spoken of demons for those foolish enough to believe in them, but in this condescension, his only goal was "teaching moral lessons" to those incapable of rational thought.[25] Spinoza thereby made Jesus into an Averroist, a teacher of the double truth.

So as not to overtax the capacities of the irrational multitude, Spinoza boiled down the moral lessons of the Bible for the sake of the plebs. Unsurprisingly, there wasn't much left in the pot, so to speak: "A unique and all-powerful God exists who cares for everyone and cherishes above all those who adore him and love their neighbor as themselves, etc."[26] Everything else in the Bible is of no doctrinal consequence, and so "we are bound to believe nothing else on the basis of the bidding of Scripture but what is absolutely necessary for executing this commandment."[27] This "commandment is the sole norm of the whole catholic faith; and all the dogmas of the faith . . . are to be determined through it alone."[28] Spinoza therefore declared that "we can judge no one to be faithful or faithless except on the basis of works. Namely, if the works are good, however he may dissent in his dogmas from the other faithful, he is still faithful. And on the contrary, if the works are evil, however he may

[24] Spinoza, *Theologico-Political Treatise,* 4.4.28–30.

[25] Spinoza, *Theologico-Political Treatise,* 5.1.14.

[26] Spinoza, *Theologico-Political Treatise,* 7.5.3–5.

[27] Spinoza, *Theologico-Political Treatise,* 14.1.14.

[28] Spinoza, *Theologico-Political Treatise,* 14.1.15.

agree in words, he is still faithless."[29]

A short creed, to say the least. Dogmatic discord is thus rendered impossible because the whole Bible boils down to a simple moral command, and whoever obeys this moral command (no matter what else he may believe or not believe about God) has fulfilled all that can be asked of him religiously. Contra Luther, Spinoza reduced the entirety of faith to works—both in terms of the method of his exegesis and the practical effect of using his method to eliminate political discord and persecution based upon religious differences. One may believe whatever he likes privately, as long as he acts morally—and this goes for atheists, a not unimportant result, given that Spinoza was continually charged with atheism.

In a Marsilian triumph, Spinoza then declared, "How salutary and how necessary this Teaching is in a republic, so that human beings might live peacefully and harmoniously—and I say, how many and how great the causes of disturbances and wicked deeds which it might prevent—I leave for everyone to judge."[30]

We are not surprised, given previous developments leading up to Spinoza, that civil peace is *the* overriding goal and Spinoza's method is the means to achieve it. Since civil peace is the goal, then Spinoza (like Hobbes) gave the state the full power to determine what religious beliefs are allowed and which are disturbers of the civil peace: "The highest right to make statutes concerning religion . . . belongs to the highest [civil] power, . . . and all are

[29] Spinoza, *Theologico-Political Treatise,* 14.1.25.

[30] Spinoza, *Theologico-Political Treatise,* 14.1.51.

bound to comply with its decrees and commands concerning religion."[31] But since Spinoza's "moral core" allegedly comes from Scripture, then the civil power defines both religion and morality (the latter equated with piety), and both are therefore "accommodated to the peace of utility of the Republic and, consequently, [must] be determined solely by the highest powers—who thus have to be its interpreters as well."[32]

We might think these "highest powers" rest in someone like Hobbes's absolute sovereign, but in fact, for Spinoza, the highest sovereign power is the political majority. So rather than a monarch defining religion and morality for the state, Spinoza gave this power to an absolutist democratic political assembly, "which, collectively, has the highest right to everything it can do," since it is "bound by no law."[33]

A perceptive reader might notice that religion and morality are thereby politicized democratically—that is, by the very vulgar masses whom Spinoza designed his method of scriptural exegesis to tame and subordinate to the truly wise. Isn't this a contradiction, at least of his intent?

In trying to sort this out, we mustn't forget that Spinoza's biblical exegetes, acting as agents of the philosophers, have removed everything from the Bible but the simplified moral core. Since the vulgar do not have the intellectual ability to question science, they lack it as well in judging what the scientific method of biblical exegesis produces. They are as

[31] Spinoza, *Theologico-Political Treatise,* 16.8.18–19.

[32] Spinoza, *Theologico-Political Treatise,* 19.1.2.

[33] Spinoza, *Theologico-Political Treatise,* 16.6.1–3.

equally incapable of doing advanced math as they are of reading Hebrew or Greek, and so they are as beholden to the exegetes as they are to the scientists.

The "scientific" exegetical method ensures that all theological doctrines are inconsequential (and therefore, a matter of personal taste). This privatization of religious belief ensures the peacefulness of the vulgar.

But to guarantee their peacefulness, Spinoza declared that each person has a *right* to whatever religious opinions he happens to have, *as long as* he is morally upright. This protects the freethinkers and atheists, as well as any and all religious beliefs. Consequently, "the best republic grants the same freedom of philosophizing to each which we have shown faith grants to each."[34]

The sum total result of Spinoza's efforts would seem to be, as Spinozan scholar Martin Yaffe states, the simultaneous creation of "liberal religion (grounded in modern-scientific biblical criticism) and liberal democracy,"[35] wherein biblical criticism serves liberal democracy by making all belief beyond the purely moral entirely subjective and hence private, *and* simultaneously protects the most radical atheistic and anti-Christian thought from political persecution.

The end result, seen clearly in biblical scholarship from the nineteenth century onward, is a union of the two aspects in tenured academic biblical scholars who are themselves either atheists or clearly subversive of orthodox

[34] Spinoza, *Theologico-Political Treatise*, 20.4.15.

[35] In Yaffe's translation of Spinoza's *Theologico-Political Treatise*, "Glossary," 254.

Christianity. In this capacity, Spinoza's academic biblical scholars act as agents of de-Christianization, thereby helping to ensure that liberal democracy will become increasingly secularized (including the secularization of the moral core itself, so that toleration of all moral views eventually follows upon toleration of all religious views).

This occurs because Spinoza's *method* is not neutral but entirely formed by his political aims. Thus, the application of the method by exegetes produces Spinoza's desired result, even if (or perhaps, especially if) its practitioners are unaware of the assumptions and aims that formed it. As proof of this, we find that Spinoza's method has so deeply defined consequent biblical criticism that it still has the desired result centuries later. Speaking in the late twentieth century, Wilfred Cantwell Smith remarked that biblical studies programs "are on the whole calculated to turn a fundamentalist into a liberal."[36] Picking up on this important point, biblical scholar Jon Levenson declared twenty-plus years after Smith that Smith's insight was "profoundly appropriate. For historical criticism is the form of biblical studies that corresponds to the classical liberal political ideal. It is the realization of the Enlightenment project in the realm of biblical scholarship."[37]

We mustn't misunderstand either Smith or Levenson here. They were not making a kind of political slur, but a profound observation. To clarify, if the modern historical-critical method as it developed over the centuries had been primar-

[36] Wilfred Cantwell Smith, "The Study of Religion and the Study of the Bible," *JAAR* 39 (1971): 132.

[37] Jon D. Levenson, *The Hebrew Bible, the Old Testament, and Historical Criticism* (Louisville, KY: Westminster/John Knox Press, 1993), 118.

ily formed by Thomas Hobbes, it would be appropriate to say instead that "historical criticism is the form of biblical studies that corresponds to absolutist monarchy," and perhaps to add that biblical studies programs "are on the whole calculated to turn a fundamentalist Independent into a staunch Royalist." As it turns out, Spinoza, even though significantly indebted to Hobbes, had the last historical laugh: Spinoza's arguments fit more neatly into the political development of liberal democracy that displaced royal absolutism historically.

That doesn't mean that the influence of Spinoza's biblical method hinged on the fact that liberal political ideas preceded it. Spinoza is rightly credited with being one of the fathers of liberal democracy, just as he is credited with the patrimony of the historical-critical method. The two developments went hand in hand as two sides of one political project in Spinoza. We now see the connection: according to political liberalism, civil peace is achieved by reducing the Bible to moral platitudes and by declaring a complete freedom of religious belief (and unbelief) as long as each citizen obeys a common moral-civil code. Biblical scholars serve that political aim by applying the method crafted by Spinoza.

It would not be too much to say that these scholars are the equivalent of "court theologians" of political liberalism, occupying the middle intellectual layer in Spinoza's intellectual hierarchy. They are below the philosopher-scientists whose abstruse mathematical reasoning they cannot fully comprehend but whose assumptions they can incorporate in their method, but they are above the vulgar many who are incapable of reading Greek, Latin, Hebrew, and Aramaic, and of wading through the continual layers of scholarship that pile up between the ordinary reader and the text itself.

In a very clever way, Spinoza both created these academic "court theologians" and multiplied their work, thereby assuring that their numbers would expand, and hence increasing their political effect on the multitude. In this regard, we recall from a previous chapter that by the late 1500s and early 1600s, the scholarly efforts put into sorting out the different biblical manuscripts, and the consequent translating and retranslating of scriptural texts accordingly, had created a Great Divide by the time of Spinoza. On one side were the popular, politically sanctioned, unscholarly translations into the vernacular, and on the other side of the Divide, the ever-burgeoning scholarly editions with increasingly dense critical apparatus.

Well aware of this, Spinoza purposely increased the Divide in the *Tractatus* by multiplying the scholarly obstacles set in the way of anyone who hoped to work his way to the original text. Not only do we have multiple manuscripts of the Old Testament, Spinoza pointed out, but even if we could determine the original, the Hebrew language itself isn't easily deciphered. So before getting to the meaning of the text, we must first examine "the nature and properties of the language in which the books of Scripture were written." But since the Bible covers centuries of time, we then need "a History of the Hebrew language."[38] Given that there are countless semantic difficulties and obscurities in Hebrew,[39] which would only be multiplied

[38] Spinoza, *Theologico-Political Treatise,* 7.2.1–3.

[39] Spinoza, *Theologico-Political Treatise,* 7.5.32–8.11.

by our attempts at sorting out its developments over time, "so many ambiguities . . . arise that no method can be given by which they are all able to be determined."[40]

As if sorting out the Hebrew isn't bad enough, the exegete must also grasp the original meaning of the authors of the various books of the Bible, and that entails an extended academic foray into "the life, mores and studies of the author of each book, who he was, on what occasion, at what time, for whom and, finally, in what language he wrote," as well as the "fortune of each book: namely, how it was first received and whose hand it fell into; furthermore, how many variant readings it had, and by which council it was accepted among the sacred ones [books]; and, finally, how all the books that everyone now confess to be sacred coalesced into one corpus."[41]

The obstacles are "so great that I would not hesitate to affirm that either we are ignorant of the true sense of Scripture in very many passages, or else we guess at it without certainty."[42] Happily, at least according to Spinoza, the *moral* lessons of Scripture are both clear and simple, and so while the Bible cannot be used by the plebs (or anyone else, for that matter) to make theological assertions, it can still function as a useful political text.

Spinoza thereby provided a double service to those who followed his method: the possibility of religious conflict based upon the Bible was entirely eliminated, and thousands of biblical scholars would have gainful employ-

[40] Spinoza, *Theologico-Political Treatise,* 7.9.1.
[41] Spinoza, *Theologico-Political Treatise,* 7.4.1–2.
[42] Spinoza, *Theologico-Political Treatise,* 7.11.6.

ment performing the endless academic tasks which, by their continual multiplication, served to ever widen the Great Divide between the faithful and the academics.

And that brings us to the work of the Catholic priest Richard Simon (1638–1712), yet another acknowledged father of the historical-critical method. A simple summary of his efforts is as follows. In order to annihilate the Protestant claim of *sola scriptura*, Fr. Richard Simon used Spinoza's method to multiply exponentially the number of academic difficulties that would have to be settled before one could finally reach the real, original meaning of the Bible, thereby showing the absolute need for *traditio* to determine the proper interpretation of Sacred Scripture.

The problem with this scorched-earth exegetical strategy was that Simon was so thorough that he seemed to undermine the authority of the Bible entirely, even for Catholics as well. Simon also inadvertently provided ample ammunition for Deists and radical atheists, who saw little or no worth in the biblical text at all after Simon shredded it exegetically. Understanding all of this is immensely important for mapping the consequent development of the modern historical-critical method: what Spinoza started Simon nearly perfected, and consequent historical-critical scholars only elaborated. The effect was not the destruction of the doctrine of *sola scriptura*, but the intellectual destruction of *scriptura* itself.

Richard Simon wrote "Critical Histories" of both the Old and the New Testament—*Histoire critique du Vieux Testament* (1678) and *Histoire critique du texte du Nouveau Testament* (1689)—but his treatment of the Old Testament was most influential. In his preface to his treatment of the

Old Testament, Simon revealed his exegetical strategy and the goal it served. The "great alterations . . . to the Copies of the Bible since the first Originals have been lost, utterly destroy the Protestant . . . Principle" of *sola scriptura*. In the non-original manuscripts that we have, there are "so many alterations" that "depended upon the pleasure of Transcribers," who "took the liberty of adding and leaving out certain letters according as they thought fit," that sorting out the original text is exceedingly difficult. As if that weren't bad enough, there is (as Spinoza noted) "the uncertainty of the Hebrew Grammar." Adding together all these difficulties and more makes it clear that "it is almost impossible to translate the Holy Scripture." And so, Simon declared triumphantly, "Those Protestants . . . who affirm that the Scripture is plain of it self [sic]," and who were "obliged to suppose it plain and sufficient for the establishing the truth of Faith without any Tradition," are therefore entirely undermined by the advance of Scripture scholarship itself. "If the truth of Religion remain'd not in the Church, it would be unsafe to search for it at present in Books" [i.e., the various books of the Bible], consequently, "if we join not Tradition with the Scripture, we can hardly affirm any thing for certain in Religion."[43]

Again, we must not miss the unintended results of Simon's efforts for the subsequent development of the

[43] We use the 1682 English translation *A Critical History of the Old Testament* done by "a Person of Quality," printed by Walter Davis, and reprinted by Classic Reprints No. 61 (Pensacola, FL: Vance Publications, 2002). Simon, Author's Preface, viii–ix. (Preface pages are unnumbered in text. To avoid confusion, we have used lowercase Roman numerals, beginning from the first page of the Preface.)

historical-critical method. He defined the proper method of approaching the exegesis of Scripture—as his titles profess—to be the *critical* deconstruction of the text into the *historical* layers of manuscripts, and the *critical* sorting out of the obscurities of the original language as expressed in the different *historical* periods covered in the Old Testament. "It is impossible to understand throughly [sic] the Holy Scriptures unless we first know the different states of the Text of these Books according to the different times and places, and be instructed of all the several changes that have happened to it."[44]

In order to make certain the task of understanding the Old Testament was impossible, Simon asserted that the "publick Writers" of the "Hebrew Commonwealth" (whom he oddly designated "prophets") were the ones in charge of "collecting faithfully the acts of what pass'd of most importance in the State."[45] It was they, as agents of the Jewish "State," who were responsible for collecting the materials that ultimately formed the Old Testament. A good bit of private judgment entered into overseeing the manuscripts, as they took the liberty of "giving a new form to these same Acts by adding or diminishing what they thought fit." Not to worry, added Simon, for these state bureaucrats "were real Prophets directed by the Spirit of God," and consequently, "their alterations . . . are of as

44 Simon, *A Critical History of the Old Testament*, Author's Preface, i.

45 Simon, Author's Preface, ii. These "Prophets, Scribes, as they are termed in the Bible or publick Writers . . . did faithfully collect the transactions that passed in the whole [Hebrew] state and kept them in Registries ordain'd for that purpose." I.1, 3.

great Authority as the rest of the Text of the Bible."[46]

But the Holy Spirit's mode of working through these "publick Writers" was, to say the least, curious. For example, the ancient biblical sources were written on "Leaves or Scrolls" that had "not been carefully enough kept" by the "publick Writers" themselves, the result being that "the order of things has been sometimes chang'd," so that we now find "disorder in some places of the Holy Scripture."[47] Furthermore, the "publick Writers" were mainly concerned with re-presenting the gist of the sacred writings for the "publick"; that is, they were "abridging . . . Scripture to give it to the People" in a way "which they thought . . . most proper for the instructing of the People," so they "have not always observed the [historical] order of the times" in the biblical narrative.[48] We are, therefore, hopelessly cut off from the original revealed texts: we have "onely an abridgment of the Acts which were preserv'd intire in the Registery of the [Hebrew] Republick."[49]

The sum result: without *traditio* arbitrarily affirming a certain set of received manuscripts, there would be no other way to determine what was truly revealed. And so, while Simon's critical-historical approach undoubtedly raised insuperable obstacles to the Protestant principle of *sola scriptura*, it simultaneously undermined the unity and authority of the Bible for Catholics as well. For Catholics,

46 Simon, Author's Preface, ii–iii.

47 Simon, Author's Preface, vi. Simon uses the example of Sarah being ninety years old in Genesis 17:17 and then later, at 20:2, she is beautiful and hence desirable enough to be taken as a wife by Abimelech.

48 Simon, Author's Preface, vii.

49 Simon, Author's Preface, v.

Scripture and Tradition worked together, each supporting the other. In trying to emphasize the absolute necessity of *traditio*, Simon undermined the entire Catholic tradition of scriptural interpretation and made of *traditio* a kind of arbitrary sovereign that imposed its particular reading on an indecipherable text. If that weren't destructive enough, since Simon significantly advanced the number of problems set out by Spinoza, he inadvertently furthered the cause of Spinoza, thereby providing even more abundant fuel for atheists, scoffers, and Enlightenment radicals, all set on the destruction of Protestants and Catholics alike.

Which brings us at last to John Toland, who was certainly one of the most colorful and duplicitous of the acknowledged fathers of the modern historical-critical method. His contribution is usually focused narrowly on his *Christianity not Mysterious*, published in 1696, which, in the estimation of most scholars, pegs Toland as something of a mild Deist. But upon closer examination of his other works, we find that he both extends and radicalizes Spinoza, using the arsenal of critical weapons and results marshalled by Simon.

The best place to begin with Toland is not his *Christianity not Mysterious*, but the various works in which he propounds his version of Averroism: *Letters to Serena* (1704), *Pantheisticon* (1720), and *Clidophorus* (1720). It is not surprising that Toland, a devout pupil of Spinoza, asserted that the philosophically enlightened are pantheist-materialists, who are ever at odds with the unwashed and unwashable vulgar masses. Thus, pantheists hold to a "Two-fold Philosophy," wherein the one is "*External* or popular, adjusted in some Measure to the Prejudices of the

People, or to Doctrines publickly authorized for true; the other *Internal* or philosophical, altogether conformable to the Nature of Things, and therefore to Truth itself." The "secret Philosophy" of pantheism must only be shared with the initiated "in the Recesses of a private Chamber, to Men . . . of consummate Probity and Prudence."[50]

According to Toland, the true philosophy never changes throughout the ages: pantheism is the eternal truth. But different religions rise and fall historically, and so the philosophers must each deal with the religion of the time and place in which they happen to find themselves—in Toland's case, Christianity, and even more particularly, Christianity in England.

Toland clearly considered himself to be among the long line of the wise, stretching back to the ancient pagans Critias, Polybius, Livy, and Plutarch, running through Marsilius, Machiavelli, Hobbes, and Spinoza, wherein the enlightened philosophers cleverly create or reform religious belief to control the masses politically. For Toland, that meant "adjusting" Christianity so that the controlled vulgar would not persecute the few wise. This "adjusting" is the goal of his exegetical efforts, and it must be done in such a way that the enlightened pantheist does not appear to "run counter to the received *Theology*" so he doesn't "run the Risque of his Life." Yet he somehow is not "altogether Silent" about his true beliefs, a feat that is achieved by his use of "equivocal Expression."[51]

[50] John Toland, *Pantheisticon: or, the Form of Celebrating the Socratic-Society*, originally in Latin in 1720; English translation, London, 1751, Samuel Paterson; Facsimile (New York: Garland Publishing, Inc., 1976), II.96.

[51] Toland, *Pantheisticon*, V, 106–108.

For those among the wise who might object to telling veiled half-truths, Toland asserted that the irrational multitude is to blame, and not the philosophers. The truth cannot be told publicly "but at the hazard of a man's reputation, employment, or life."[52] The philosopher is therefore compelled, in his public writings about religion, to "produce shiftings, ambiguities, equivocations, and hypocrisy in all its shapes."[53] These words are from Toland's esoteric work, *Clidophorus, or Of the Exoteric and Esoteric Philosophy*, obviously not meant for the multitude since it makes clear the "key" (*kleis*, hence *Clido*) of the real meaning and character of Toland's entire project.

In *Clidophorus*, Toland revealed that the wise among the Egyptians, "the wisest of mortals," held to a double philosophy, one for the few (unsurprisingly, pantheism) and one for the vulgar many. As proof, Toland pointed to the inscription of a statue of Isis at Sais (as reported by Plutarch), "I AM ALL THAT WAS, IS, AND SHALL BE."[54] For the philosophers, that statement encapsulated the truth that nature is all that there is, and since it is eternal and the ground of all that is, nature is equivalent to a god, or rather, *is* god. The public worship of Isis as a goddess, which spread as a popular religion all over the ancient world, was the exoteric face of pantheism, designed by the Egyptian philosophers.

Of course, the inscription sounds strikingly like the

[52] John Toland, *Clidophorus*, in *The Theological and Philological Works of the Late John Toland* (London: W. Mears, 1732; facsimile edition by Elibron Classics, 2005), II, 67.

[53] Toland, *Clidophorus*, II, 68.

[54] Toland, *Clidophorus*, III, 71.

revealed name of God in Exodus 3:14, "I AM WHO I AM." This is no accident, Toland informed his fellow philosophers, because Moses was part of the Pharaoh's inner circle since he was a baby, and so he was himself a pantheist and a devotee of the double philosophy! The religion of Judaism was consequently the exoteric form of Moses's esoteric, Egyptian pantheism. And so "MOSES, the most illustrious Lawgiver of the Jews . . . departed somtimes [sic] from the accurate truth of divine and natural matters . . . to accommodate his words, when speaking of GOD himself, to the capacity and preconceiv'd opinions of the vulgar."[55]

Hence, the Old Testament, or at least the Pentateuch, cannot be taken at face value, at least by philosophers; rather, they must discern the veiled truth underlying the surface religion of the vulgar. The same is, in some way, true of the New Testament because Jesus Christ spoke, in the most part, in parables, and parables are ingenious modes of equivocation, which allowed Jesus to veil his "true doctrine" so as "*not to cast . . . pearls before swine.*" Toland also included St. Paul and the Apostles as double-speakers of the truth—just like Toland.[56]

The question that arises, then, is what form should Christianity take in Toland's own time? The short answer: *Christianity not Mysterious*, which was Toland's attempt at an exoteric presentation of Christianity. Ironically, this text is taken by almost all later academics to be a presentation of his actual views (and one that informed the approach of

[55] Toland, *Clidophorus*, VI, 78.

[56] Toland, *Clidophorus*, VI, 78–79.

later historical-critical scholars).

To understand this, we must further examine his *Clidophorus*, the self-proclaimed "key" to his writing. If Moses, Jesus, St. Paul, and the rest of the Apostles were rightly informed philosophers, then what happened to Christianity? For Toland, the unenlightened and conniving priests wrested control of it from the philosophers and, even worse, used their ill-gained religious power to bilk the vulgar masses of their wealth by spreading superstition in the form of *mysteries* of the faith. Since the priests feared that the philosophers might expose them, they turned the duped masses *against* the illumined pantheists.[57] As a result, Toland and other true philosophers must live in fear of "being accus'd of impiety by the Priests" and hence "expos'd in their turn to the hatred, if not to the fury of the Vulgar."[58]

The philosophers must regain control of religion so that (in this instance) Christianity can be transformed back into an exoteric religion that protects the esoteric beliefs of the true philosophers. The way to do that, for Toland, was to remove the source of the priests' power over the vulgar. Their priest-crafty ruse was made possible by their claim that something *above* reason made necessary the mediation of a priesthood. And so Toland set out to show the opposite (as the full title makes evident): *Christianity not Mysterious: or, a Treatise Shewing, That there is nothing in the Gospel Contrary to Reason, Nor Above it: And that no Christian Doctrine can be properly call'd a Mystery.*

57 Toland, *Clidophorus*, XII, 94.

58 Toland, *Clidophorus*, XII, 94.

So as to make clear, at least to some, the character of this work, Toland noted in the Preface "the deplorable Condition of our age" is such that "a Man dares not openly and directly own what he thinks of Divine Matters . . . but he is either forc'd to keep perpetual Silence, or to propose his Sentiments to the World by way of Paradox under a borrow'd or fictitious name."[59] Toland at first published anonymously rather than using a borrowed or fictitious name, but he soon owned up to the work as his. We also have every reason to believe that *Christianity not Mysterious* is also an exoteric work where his real aims were masked "by way of Paradox"—that is, presented in a veiled way for "the Vulgar."[60]

Toland's argument was straightforward. Truth, for Toland, is defined according to Cartesianism. "*Reason* is the only Foundation of all Certitude" and is defined in terms of "*clear and distinct Ideas.*" There is "nothing reveal'd, whether as to its *Manner* or *Existence*," that is "exempted from its [i.e., reason's] Disquisitions." Therefore, "*what is evidently repugnant to clear and distinct Ideas, or to our common Notions, is contrary to Reason*" and "*the Doctrines of the Gospel*, if it be the Word of God, *cannot be so.*"[61]

We must remember that, going back to Descartes and through Spinoza, reason has been redefined in accordance

[59] Toland, *Christianity not Mysterious*, in *John Toland's Christianity not Mysterious: Text, Associated Works and Critical Essays*, ed. Philip McGuinness, Alan Harrison, and Richard Kearney (Dublin: The Lilliput Press, 1997), Preface, 5.

[60] Toland, *Christianity not Mysterious*, Preface, 10.

[61] Toland, *Christianity not Mysterious*, Section Two, "That the Doctrines of the Gospel are not contrary to Reason," 31, and "The State of the Question," 17.

with the assertion that nature itself is entirely reducible to mathematical-material extension, and since nature is eternal, it is divine. Mystery and miracle are therefore banished because there is nothing above god-nature, and god-nature cannot contradict itself. Rationality was redefined accordingly: to be rational means to hold that nature is eternal, divine, and entirely reducible to mathematical-material extension. Thus, following Spinoza, Toland's pantheism is the ultimate source of his assertion that anything smacking of mystery or miracle in the New Testament must be exegetically reformulated or removed. The goal, again, was to cut off anything that priests could claim was above reason: there is nothing above reason because there is nothing above nature so-defined.

In a clever, if disingenuous, rhetorical move, Toland informed his exoteric audience (the vulgar) that it is precisely the pretense of mystery in the Bible that allows "cunning Priests" to dupe and then manipulate them, and consequently lets the priests extract money from the vulgar and maintain power over them as well. The crafty priests' appeal to mystery, of truths above reason and realities above nature, is merely a tool "*to stop the Mouths of such as demand a Reason where none can be given, and to keep as many in Ignorance as Interest shall think convenient.*"[62]

There was originally no mystery in Christianity at all, Toland assured readers. It was a pure, rational, natural religion without any superstition or mystery at all. Jesus Christ did not come to declare his divinity and set up a sacramental priesthood but only to preach "the purest Morals"

[62] Toland, *Christianity not Mysterious*, Section Three, ch. 4, 79.

and teach "reasonable Worship." So he "stripp'd the Truth of all those external Types and Ceremonies" practiced by the Jews of his day. But this pure and original form of Christianity was soon befouled by two streams: converted Jews and converted Pagans, each bringing mystery, ceremony, and hence degeneration to the pure Gospel. The degenerate, mystery-filled form of Christianity, ruled by priests, became the official version of Christianity adopted by Christian emperors from Constantine forward, thereby shielding mystery-mongering priests under political, imperial authority.[63]

The obvious exegetical method to follow upon these assumptions entailed the removal of all mystery from the text to leave only what natural reason could affirm. Of course, the assumption and the method would thereby reduce the Bible to the same status as any other ancient work—and this would soon enough become a hallowed exegetical principle of the historical-critical method. As a result, supernatural faith is not required for the proper interpretation of Scripture. We thus regularly hear, in later biblical scholars, the echo of Toland's words: "Nor is there any different Rule to be follow'd in the Interpretation of *Scripture* from what is common to all other Books."[64]

Toland's long-term effects aside, there is no doubt his narrative was meant to appeal to Protestants of his day who likewise believed that Catholicism represented a decline from the pure, original church, one deformed by the embrace of Jewish Law, ceremony, and sacrament, and

[63] Toland, *Christianity not Mysterious*, Section Three, ch. 5, 92–94.

[64] Toland, *Christianity not Mysterious*, Section Two, ch. 3, 44.

further degraded by the inclusion of pagan elements. But in this appeal, he was steering Protestants toward a new rationalistic form of Christianity amenable to Toland's aims.

As we've seen, there could be nothing more pagan—or more unfavorable to Christians, Protestant or Catholic—than Toland's esoteric pantheism hidden underneath. On the exoteric surface, the Gospel was shorn of all mystery and turned into a rational, civil religion, hostile to the priesthood and aimed purely at morality. On the esoteric level underneath, the crafty priests were divested of all religious and political power, thereby allowing the pantheistic philosophical elite to rule the vulgar, whose religion was now entirely defined in terms of a morality that functioned to buttress political order.

What *kind* of political order did Toland aim to support? The answer to that question will reveal in what way he politicized the Bible: in much the same way as Spinoza—that is, in terms of a liberal political order that allowed each citizen (including pantheists!) to believe whatever he wanted as long as he was a moral, and hence law-abiding, citizen.

Of course, the primary aim was, first and foremost, to reform his own home country, England. Although Toland was born a decade after the monarchy was reestablished in England, his sympathies lay with the radical republicans, the regicides who believed that England should be ruled by what amounts to a democratic assembly. The Glorious Revolution of 1688 reaffirmed England's monarchy, albeit under control of the commercial class in Parliament. Toland's aim then became to bend the Glorious Revolution, insofar as he could, to the principles of the more radical republican cause.

In this regard, his *Letters to Serena* (1704) mentioned above was part of his adamant political support of the Hanoverian succession. At issue in the succession was what to do if the Stuart line of monarchs came to an end without an heir, one option being that succession would pass to the Protestant House of Hanover in Germany (Sophia of Hanover being the granddaughter of King James I).

The Act of Settlement in 1701 declared for the House of Hanover, and Toland set about immediately insinuating himself with Sophia and her daughter Sophie (the queen of Prussia), mentoring them to rule England according to his own more radical vision. *Letters to Serena* is an esoteric work that reveals Toland's attempts to initiate Sophia and Sophie into the mysteries of esoteric pantheism so that England's new rulers would be true philosophers, using liberal civil religion of the sort outlined by Toland to control the vulgar masses.

The union of this political aim with the tools of biblical scholarship can be seen quite clearly in Toland's *Nazarenus*, of which he produced two versions, one esoteric and the other exoteric. In Justin Champion's words, Toland's "*Nazarenus* was an attempt to reform the established church in England" so as to show "the compatibility of a national church and the toleration of religious diversity," thereby creating "a pluralistic civil religion" based upon "a relativistic understanding of religion."[65]

[65] John Toland, *Nazarenus*, ed. Justin Champion (Oxford: Voltaire Foundation, 1999), Champions's Introduction, 97, 102.

We already see the importance of *Christianity not Mysterious* for the arguments of *Nazarenus*. Theological relativism is the foundation of the pluralism: reason defines the truth, so all nonrational religious beliefs are equally false. As long as these beliefs are held privately *and* one is publicly moral, it doesn't matter what one believes (provided that one extends this courtesy to everyone else's irrational, private beliefs). The civil religion therefore consists in holding to a common public morality *and* to a common belief that one's personal religion is entirely nonrational and private.

Toland's strategy for supporting this exegetically was to "show" that the reconstructed form of Christianity he desired for England was actually the *original* form of Christianity—a move not unrelated to the Protestant attempts (against Catholics) to show that the primitive church coincided with their particular confessions, or the attempts of English messianic nationalism to connect the primitive church of the Apostles to the primitive national church of the English.

Toland set about this project in a rather convoluted way, by attempting to demonstrate, using every scholarly means at his disposal, that the noncanonical Gospel of Barnabas revealed the beliefs of the first Christians, the "Nazarens" or "Ebionites." Unsurprisingly, these Nazerens, the original Jewish converts, held to an entirely non-mysterious form of Christianity; hence, they "*affirm'd* JESUS *to have been a mere man, as well by the father as the mothers side, namely the Son of* JOSEPH *and* MARY; *but that he was just, and wise, and excellent, above all other persons, meriting to be peculiarly call'd* THE SON OF GOD, *by reason of his most virtuous life*."[66] While the Apostles affirmed the beliefs of the Nazerens—or more accurately, tolerated them—St. Paul (the apostle to the Gentiles) insisted on the affirmation of Christ's divinity (a contaminating import from Hellenism itself). Hence, the source of the scriptural conflict between the tolerant Apostles and the intolerant St. Paul, the latter being the source of deformation.[67]

The lesson drawn by Toland nicely fit his aim of redefining Christianity as a non-mysterious, liberal civil religion. In his words, "*Toleration* . . . is no less plainly a duty of the *Gospel*, than it is self-evident according to the Law of Nature; so that they who persecute others in their reputations, rights, properties, or persons, for merely speculative opinions, or for things in their own nature indifferent, are so farr equally devested both of Humanity and Christianity."[68]

Recalling a common theme running all the way back to Marsilius, Toland's civil religion was intended to bring civil peace. Using scholarship to "establish" that the original Christians were tolerant was Toland's way of protecting pantheist philosophers from persecution by priests or the vulgar, removing the priests from power by undercutting anything supernatural and taming the vulgar by convincing them that they protected their own particular religious

[66] Toland, *Nazarenus*, I.ix, 152–153.

[67] How Toland could reconcile this with his notion from *Clidophorus*, noted above, that both the Apostles and St. Paul were doublespeakers, can perhaps be resolved by noting that *Clidophorus* was an esoteric text, and this version of *Nazarenus*, an exoteric text.

[68] Toland, *Nazarenus*, I.xii, 161; I.xiv, 170; I.xvi, 178; I.xviii, 181; I.xx, 193.

beliefs by keeping them private and behaving themselves publicly.

One might well ask, given the radical nature of Toland's esoteric and exoteric works, whether his reformulation of Christianity was likely to fool Christians. Or, to be more exact, since he was publicly suspected of the most radical beliefs from very early on in his life, whether his efforts actually resulted in signaling Christians of his deep heterodoxy rather than convincing them to join his attempt at creating a new orthodoxy.

We don't have to conjecture. For most Christians at the time, Toland was classed along with Hobbes and Spinoza as faith-wreckers who spread atheism. The spread of atheism would, of course, present an obvious problem for Christians. But it presented a problem for those who desired to *use* religion as well. The spread of the likes of Machiavelli, Hobbes, Spinoza, and Toland, aided by the devastating historical-critical deconstruction of the Bible by Simon, meant atheism's eventual reach to the vulgar masses themselves, thereby undermining the use of religion as an instrument of political control. Indeed, it could certainly make the vulgar masses completely unruly. As we've noted in a previous chapter, clear signs of the chaos that would result from spreading radical philosophy to the masses were evident in the English Civil Wars, and no one saw these signs with greater clarity than John Locke. As Locke realized, if Scripture scholarship were to advance the underlying secular goals we've seen from Marsilius forward, then it would have to be much more moderate and circumspect in its approach to the Bible.

Before turning to Locke, we may call the reader's

attention to some important points from this chapter in regard to the radicals Spinoza and Toland. First and foremost, there are clear connections between what they argued in the late seventeenth and early eighteenth centuries, and what our contemporary scholars such as Robert Funk, Dominic Crossan, the various scholars of the Jesus Seminar, and Bart Ehrman assert today. In short, these figures writing just prior to the Enlightenment reveal the philosophical assumptions that seem to be entirely invisible to contemporary historical-critical scholars.

As a consequence, that miracles cannot occur is now assumed without argument and taken to be the unquestioned and unquestionable beginning point of any competent biblical exegete. For this reason, Christianity must be rendered *not Mysterious*, a task that defines the entire efforts of the biblical exegete and inevitably results in the reduction of Jesus to a mere man. In accepting this beginning point as the foundational assumption of the historical-critical method, our contemporary historical-critical scholars do not seem to be very *critical* of the philosophical assumptions of Spinoza and Toland, because they are unware of the *history* of modern philosophy and its politicizing aims. Do they truly know whether nature can be ultimately defined in terms of mathematical-materialist reductionism? Would they subscribe to pantheism so as to somehow keep the divine but exclude the miraculous? Do they believe that the vulgar rabble should be cleverly manipulated by those in political power? Do they understand that their chase after exegetical minutiae was, as an academic project, cleverly designed to create a dense intellectual fog that allowed for political-biblical manipulation by the elite?

One wonders what answers our contemporary scholars would give *if* they would become sufficiently historical and critical of their own assumptions. It is beyond the scope of this present work to search for clues to possible answers from our own radicals. Instead, we must continue our analysis by going to John Locke, a moderate reacting to radicals of his own time.

Chapter Eleven

JOHN LOCKE, THE MODERATE RADICAL

To CAPTURE JOHN LOCKE'S EFFORTS in short form, we might say that Locke reacted politically and exegetically *both* to royalists *and* to the republican radicals of his time.[1] Locke was an avowed enemy of royal absolutism, and thus a staunch supporter of the parliamentary rule of England's propertied class against the king. But he also rejected the radical republicanism that had broken out and caused so much democratic chaos from below during the English Civil Wars.

Royal absolutists and democratic radicals sincerely claimed scriptural support. But as we've seen, the same *political* division existed among those who viewed the Bible solely as an instrument of political rule, Hobbes on the side of the royal absolutists, and Spinoza and Toland on

[1] For a more in-depth analysis, see Hahn and Wiker, *Politicizing the Bible*, ch. 11, "The English Civil Wars, Moderate Radicals, and John Locke."

the side of the radical republicans and liberal democracy.

Locke steered between the two extremes, taking the politically moderate course of supporting the rule of the propertied class, the new commercial class that had largely defined Parliament's House of Commons before the Civil Wars. That would mean, for Locke, a politicizing of the Bible in support of a commercial oligarchy. Recalling once again Levenson's apt quote—"historical criticism is the form of biblical studies that corresponds to the classical liberal political ideal"—we may say that in Locke's method of scriptural exegesis the form of biblical studies corresponds to *classical* liberalism of the kind later associated with Adam Smith (rather than, as with Spinoza, *democratic* liberalism that we might associate with the political Left).

In order to make good this assessment, we need to examine Locke in some detail, beginning with his background. John Locke was born in 1632, not long before the Civil Wars would break out in England. Both his parents were of the more liberal kind of Puritan, and his father would fight in the Civil War on the side of the Parliamentarians. When King Charles I was beheaded in January of 1649, young Locke was a student at the prestigious Westminster School, and he was at Oxford during the most radical phase of the Commonwealth period and consequent dictatorship of Cromwell. He had not only no sympathy for the defeated royalists but also complete antipathy for the democratic radicals. Locke therefore staked his claim among the commercial-class Parliamentarians—soon to be dubbed "Whigs"—who wished to tame both the king and the leveling democratic rabble.

For Locke, this was not merely a theoretical philosophical project engaged from a comfortable armchair; he was an integral political participant as well. To give some more needed background, the restoration of the monarchy in 1660, in the person of Charles II, did not bring an end to the political and religious conflicts that marked the Civil Wars. Things were still greatly unsettled, with radical republicans pushing to reestablish the Commonwealth and put an end to the established (now reestablished) state Anglicanism, and Catholics surfacing again as a significant threat from the other side.

In regard to the latter, Charles II had strong Catholic leanings, which soon became apparent in his political actions and appointments to positions of power. Things were even more interesting behind the scenes. Charles actually signed the secret Treaty of Dover in 1670, wherein (for a generous subsidy) he promised the Catholic royal absolutist King Louis XIV of France that he would convert to Catholicism privately and openly support France's ambitions on the Continent. At a suitable time, Charles would then make his Catholicism known publicly, which, since he was by virtue of Henry VIII's Act of Supremacy the head of England's church, would put an end to the Anglican Church.

Locke, along with his mentor and patron the Earl of Shaftsbury, was a member of the Green Ribbon Club, a political club dedicated to unseating Charles II, not by argument but by armed rebellion. Despite many historians wanting to protect Locke from tarnish, the truth is that Locke was also part of the famous Rye House Plot in 1683 that aimed to assassinate Charles and his brother James (the future, even more Catholic James II).

When the Rye House Plot was discovered, Locke escaped punishment by hurrying off to the Continent. While there, he continued to plot against the king from across the channel as part of the Monmouth Rebellion (1685). Finally, he was centrally involved in the Glorious Revolution of 1688 that ousted James II and (at the behest of Parliament) put William and Mary on the throne. Locke himself returned triumphantly from exile in 1689, accompanying the soon-to-be-queen Mary as she sailed to England on the *Isabella*.

Ironically, given Locke's ultimate moderate leanings, he spent his time in exile in the Netherlands among the most radical elements, living for two years with the Quaker Benjamin Furly, who had one of the largest libraries of subversive, heterodox literature of the time. Though Spinoza himself had died in the previous decade, Locke became well acquainted with the circle of Spinozists, reading the *Tractatus* as well as a wealth of literature spun from it, including the works that dealt directly with biblical scholarship.

It seems—if we might offer a reasonable conjecture, given the nature of his later writings—that Locke's experience of political radicalism in the English Civil War and of intellectual radicalism in the Netherlands brought him to embrace, in reaction, his characteristically more moderate political and intellectual position. By designating him as "moderate" here, we mean that he was what might be called a "moderate radical"—that is, one who had foundational intellectual agreements with the radicals but believed that it was dangerous and destructive to political order (i.e., immoderate) to reveal these agreements openly.

But even this doesn't quite take us to the heart of Locke. We recall the deep intellectual connection in the affirmation of full-blown materialism in Hobbes (who used it to support royal absolutism) and Spinoza (who used it to support liberal democracy). The problem was that the materialism was so obvious in both that they were immediately taken to be two atheist peas in the same materialist pod. And so, while each intended to use Scripture for political control, their atheism seemingly destroyed their ability to do so.

For Locke, who accepted the materialism, the problem to be solved was how to retain the efficacious political use of religion. The answer seems to have been to offer a more moderate account of both materialism and politics that (at least by contrast to either Hobbes or Spinoza) supported a more orthodox (or less heterodox) method of Scripture scholarship.

In regard to the English political situation, Locke had to steer between Hobbes's support of absolute monarchy and the Spinozist Toland's support of radical republicanism, and that meant a considerably more careful approach to his treatment of the Bible so that it could retain its usefulness as a political instrument of commercial-class Parliament rule. (Although Toland's works, for the most part, were published after Locke, Locke was well acquainted with Toland's ideas beforehand.)[2]

[2] There is strong evidence that Locke's *Reasonableness of Christianity* was actually written in reaction to John Toland's much more radical *Christianity not Mysterious* after Locke had read a significant portion of Toland's unpublished manuscript, Locke then rushing his more moderate *Reasonableness* into print before Toland's work could appear.

The best place to begin to understand Locke's rather complex position as a moderate radical might be his continuity with the belief (stretching all the way back to Critias and running up through Marsilius, Machiavelli, Hobbes, Spinoza, and on to Toland) that the wise understand the vulgar masses cannot be politically controlled without religion. On this point, Locke penned an uncharacteristically blunt assessment in his *Reasonableness of Christianity*. Published anonymously in 1695, *Reasonableness of Christianity* is taken to be his main contribution to the development of the historical-critical method. In the course of the argument, we are informed that morality "must have its authority either from reason or revelation."[3] Even if philosophers could come up with a perfectly rationally demonstrable account of ethics, "yet [it] would not have been so effectual to man" as revelation, and for a very familiar reason:

> The greatest part of mankind want leisure or capacity for demonstration, nor can carry a train of proofs. . . . And you may as soon hope to have all the day-laborers and tradesmen, the spinsters and dairymaids, perfect mathematicians, as to have them perfect in ethics this way. Hearing plain com-

See John Biddle, "Locke's Critique of Innate Principles and Toland's Deism," *Journal of the History of Ideas* 37, no. 3 (1976): 411–422. Locke knew Toland personally, and had actually hired him to transport clandestine, radical literature from the Continent, but later cut off relations because of Toland's growing radical reputation.

3 John Locke, *The Reasonableness of Christianity as Delivered in the Scriptures*, ed. George Ewing (Washington, DC: Regnery, 1965), 242 (paragraph number in the Ewing edition).

> mands is the sure and only course to bring them to obedience and practice. The greatest part cannot *know*, and therefore they must *believe*.[4]

Thus, against those of more radical, democratic tendencies that assumed the Enlightenment could reach the masses, Locke claimed that "the instruction of the people were best left to the precepts and principles of the gospel." Consequently, in order to be effective in buttressing morality, one cannot (like Hobbes, Spinoza, and Toland) eliminate the miraculous, because miracles are precisely what give the biblical text the authority to act as a moral prop for the many. As Locke explained, the "healing of the sick, the restoring sight to the blind by a word, the raising and being raised from the dead, are matters of fact, which they can without difficulty conceive, and that he who does such things, must do them by the assistance of a divine power."

> These things [i.e., miracles] lie level to the ordinariest apprehension; he that can distinguish between sick and well, lame and sound, dead and alive, is capable of this doctrine. To one who is once persuaded that Jesus Christ was sent by God to be a King, and a Savior of those who do believe in him; all his commands become principles; there needs [to be] no other proof for the truth of what he says, but that he said it. And then there needs no more, but to read the inspired books to be instructed; all

4 Locke, *The Reasonableness of Christianity*, 243. See also 252.

> the duties of morality lie there clear, and plain, and easy to be understood.[5]

Consequently, even though the new materialism would seem to eliminate the miraculous, exegetically eradicating miracles in one's treatment of the Bible would undermine its moral efficacy for the non-philosophic. Moderation is called for. Locke therefore didn't eliminate miracles in his treatment of Scripture in *Reasonableness of Christianity*.

While he didn't cut miracles out, he did whittle down the theological essence of the Bible (in nearly exact duplication of Hobbes and Spinoza) to one doctrine necessary for salvation: "All that was to be believed for justification," so the Bible revealed according to Locke "was no more but this single proposition: that 'Jesus of Nazareth was the Christ, or the Messiah.'"[6]

A wide theological latitude was therefore given to those who behave themselves morally, and so theological divisions that could cause political turmoil would be neutralized. Such was Locke's prescription against the reestablished state Anglican Church that Charles II and James II had hoped to turn Catholic, as well as the church that royalists wished to use to reinstate absolute monarchy, and finally the church that radical republicans wanted to abolish completely. In Locke's view, an established Anglican state church was a good thing, as long as it steered clear of Roman Catholicism and absolute monarchy on the one side, or the religious and political excesses of radical

5 Locke, *The Reasonableness of Christianity*, 243.

6 Locke, *The Reasonableness of Christianity*, 50.

republican Independents on the other. In between these extremes, Locke's version of the Anglican Church should open its welcoming, latitudinarian arms exceedingly wide. (Just for the record, he was often accused of being a Socinian, i.e., a kind of Unitarian, but never of moral insobriety.)

Such was the argument for Locke's famous *Letter Concerning Toleration*, written in Latin by Locke in 1685 while in exile and published three months after his return to England with Queen Mary. Locke set out to convince readers in England that "Toleration" was "the chief Characteristical Mark of the True Church,"[7] an assertion that, of course, had to be backed up exegetically so that the defining goal of Locke's method of scriptural interpretation was to establish political toleration, shearing away anything that didn't fit.

The argument at the heart of this effort is essential to our understanding of Locke's goal of establishing toleration in the established state church of England. Locke asserted, first of all, that any definite claim about Christian orthodoxy was really a disguised desire for political power. Second, he claimed that toleration was actually another form of charity—that is, toleration is demanded by the Gospel call to "Charity, Meekness, and Good-will in general towards all Mankind, even to those that are not Christians" or those whom one does not consider true Christians. All that the Gospel demands is that each one attend to the correction of "his own Lusts and Vices."[8]

7 John Locke, *A Letter Concerning Toleration*, trans. William Popple (London, 1689), reprinted and edited by James Tully (Indianapolis, IN: Hackett Publishing Company, 1983), 23.

8 Locke, *A Letter Concerning Toleration*, 23.

The deepest reason for toleration is that faith itself is fundamentally personal, a kind of fideism that is entirely a matter of "the inward perswasion of the Mind."[9] Since what brings inner "perswasion" is entirely subjective—recalling Spinoza's assertion that irrational religious belief is a matter of what moves each sub-rational person's imagination—"every man . . . has the supreme and absolute Authority of judging for himself" the substance of his faith *as long as he behaves himself morally.*[10] We are here very close to Spinoza, but that would lean England, politically, toward the chaotic radical republicans. Therefore, England should allow all inward "perswasions" except those of radical Levelers, Diggers, Quakers, and outright atheists—Locke excludes atheists since the "taking away of God, tho but even in thought, dissolves all."[11] Guarding the other side, Locke also disallowed the "perswasions" of Catholics and Anglican absolute monarchists as well.

Precisely because faith is completely defined by irrational inner persuasion, no government can force or impose belief as long as citizens remain within the acceptable latitudinarian limits. To make absolutely certain that theological disagreements do not cause political turmoil, Locke defined the sole political goal to be entirely this worldly and material, thereby creating another kind of Great Divide, one existing between a fideistic, irrational, private form of Christianity and a soulless, entirely secular political realm. Politics therefore has no connection to

[9] Locke, *A Letter Concerning Toleration*, 26–27.
[10] Locke, *A Letter Concerning Toleration*, 47.
[11] Locke, *A Letter Concerning Toleration*, 50–51.

God, heaven, hell, or the soul but is completely defined by the protection and pursuit of "Life, Liberty, Health, and Indolency of Body; and the Possession of outward things, such as Money, Lands, Houses, Furniture, and the like."[12] (In short, just what Marsilius had argued for in his truncated, soulless view of politics.)

Locke's system seems therefore to offer protection for religious believers. No one can compel "inward persuasion," so "the Magistrate's Power extends not to the establishing of any Articles of Faith, or Forms of Worship, by the force of Laws."[13] The "power of Civil Government relates only to Mens Civil Interests"; that is, it "is confined to the care of the things of this World, and hath nothing to do with the World to come."[14]

The price to be paid for this kind of protection might be considered, by some, to be rather high: Christianity must give up any claim to universal truth, and so also, the Great Commission to make disciples of all nations, since the secular nation that protects privatized belief does so only if belief remains privatized. The only bridge across this iteration of the Great Divide is the moral support provided by Christianity for the secular state, a state delimited by the bodily, material concerns of the new industrial-commercial class that (so hoped Locke) would rule England through Parliament. The morality that Christianity must therefore provide is not just any morality, nor is it really deeply Christian; rather, it is a morality molded to the goals of the

[12] Locke, *A Letter Concerning Toleration*, 26–27.

[13] Locke, *A Letter Concerning Toleration*, 27.

[14] Locke, *A Letter Concerning Toleration*, 28.

industrial-commercial state. Both the Bible and morality itself will have to be politicized accordingly.

In his *Two Treatises on Government*, Locke illustrates his political-theological politicizing goals. Both treatises were written in exile and then published anonymously in 1689. The *First Treatise* set out his arguments against Divine Right and/or Hobbesian absolutist monarchy, and the *Second Treatise* (the more famous and influential of the two) contains Locke's oligarchic account of politics, complete with supportive biblical arguments, for rule of the commercial class.

The full subtitle of the *First Treatise* is *The False Principles and Foundation of Sir Robert Filmer and His Followers Are Detected and Overthrown*. Filmer was a sincere (as opposed to Hobbesian) advocate of Divine Right monarchy, who prior to the Civil Wars had argued that Scripture itself was the ultimate support of the Tory Anglican cause, because God gave dominion to Adam as the patriarch of all mankind (which meant political dominion ever after), and also gave absolute rule to all fathers. Kingship was the exalted form of patriarchy rooted in both.

Locke resurrected and then pommeled Filmer's arguments with his own counter-exegesis of the Bible, undermining all notions of patriarchal rule, including that of fathers, and insisting that (for example) God's charge of dominion given to Adam was not over men (as Tory Anglicans would have it) but over property (as Locke and the Whig commercial class would have rule defined). This argument prepared the way for Locke's overriding aim in the *Second Treatise*: to demonstrate that "the great and chief end . . . of men's uniting into commonwealths and putting themselves under government is the preservation of their property."[15]

What has always struck readers of Locke's *Second Treatise*—and thereby caused nearly endless controversies—was the strange and seemingly incompatible mixture of biblical and natural law arguments on the one hand, and Hobbesian arguments on the other—the latter appearing to undermine the former. To take a key example, rather than begin his account of our natural, original condition in Genesis (as the Bible does) or with human beings defined as essentially political animals (as the natural law states), Locke immersed his readers immediately into a Hobbesian pre-political state of nature peopled with isolated individuals. He then informed his audience that this natural state is "a state of perfect freedom" where men may "order their actions and dispose of the possessions and persons as they think fit, within the bounds of the law of nature, without asking leave or depending upon the will of any other man."[16]

This sounds almost identical to Hobbes but with important alterations that shift the political emphasis from absolutist monarchy to the oligarchic rule of the commercial class, and replace Hobbes's seeming atheism with a more moderate religious treatment. To begin with the latter, Locke added to his state of nature what Hobbes subtracted: God. In Hobbes's God-less state of nature, since there is no good or evil, each individual can claim a

[15] John Locke, *Second Treatise* (hereafter ST), in *Two Treatises of Government*, ed. Thomas Cook (New York: Hafner Press, 1947), IX.123.

[16] Locke, ST, II.4.

natural right to do with himself and others as he pleases. For Locke, this account would support the irreligious anarchy that he had experienced during the Civil Wars, as well as absolute, arbitrary monarchy to cure it. Locke maintained, by contrast, that what limited actions in this original state was the fact that (as Holy Writ informs us) all men are "the workmanship of one omnipotent and infinitely wise Maker" so that "they are his *property* [emphasis added] whose workmanship they are." Because each pre-political individual is God's property, "there cannot be supposed any such subordination among us that may authorize us to destroy another."[17]

But that is not what Scripture says. That Locke defined human beings as God's *property* rather than as made in the image of God signals Locke's central politicizing aim as it governs his exegesis of the Bible: to ground politics in property ownership and offer biblical support for the rule by the commercial class.

He reinforced this aim on several levels, first by asserting that each man "has a property in his own person," an extension or duplication of the claim that we are God's property. Since we "own" ourselves, then we have a natural right to preserve ourselves in any way we please (a Hobbesian premise). Extending Hobbes, Locke argued that our striving for self-preservation is expressed, for each individual, by his labor. For each individual, "the Labour of his body and the work of his hands . . . are properly his," for whatever "he removes of the State that Nature hath provided, . . . he hath mixed his Labour with, and joined

[17] Locke, ST, II.6.

to it something that is his own, and thereby makes it his property."[18]

Giving this argument scriptural support, Locke claimed that property ownership through labor is the proper expression of God's granting of dominion, and hence the proper pre-political foundation of politics. While "God gave the world to men in common," Locke maintained, "He gave it to the use of the industrious and rational—and labour was to be his title to it—not to the fancy or covetousness of the quarrelsome and contentious."[19] In other words, the earth was given by God to the *industrious commercial class*, rather than the aristocratic inheritors of property, who never labor at all, or the rabble, who avoid labor whenever possible and want to snatch the property of the commercial class.

That this new foundation demanded a considerable reformulation of Holy Scripture is evident in Locke's silence about the Fall, wherein the Bible informs us that labor was taken to be part of the punishment for sin, sin which wounded both human nature and nature. Against this central doctrine of orthodox Christianity, Locke stripped labor of any sense of connection to sin and, moreover, asserted that human labor turns nature, which is of itself almost entirely a useless waste, into something truly good. "It is labour . . . which puts the greatest part of the value upon land, without which it would scarcely be worth anything," in Locke's estimation, "ninety-nine hun-

[18] Locke, ST, V.26–27.

[19] Locke, ST, V.34.

dredths" of the worth being due to human labor.[20] This, too, is a twisting of Scripture: rather than nature being fundamentally good and labor being a curse, Locke substitutes the very modern notion that industrious labor is the key to advancing the human material, earthly good (and hence, the new foundation for political life, as supported by Locke's politicizing approach to Scripture).

Another sign of the tension between Scripture and Locke's account of the state of nature—one directly related to his account of labor giving nature value—is Locke's implicit denial of any limit of material acquisition of property for the industrious. Locke is silent about the many warnings in the New Testament regarding the effect of riches on the human soul. It is true that in his account of the state of nature, he first set a limit to how much property one could acquire: "As much as one can make use of to any advantage of life before it spoils, so much he may by his labor fix a property in," for "nothing was made by God for man to spoil or destroy."[21] But, we find out later in his argument, since gold and silver do not spoil, then one "might heap as much of these durable things as he pleased; the exceeding of the bounds of his just property not lying in the largeness of his possession, but the perishing of anything useless in it."[22] And so "thus came in the use of money—some lasting thing that men might keep without spoiling and that by mutual consent men would take in exchange for the truly

[20] Locke intones this assertion at regular intervals. Locke, ST, V.36–37, 40, 43.

[21] Locke, ST, V.31.

[22] Locke, ST, V.46.

useful but perishable supports of life."[23]

Industrious human labor ensures the right to acquire property, and money extends indefinitely the amount of property one can own.[24] The right to property is not limited to one's personal labor but includes the labor of animals and other human beings in one's service, and the surplus of goods produced—however large that surplus may be—can be exchanged for unlimited amounts of gold and silver, without violating any moral limit and with the full blessings of God. Again, Locke therefore had to steer clear of any scriptural passages that would seem to warn of the dangers of mammon to the soul's eternal destiny, thereby politicizing the Bible accordingly so that it fit his political aim of undergirding rule by England's new commercial industrial class—just as he had to set aside any concerns for the poor over the industrious and wealthy, or anything that would support kingship and rule by those who inherit their estates rather than labor for them.

It is certainly worth noting that Locke's famous and immensely influential *Essay on Human Understanding* is significantly politicized—that is, bent to his political aims—as well. Echoing Machiavelli's rejection of philosophical contemplation and consequent reduction of human efforts to the earthly, material realm, Locke declared that God did not make human reason to be capable of penetrating elevated metaphysical or theological truths. Rather, "men have

23 Locke, ST, V.47.

24 An extension made clear in Locke earlier in his argument when he included in one's own labor, and hence right to property, "the grass my horse has bit, the turfs my servant has cut, and the ore I have digged in any place." Locke, ST, V.28.

reason to be well satisfied with what God hath thought fit for them, since he has given them," in regard to their rational capacities, the ability to seek "whatsoever is necessary for the conveniences of life and information of virtue; and has put within the reach of their discovery, the comfortable provision for this life and the way that leads to a better."[25] Just as we are God's property and he gives us dominion to amass our own, God limited our reason to the practical economic concerns of the property-owning industrial class.

Importantly, reason so defined also limits faith, first of all, in the obvious sense that reason cannot rise above the provisioning for the flesh. God created us as *homo economicus* rather than *homo sapiens*. Secondly, according to Locke, reason judges revelation. Just as human secular politics is supreme in its realm, and theological matters may not interfere with civil peace, so also in any conflict between reason and revelation,

> *reason* is the proper judge; and *revelation*, though it may, in consenting with it, confirm its dictates, yet cannot in such cases invalidate its decrees; *nor can we be obliged, where we have the clear and evident sentence of reason, to quit it for the contrary opinion, under a pretence that it is a matter of faith*, which can have no authority against the plain and clear dictates of *reason*.[26]

[25] John Locke, *An Essay Concerning Human Understanding*, ed. John Yolton, abr. ed. (London: J. M. Dent, 1993), I.i.5. Yolton's is an abridgement of Locke's fifth edition published in 1706, the last published by Locke.

[26] Locke, *An Essay Concerning Human Understanding*, IV.xviii.6.

While the considerably thinned-out version of the Bible can support Locke's political realm morally, it may never criticize or contradict it. In Locke's words,

> There can be no evidence that any traditional revelation is of divine original, in the words we receive it and in the sense we understand it, so clear and so certain as that of the principles of reason; and therefore *nothing that is contrary to, and inconsistent with, the clear and self-evident dictates of reason has a right to be urged or assented to as a matter of faith, wherein reason hath nothing to do.*[27]

In terms of what these assertions would mean for creating a biblical method, the Bible would have to be exegetically remade accordingly. We are back at *The Reasonableness of Christianity*, Locke's Whig interpretation of Scripture. Readers interested in delving more deeply into this mode of exegesis could read Locke's influential *Paraphrase and Notes on the Epistles of St. Paul*, also very influential with historical-critical scholars of the eighteenth century.

For our purposes, we have covered enough of Locke's works to understand how his moderate radicalism in support of the rising industrial commercial class defined his approach to interpreting the Bible.With Locke we have arrived at the eighteenth century, the Century of Enlightenment, the century often referred to by historians of philosophy as Locke's century, the century to which our

[27] Locke, *An Essay Concerning Human Understanding*, IV.xviii.10.

own modern historical-critical scholars look as the source of their approach to biblical exegesis. Locke was the great philosopher of the Enlightenment, the intellectual mentor of the more moderate Enlightenment thinkers both in England and on the Continent, as contrasted with Toland, who well represents the radical Enlightenment, those who carried Spinozism forward.

Given this preparation—which actually extends all the way back to the early 1300s, as our analysis over these chapters has made clear—we may now work our way into territory more familiar to the contemporary historical-critical exegete. As the reader will soon discover, it is not new territory at all, but flows directly from the developments we have traced over the previous four centuries and right down to the present day.

Chapter Twelve

COMING BACK TO THE BEGINNING

We have arrived at the beginning; that is, we have worked our way up to the so-called century of Enlightenment, the eighteenth century, the time that most contemporary historical-critical scholars regard as the century of origin for their approach to Scripture, the century before the great intellectual peak of their method in nineteenth-century Germany.

Recall from our first chapter that the scholars of the Jesus Seminar looked back to Hermann Samuel Reimarus (1694–1768) and David Friedrich Strauss (1808–1874) as representative grandfather and father of the "scientific" method of interpreting Scripture. To this short list, we could justly add other acknowledged luminaries spanning both centuries: in the eighteenth century figures such as Johann David Michaelis (1717–1791), Johann Salomo Semler (1725–1791), and Gotthold Lessing (1729–1781), and in the nineteenth century Johann Gottfried Eichhorn (1752–1827), W. M. L. de Wette (1780–1849), and Julius Wellhausen (1844–1918). All of these figures would be acknowledged by any contemporary historical-critical scholar as significant architects of their method.

What is enlightening, in this claim of pedigree, is how *derivative* these figures actually are. Upon reading them, we find that they carried forward the developments we've covered in the period between 1300–1700, rather than offering anything strikingly original.

Just to give a few indications of illuminating connections to the "pre-Enlightenment" period, Reimarus did his dissertation on Machiavelli, read Toland's works avidly, and was certainly influenced by Spinoza as well. Semler and Michaelis praised Richard Simon as heralding a new age in biblical criticism, with Semler publishing German translations of Simon's critical histories of the Old and New Testament in the mid-1770s. In 1776, Semler produced a new edition of the radical Spinozist Lodewijk Meyer's *Philosophia S. Scripturae Interpres* (1666), a book attacking superstition in the name of reason that since its publication had been routinely classed with Spinoza's *Tractatus* and Hobbes's *Leviathan* as great destroyers of biblical faith. For this clearly heterodox book, Semler provided a preface and extensive notes. Semler greatly influenced Lessing, who in the 1770s published Reimarus's rationalist attack on Christianity in the Wolfenbüttel Fragments, and Lessing himself was also deeply indebted to Spinoza. Michaelis was greatly influenced by Locke's *Paraphrases*, even writing the preface to the German translation published in the late 1760s. The tilt toward the more radical is obvious in this list, with Michaelis being the exception.

If we attend more closely to the lives and arguments of these great German figures, we see their evident connections to the previous centuries. As just noted, Hermann Samuel Reimarus not only read Toland but also "lived" his arguments, in particular Toland's key distinction between the exoteric (public) and esoteric (private). Publicly, Reimarus allied himself with the moderate deism of Christian Wolff (who, in turn, was indebted to Locke's arguments), but privately he was a Spinozist. We know about Reimarus's private beliefs because they were made public by Gotthold Lessing in the 1770s, a decade after Reimarus's death. Lessing published only parts of Reimarus's esoteric writings, which came to be known as the Wolfenbüttel Fragments, and it was this private side of Reimarus that became so immensely influential in the further development of the historical-critical method in Germany.

Reading Reimarus, one finds almost exact parallels to Toland's *Christianity not Mysterious*.[1] As with Toland, and Spinoza before him, the goal was to remove the miracles from Scripture, cutting off any supernatural aspects of the Bible, and then to retool what remained to fit the political goal of toleration. Reimarus thereby redefined Jesus as a mere mortal, a Jewish prophet divinized by his followers (the same claim set out, as we've seen in the first chapter, by scholars in our own time).

The publication of Reimarus's secret musings by Lessing caused an uproar, in great part because they were rightly recognized as *one more* instance of the notorious Spinoza's growing influence. In fact, Lessing himself was rightly accused of being a Spinozist. He was greatly

[1] See the Introduction to Charles Talbert, ed., and Ralph Fraser, trans., *Reimarus: Fragments* (Chico, CA: Scholars Press, 1985), 16–17.

influenced by another German Spinozist, Johann Lorenz Schmidt, who translated Spinoza's *Ethics* and then smuggled it into Germany, the *Ethics* being the text wherein Spinoza set forth his pantheism.

In Lessing's own work—which was as influential as Reimarus's, if not more so, for the development of the historical-critical method—we find that the familiar Averroistic-Spinozan Great Divide between the Enlightened and the vulgar has been transformed into a historical schema, where humanity moves from its pre-critical, infantile, vulgar period to enlightenment. Prior to Newton, everyone (or nearly everyone) was in the condition of the vulgar: unenlightened by modern science and therefore prone to believe in the supernatural and miraculous. Not so for Lessing. As he stated matter-of-factly, "I live in the eighteenth century, in which miracles no longer happen."[2] Between those on the prescientific side of the line and those on the enlightened side, there exists a Great Divide, an "ugly, broad ditch" about which Lessing famously declared, "I cannot get across, however often and however earnestly I have tried to make the leap."[3] On the far side of the ditch are those who still believe in Christ as the miracle-performing God-man; on Lessing's side, one finds only the Jesus of history, a Jewish man.

The existence of Lessing's Ditch, as it soon came to be called, meant that something like Spinozism had to be applied to the interpretation of the Bible as the only

[2] Gotthold Lessing, "On the Proof of the Spirit and of Power," in *Lessing's Theological Writings*, trans. and ed. Henry Chadwick (Stanford, CA: Stanford University Press, 1956), 52.

[3] Lessing, "On the Proof of the Spirit and of Power," 55.

reasonable, possible response of someone in the eighteenth century (and then the nineteenth, twentieth, and twenty-first centuries as well). There was no going backward; science demands Spinozism, the full removal of the miraculous.

Lessing's historical lesson did not receive a warm reception by those unenlightened Germans who still stubbornly remained on the other side of the ditch in the late 1700s. So Lessing (following Spinoza, Toland, and Locke) argued for political toleration of the enlightened by the not yet enlightened who still had political control. His hope was that "scientific" biblical scholarship would eventually tame and transform the unenlightened: progressive, historical enlightenment would bring everyone over the ditch.

As we recall from our first chapter, over two centuries after Lessing, historical-critical scholar Robert Funk was still sounding the same battle cry: "We can no longer simply repeat the old creeds and *pre-Enlightenment* shibboleths and expect thinking people to regard them as illuminating and persuasive." Alas, for the exasperated Funk, unthinking, precritical holdouts clinging to the Divine Jesus still mulishly remain on the wrong side of Lessing's Ditch, the Great Divide. And so historical-critical scholars must double down on enlightening exegesis.

Returning again to the eighteenth century, we find another disciple of Spinoza, Johann Salomo Semler, who, as noted, spent considerable intellectual effort in transporting the most radical thought to Germany. Yet, as with Reimarus, and perhaps even more so, Semler lived a double life. He was at the very same time a staunch *public* supporter of the position that Prussia's university faculty, who were servants of the Prussian state, had a duty to uphold the orthodox theological positions of the populace being ruled (in this case, Lutheran orthodoxy). Privately echoing Toland, Semler declared that Jesus was a mere man, a moral teacher who himself taught his audience at two levels, the exoteric teaching for the great masses and the esoteric for the inner circle of disciples. The Bible, of course, was a mixture, so the enlightened exegete had to separate the "Word of God" (the rational, demythologized enlightened elements) from "Scripture."[4]

The contradiction between Semler's call for academics to toe the orthodox Lutheran line and his private views couldn't be more stark: not only did he privately reject the miracles of Christ the God-man as well as his divinity, but, predictably, he also reduced the entire enlightened Gospel to moral admonitions, exalting "works righteousness." As if that weren't enough divergence from Lutheran orthodoxy, Semler argued that since the biblical canon as we received it was defined by the early Church, then it is the result of the pre-critical, irrational judgments of that unenlightened time. Consequently, the question of canonicity should be reopened so that rational historical-critical scholars could choose from among the canonical and noncanonical books to create an acceptable Bible defined by the enlightened. In Semler's words, after a proper critical inquiry, "one finally discovers that the canonical books . . . as little contain the

[4] See John Hayes, "Historical Criticism of the Old Testament Canon," in *Hebrew Bible / Old Testament, The History of Its Interpretation*, Vol. II, *From the Renaissance to the Enlightenment*, ed. Magne Sæbø (Göttingen: Vandenhoeck & Ruprecht, 2008), ch. 42, 1003.

universal unalterable complete sum of the Christian religion as those other books not in the canon: the Epistle of Barnabas, the writings of Hermas and of Clement in Rome."[5] At best, the received canon tells us something about the historical time of the early Church and its actors in terms of the exact particularities of their unenlightened views.

Of course, this sounds much like Toland, but also like our contemporary historical-critical scholar Bart Ehrman, who for very similar reasons also calls for an opening of the biblical canon by the academic elite, as evidenced in his *The Lost Christianities: The Battles for Scripture and the Faiths We Never Knew* (2003). Of course, we are not surprised to find (in accord with Toland, Reimarus, Lessing, and Semler) that Ehrman also published a book demonstrating the now well-worn thesis that Christianity as a religion is based upon a mistake: *How Jesus Became God: The Exaltation of a Jewish Preacher from Galilee* (2014). As the title proclaims, the unenlightened must realize that Jesus was only a man.

As noted, David Friedrich Strauss is also considered a giant of the formation of the historical-critical method in nineteenth-century Germany, but we are not surprised to find that he too is derivative. Strauss's most famous work was *The Life of Jesus Critically Examined*, published in German in 1835, and translated into English, interestingly enough, by the famous authoress George Eliot (Marian

5 Quote from Semler's *Neue Versuche die Kirchenhistorie der ersten Jahrhunderte mehr aufzuklären* (1788) in J. C. O'Neill, *The Bible's Authority: A Portrait Gallery of Thinkers from Lessing to Bultmann* (Edinburgh: T & T Clark, 1991), 46.

Evans) eleven years later, thereby rocking both sides of the English Channel. In the introductory chapter, entitled "Development of the Mythical Point of View," Strauss informed readers that an "account is not historical" if "the narration is irreconcilable with the known and universal laws which govern the course of events." Why? Because "the absolute cause never disturbs the chain of secondary causes by single arbitrary actions of interposition."[6]

We are not told *why* the absolute cause is unable (or unwilling) to disturb the creation he caused. We are simply informed that miracles cannot happen, and anything in the text that smacks of the miraculous must therefore be mythical. To examine Jesus's life critically therefore meant, for Strauss, to remove the mythical and reveal the historical.

We are certainly on familiar turf here, reaching all the way back through Toland and Spinoza to Hobbes, and back even further through Machiavelli and Marsilius to the ancient pagan assumption that philosophers know that the miraculous and mythological have no basis in reality (even if they might be useful instruments of political control).

Strauss's conclusion allows us to see the influence of Spinoza's pantheism, however indirectly it may have been filtered through Hegel: a divinizing of humanity that substitutes our own efforts in mastering nature via technological science (recalling Descartes's project) for those of the mythical God-man in bringing about our own earthly salvation—the ultimate politicization of the

[6] David Friedrich Strauss, *The Life of Jesus Critically Examined*, 4th edition, ed. Peter Hodgson (Philadelphia, PA: Fortress, 1972), Introduction, section 16, 87–88.

Bible. It is worth quoting at length.

> In an individual, a God-man, the properties and functions which the church ascribes to Christ contradict themselves; in the idea of the race, they perfectly agree. Humanity is the union of two natures—God become man, the infinite manifesting itself in the finite, and the finite spirit remembering its infinitude; it is the child of the visible Mother and the invisible Father, Nature and Spirit; it is the worker of miracles, in so far as in the course of human history the spirit more and more completely subjugates nature, both within and around man, until it lies before him as the inert matter on which he exercises his active power; it is the sinless existence, for the course of its development is a blameless one, pollution cleaves to the individual only, and does not touch the race or its history. It is Humanity that dies, rises, and ascends to heaven, for from the negation of its phenomenal life there ever proceeds a higher spiritual life; from the suppression of its mortality as a personal, national, and terrestrial spirit, arises its union with the infinite spirit of the heavens. By faith in this Christ, especially in his death and resurrection, man is justified before God; that is, by the kindling within him of the idea of Humanity, the individual man participates in the divinely human life of the species.[7]

[7] Strauss, *The Life of Jesus Critically Examined*, "Concluding dissertation," section 151, 780.

Strauss would soon give up any pretense of Christianity and embrace an entirely secular worldview, the usual end of the radical side of the Enlightenment.

What about the more moderate branch, the one associated with Locke and then (as noted above) Johann David Michaelis? We might sum up Michaelis's considerable influence by saying that he transformed biblical studies in order to make it relevant to an age that had grown weary of confessional controversies.[8] One response to such controversies, as we have seen, was the introduction of skepticism that undermined the authority of the Bible, skepticism that had penetrated Germany. Michaelis offered an alternative, a more traditional response that shifted the focus of biblical studies from a confessional, theological enterprise to a cultural, political, academic effort aimed at using the Bible to support German political aims. In Michael Legaspi's words, Michaelis steered away from the "kind of aggressive heterodoxy associated with the radical or early Enlightenment," and instead was among those championing "a conservative progressivism that took the cultural obsolescence of confessional Christianity for granted and aimed at the creation of an irenic social order based upon reason, morality, and the growing power of the state."[9] He did not—as the radical Enlightenment sceptics—undermine the authority of Scripture; rather, in Legaspi's words, he

[8] For a more thorough analysis of Michaelis, see Scott Hahn and Jeffrey Morrow, *Modern Biblical Criticism as a Tool of Statecraft (1700–1900)* (Steubenville, OH: Emmaus Academic, 2020), chs. 3–4.

[9] Michael Legaspi, *The Death of Scripture and the Rise of Biblical Studies* (Oxford: Oxford University Press, 2010), ix–x.

"redeployed" it.[10] Ironically, Michaelis's good-faith effort actually furthered the secularization and politicization of Scripture

At the center of Michaelis's "conservative progressivism" was the German University, an institution entirely subservient to the state (meaning, of course, that all faculty, including those in religion, were civil servants—an idea that goes all the way back to Marsilius of Padua). In continuity with Marsilius (and Locke as well), the goal of biblical exegesis for Michaelis was irenic—that is, to aid in bringing about and maintaining political peace, largely through an emphasis on the moral (rather than theological) teachings of the Bible.

Thus, in Volume I of his influential multi-volume *Raisonnement über die protestantischen Universitäten in Deutschland*, Michaelis argued that the proper teaching of irenic, enlightened biblical studies is necessary because without it, "theology is beset by barbarism and ignorance," which opens the door for "religious frauds to deceive the citizens," the result being that "they will not spread reasonable and useful morality but, instead of these, traffic in many useless, incomprehensible, or erroneous propositions," which breed "useless quarrels . . . capable of unsettling the state." This "danger" will be avoided "if theology is drawn from the Bible with sufficient linguistic competence and if it is enlightened by philosophy." If this enlightened approach is taken, "it will train still more effectively the obedient citizen who, because of his duties,

[10] Legaspi, *The Death of Scripture*, xii.

treats it [i.e., theology so understood] as a law."[11]

Biblical studies therefore had a place in the modern German university. Its aim was not to produce fervent believers, or even towering academics, but competent, solid citizens and civil servants. This fit into a more comprehensive goal of the university: to contribute to the glory of the state (and that meant the university's biblical studies departments were departments of state).[12]

As with the moderate Locke, this transformation of theology, though "progressive," guarded against the most damaging intrusions of the radical Enlightenment. So, for example, Michaelis provided a famous refutation of Reimarus's denial of the resurrection of Jesus Christ, and along with other like-minded academics at the University at Göttingen, defended Christianity against the attacks of Enlightenment atheists.[13] Here we have a parallel to Locke's moderate defense of Christianity against the likes of radicals such as Toland.

Along with our previous thinkers from Hobbes forward, Michaelis was intent on undermining the Judaic elements in the Bible, but for different reasons that were specific to the German political context of his time. Michaelis was not trying to destroy the authority of the Bible by chipping away at the Old Testament, as were the skeptics. Rather, he was attempting to remove any cultural support in Protestant Germany for Jews (whom he feared were weakening the state), and to blunt any Catholic-friendly elements

[11] Quoted in Legaspi, *The Death of Scripture*, 35–36.

[12] Legaspi, *The Death of Scripture*, 34.

[13] Legaspi, *The Death of Scripture*, 40–50.

in Scripture that would lend credence to Catholicism in Protestant-dominated Germany.

To do this, Michaelis brought his profound philological and historical learning to the task of transforming Old Testament studies from a confessional, theological discipline to a kind of academic study of a great ancient culture (one comparable to the study of Greek or Latin culture in Classical Studies). To study the Hebrew Bible properly, on this view, one had to study the ancient Hebrews, their language, and their defining text in the same way, academically, that one would study any ancient culture. Michaelis thereby—almost single-handedly—created Hebrew Studies, an academic discipline that (since it rested on the study of ancient culture, history, and philology rather than theology) did not depend on the beliefs of its practitioners. Michaelis thereby contributed to the secularizing tendency of historical criticism that would result in the academic treatment of the Bible as the equivalent of, say, Homer's *Iliad* or Virgil's *Aeneid*.

But, we repeat, Michaelis's goal was not that of someone like Spinoza. The development of Hebrew Studies would (he thought) elevate the study of the Old Testament to the more esteemed academic level of Classical Studies, even while it emphasized moral lessons that would buttress the political order of Germany and suppress theological controversies that upset it. In the same way that one could learn moral wisdom from ancient Greek and Latin texts, the Old Testament could "become another classical text from which Germans could learn specific (Hebrew) wisdom and virtue that would better the German people and culture."[14]

We mustn't forget Michaelis's other political aims. Hebrew Studies isolated the study of ancient Jews and ancient Hebrew culture from later developments in Judaism and from Roman Catholicism, thereby undermining biblical support for contemporary Jews and Catholics. This academic goal was not innocent but, as several scholars have noted, clearly anti-Semitic and political. Michaelis even argued that Jews, instead of being incorporated into German society, should be resettled as a colony on an island where they could engage in the useful production of sugar[15] (a not at all veiled parallel to the treatment of African slaves).

As with Machiavelli, Hobbes, and Toland, one can see Michaelis's political presuppositions come through in his account of Moses. As a conservative, he argued against the radicals who undermined Mosaic authorship of the Pentateuch, but he did so by presenting Moses as a kind of enlightened, monotheistic, poetic genius, a Jewish Homer and a great political founder who tailored the Jewish law to the particularities of the situation of the Jews at the time (an approach that was heavily indebted to the political philosopher Montesquieu[16]).

Thus, "God never meant [the Mosaic Law] to bind

[14] Hahn and Morrow, *Modern Biblical Criticism as a Tool of Statecraft (1700–1900)*, 76.

[15] Legaspi, *The Death of Scripture*, 98.

[16] See Legaspi, *The Death of Scripture*, 141, and even more importantly, Jonathan M. Hess, "Johann David Michaelis and the Colonial Imaginary: Orientalism and the Emergence of Racial Antisemitism in Eighteenth-Century Germany," *Jewish Social Studies* 6, no. 2 (Winter 2000): 56–101.

any other nation but the Israelites."[17] It was a particular law defined by the enlightened philosopher-founder Moses, one that rested on consideration of the particular time and place of the Jews. Since the Mosaic Law was designed only for ancient Jews, it could not support modern Jews. Hebrew Studies thereby contributed to Michaelis's anti-Semitic political vision (and, one should add, the later efforts, a century after Michaelis's death, to remove the influence of Catholics in Germany's *Kulturkampf*, since it undermined the priestly foundation for Catholicism in the Old Testament).

Johann Gottfried Eichhorn studied under Michaelis at Göttingen and was greatly influenced by Semler. He is most famous as a precursor to Julius Wellhausen, and the latter's division of the Pentateuch into historical layers, from earliest to latest (ranging from the tenth to sixth centuries BC): Jehovist (or Yahwist), Elohist, Deuteronimist, and Priestly, or JEDP, as it's popularly known. This Documentary Hypothesis was aimed at showing that the Pentateuch was not written by one man, Moses, but consisted of historical layers that the enlightened exegete could identify.

For Eichhorn, the earliest layer, the Jehovist, revealed the first Israelites as myth-makers, who (despite their pre-enlightened condition) yet uttered philosophical truths in mythical form. The kernel of purely rational, natural truths—those which accorded with the enlightened notions of Eichhorn—could be recovered by the exegete, and therefore the mythical truths could be retooled and

[17] From Michaelis's *Mosaiches Recht*, as quoted in Legaspi, *The Death of Scripture*, 141.

made relevant. This allowed Eichhorn to reach over Lessing's Ditch and reconstruct the Bible as leading up to the Enlightenment (if the myths were properly interpreted). For Eichhorn, the prophets were not divinely inspired but spoke with such authority and power that their utterances were taken to be divine. They are the most salvageable part of the Old Testament. The priests, however, with their superstitious ceremonialism, were late obscurantists of this promising rational beginning.

Wellhausen worked Eichhorn's assumptions into a more elaborate account of JEDP, wherein the earliest Jews represented the purest natural, spontaneous religion, a religion without law that welled up from their direct connection to nature—an idea obviously indebted to the Romantic movement, and found in figures from Jean-Jacques Rousseau (1712–1778) to Johann Gottfried Herder (1744–1803). For Wellhausen, this original natural religion was at one and the same time a prototype of Lutheranism, and, even more deeply, of the original Teutonic natural religion (thereby fusing two aspects of German messianic nationalism reaching back five hundred years). In this regard, we may witness his account of the earliest religious life of the Israelites. In his *Prolegomena to the History of Ancient Israel* (1883), Wellhausen declared that,

> In the early days, worship arose out of the midst of ordinary life, and was in most intimate manifold connection with it. A sacrifice was a meal, a fact showing how remote was the idea of antithesis between spiritual earnestness and secular joyousness. . . . Religious worship was a natural thing in

> Hebrew antiquity; it was the blossom of life, the heights and depths of which it was its business to transfigure and glorify.[18]

The Deuteronomic Law came later, sullying this original, natural religion with the law, and far worse than this, then came the even later priestly accretions. Recovering the early Jehovist epoch was a way to reinforce Germany's striving for political identity, where the common political religion grounded national unity, both ancient and modern, Jehovist and German. This striving, for Wellhausen, was therefore not unconnected to Germany's nationalist wars, from Bismarck's efforts at unification to Germany's quest for empire in World War I.[19] One cannot properly assess Wellhausen's historical-critical account of the Old Testament without keeping in mind the infusion of politicized aims that defined it.

With Wellhausen, we enter the twentieth century, the century with which we began (along with the twenty-first) in our introduction. We are back to the beginning and have learned quite a lot about the *politicization* of the Bible. Let's go over some of the main points and add important reflections.

First of all, when we enlarge our vision historically, we find a much deeper and broader understanding of what

[18] Julius Wellhausen, *Prolegomena to the History of Ancient Israel* (Cleveland: Meridian Books, 1957), ch. II.iii, 76–77.

[19] For an overview and assessment of the connection of Wellhausen's thought to Germany's military endeavors, see Paul Michael Kurz, "The Way of War: Wellhausen, Israel, and Bellicose *Reiche*," *Zeitschrift für die alttestamentliche Wissenschaft* 127, no. 1 (2015): 1–19.

politicizing is. The politicization of Scripture is one part of a much larger historical movement to purposely reduce human nature and human experience to a less-than-human level. It began with Marsilius stunting Aristotle's account of human beings, from rational animals who were somehow divine in their capacities and whose highest goal was to search the heavens to mere animals whose aims were entirely limited to the bodily concerns of animals. This lowered aim was the deepest cause of his attempts at politicizing the Bible; that is, the assumption that there was nothing above material existence was the source of his redefining religion as a mere political instrument. After all, if there is nothing above material existence, then the worship of an immaterial God by human beings claiming they are made in the image of God—when they are really only animals—is foolish. But that doesn't keep the belief itself, however foolish, from being useful for some wiser animals to control other foolish animals politically.

Hence, following the ancient pagans, who shared this lowered view of human nature and the political instrumentality of religion, Marsilius made the first modern steps toward politicizing the Bible. We would more properly say that Marsilius first politicized human beings—that is, made of them nothing more than an animal that gathers together socially and has no higher aim than peaceful, comfortable existence for as long each one's earthly life lasts.

Now it should be obvious that, even though Marsilius lived almost four centuries before Newton and the consequent Enlightenment, nothing more than his fundamental conviction is needed for the assertion that there cannot be any miracles and that if a certain Jesus Christ existed, then he could not have been anything more than a man (and if so, nothing more than yet another animal of the species, however interesting). And if he was, in fact, a mere man, then one can only assign to the realm of mythology the parts of the Bible that speak otherwise. *Nothing more than this fundamental conviction of humanity's reduced nature is necessary to produce nearly all the assumptions and conclusions of the modern historical-critical method*, and it is this fundamental conviction that was carried forward, deepened, and elaborated by the likes of Machiavelli, Descartes, Hobbes, Spinoza, Toland, and Locke.

We must note an important related point about the beginnings in Marsilius. By mythology, as related to his account, one cannot mean "nonscientific" in the modern sense, because the advent of modern science, even in its earliest infancy, is at least three centuries away from the early 1300s. "Myth" actually means something like this: the kind of thinking that goes with human beings assuming that they are a special creature whose capacities and aims cannot be reduced to quotidian animal existence, including accounts of cosmology that are inferred from this foolishly assumed special status. On this account, thinking that human beings are defined by something more than quotidian animal existence is the first step to foolishly assuming that human life may have an ultimate destiny beyond such existence, and even more, that there is a divine being or beings that exist entirely free from such worldly existence.

That brings us to Machiavelli, who gave us our first, truly modern example of (deeply politicized) exegesis in his treatment of Moses, one that resurfaces again, in multifarious forms, among later historical-critical scholars. But the thing to note about Machiavelli, given what we have just said, is that before he politicizes the Bible, he first of all politicizes philosophy. That is, Machiavelli attacks Plato, whose profound analysis of politics in terms of the immaterial soul's order resulted in spiritualized political philosophy, an approach that defines political life in terms of the trans-political, supra-political capacities of the soul. For Machiavelli, that goal was illusory, along with any notion of the "idea of the good" to which political life must conform. This life, this transient bodily life, is all there is, intoned Machiavelli, and so our understanding of politics must be reduced accordingly, uncontaminated by any notions of ideas of the good, of the soul, or of anything else that provided obstacles to effective political force by very worldly and worldly-wise rulers.

In this, Machiavelli (following Marsilius) politicized political philosophy, purposefully reducing its aims to conform to a thoroughly secularized, materialist account of reality (recall how influential Lucretius was for Machiavelli). This first, more fundamental instance of politicizing led Machiavelli to politicize the Bible, and so to remove the miraculous from Scripture and turn Moses into a Machiavellian prince who used religion to ruthlessly control the obstinate but gullible Jews fresh out of Egypt.

Again, this occurred nearly two centuries before Newton and the Enlightenment. It did not result from the victories of modern science, but preceded them. And so as with Marsilius, nothing more than Machiavelli's "prescientific" assumptions were necessary for him to become a great-grandfather of the modern historical-critical method and to treat Moses as a purely non-miraculous political leader.

Also, as we have seen, both political conditions and reforming efforts aided these new secular goals defined by Marsilius and Machiavelli (and those whom they directly influenced, such as the court surrounding the most Machiavellian Henry VIII). Certainly, the situation was quite complex, and the faithful aided and abetted the secularizing philosophers in their politicizing efforts. A string of corrupt popes, from the Avignon Papacy up through the Renaissance, lent credence to the notion that religion was just a sham used for political control and self-enrichment. Further, the reforming efforts of Ockham, Wycliffe, and Luther all contributed, directly or indirectly, to the secular political control of the church and of the Bible along with it so that, despite the sincere intentions of these Christian reformers, they played into the hands of those who would reduce the Bible to a political tool. As we have found out, even the Reformation's defining principle of *sola scriptura* was already invoked for quite different purposes by Marsilius (and would be again, later on, by Hobbes and even Spinoza). The history of these interactions from the 1300s to the early 1500s is, to say the least, exceedingly complicated, but let us remind ourselves again that we are still two centuries prior to the scientific revolution.

That brings another very important point to our attention: the Great Divide preceded the modern scientific revolution as well. This particular division of the human race into the wise and foolish, those who know that the Bible is yet another book of ancient mythology and those who are too dim to realize it, can be traced back from Machiavelli and Marsilius to the ancient pagan authors who believed the very same thing about any and every religion, even though they had no connection to the particular "mythology" that arose among the Jews.

Interestingly, it is a philosophical inversion of another form of the Great Divide, one found in Plato and Aristotle, where human beings are divided into those who live according to the highest goods of the soul and those who live as if they were no more than mere animals. For Marsilius and Machiavelli, the latter were really the wise ones, and the former were fools.

And so, looking very carefully at this long "prescientific" history, what we find is a philosophical revolution at the root of the transformation to modern secularism, and the exegetical approach to biblical scholarship that will emanate from and reinforce it. That is the importance of our analysis of Descartes and even more of Hobbes, whose treatments of religion in general and Christianity in particular result from their complete embrace of ancient Democritan-Epicurean-Lucretian materialist atomism.

Descartes defined Christianity fideistically and then set it aside so he could present a completely mathematical-materialist philosophy that, if applied to Scripture (a task he left for his followers), would result in the removal of all that fails the twin criteria of clarity and certainty. What would have to be excised is pretty much everything latter historical-critical scholars said must be removed, because clarity and certainty were defined in terms of materialist reductionism. Hobbes was more ruthless in his application of materialism to the faith, all to support the power of his absolute political sovereign.

Descartes and Hobbes illustrate a very important point, even if it is often overlooked. They were both instrumental, in the first half of the seventeenth century, in laying the *philosophical foundation* for the modern materialist approach of science that would come into full flower by the end of the seventeenth century. Their view of what science *should be* was derived from their preexisting commitments to a kind of materialist reductionism that itself was not new, not discovered as the result of patient scientific discovery, but a reductionist assumption that came from the pagan philosophers Democritus, Epicurus, and Lucretius.

Spinoza and Toland, as we have seen, were simply carrying forth Hobbes's materialism and his project of completely subordinating Christianity to the political sovereign (hence, politicizing the Bible accordingly). Different sovereigns would be in charge of this politicizing: not absolute kings but absolute liberal democratic ruling bodies (who unknowingly served the materialist philosophical elite). Similarly, in Locke we find the same underlying commitment to subordinate the Bible to political ends, and we have made a strong case that he too was politicizing the Bible in accordance with materialist doctrines—in his instance, to support the commercial class rule of Parliament.

Hobbes, Spinoza, Toland, and Locke (along with Richard Simon, who, whatever his intentions, furthered Spinoza's radical attack on the Bible) are all acknowledged grandfathers of the historical-critical method, ones that bring us right up to the critical century, the century of Enlightenment, the 1700s. When, in this chapter, we examined key fathers of the historical-critical method in the 1700s and 1800s, we found continuity with the previous four hundred years, not a sudden intellectual revolution demanded by a scientific revolution. That brought us to recall the assortment of contemporary historical-critical scholars we covered in the first chapter who, likewise, give us nothing new (despite their claims to be on the cutting edge).

Understanding the sweep of these centuries, we can then grasp why—to repeat the essential point—*the scientific revolution of the late seventeenth century is unnecessary to produce the scholarship of the twentieth and twenty-first.* We need nothing in hand other than a well-read copy of the materialist classic Lucretius's *De Rerum Natura*, written a bit over a half-century before the birth of Jesus Christ, to assure us that Jesus must have been a mere man, and then Critias, Polybius, and so on to tell us what we should then do with religion to secure political order.

Some other reflections are in order. We recall the very Lucretian point, taken over from Epicurus, that the removal of religion would lead to peace of mind, an assumption taken over by Marsilius, Hobbes, Spinoza, Toland, and Locke in their belief that the politicization of Christianity would lead to lasting civil peace. This belief seemed to be affirmed in the destruction caused by the Thirty Years' War and the English Civil Wars. However, upon closer scrutiny, these sets of wars had far deeper political causes, ones that were exacerbated by religious differences but not reducible to them. This calls into question that important driving assumption that politicizing the Bible would result in an end to war. As if that weren't enough, we have as witness the fact that the greatest and most destructive wars of all time were those in the twentieth century, and they were nationalist in origin. And finally, the communist regimes in the Soviet Union, China, and elsewhere slaughtered tens upon tens of millions—far, far more than any religious conflict.

All of this destruction was caused by the most secularized nations in human history, ones that either heavily politicized Christianity for political purposes (such as Germany) or set about destroying the influence of Christianity once and for all (such as the Soviet Union and China). It is not too much to suggest that modern historical-critical scholarship contributed to this destruction, rather than acted to prevent it, and it did so either by reconstructing the Bible for nationalist aims (such as those of Wellhausen) or by destroying the possibility of biblical belief, thereby creating the vacuum for atheistic philosophies like Marxism, and hence the political devastation wrought by communism.

We may end these reflections on a moral note. We recall that one persistent, intended effect of politicizing the Bible was to remove all doctrinal content, leaving only a moral core which, so it was alleged, would allow the Bible to function as a moral prop for the secular state without upsetting political order with doctrinal disputes. Taken at face value, the assumption here was something like this, if we put it into words: we see that there's no end of wrangling about theological differences, but we all at least have a common moral agreement, so let's keep our separate doctrines to ourselves and live together on the common moral ground.

But today we realize that this was all either naïve or disingenuous. The morality derived from secularized culture and the morality derived from the Bible do not share common ground, as our current, extremely heated debates about abortion, infanticide, eugenics, homosexuality, homosexual marriage, and transgenderism make clear. Evidently, the subtraction of the doctrinal aspects of Christianity result, after several generations, in the substitution of secular morality for Christian morality. The fundamental differences between the two now divide our society far more deeply, vividly, and intractably than previous disputes among rival Christian parties. Needless to say, historical-critical scholarship, in undermining doctrine, has contributed mightily to the cultural substitution of secular morality for Christian morality.

This is, for the Christian, all rather distressing. It might seem that academic biblical scholarship is entirely redefined by the historical-critical method and its assumptions. While this is largely the case, it is, happily, not entirely the case, and so we leave our readers with a list of very helpful books by actual *believing* biblical scholars, those who maintain the highest academic standards except the artificial one that assumes that biblical scholars must leave faith and doctrine at the university door.

RECOMMENDED READING

Sources about the Bible

Bergsma, John. *Bible Basics for Catholics: A New Picture of Salvation History*. Notre Dame, IN: Ave Maria Press, 2012. An excellent basic overview of the Bible from a Catholic perspective.

____. *New Testament Basics for Catholics*. Notre Dame, IN: Ave Maria Press, 2015. An excellent basic overview of the New Testament from a Catholic perspective.

Bergsma, John, and Brant Pitre. *A Catholic Introduction to the Bible: The Old Testament*. San Francisco: Ignatius Press, 2018. An excellent overview of every book of the Old Testament from a Catholic perspective.

Gray, Tim, and Jeff Cavins. *Walking with God: A Journey Through the Bible*. West Chester, PA: Ascension Press, 2018. A very readable overview of the Bible from a Catholic perspective.

Hahn, Scott, ed. *Catholic Bible Dictionary*. New York: Doubleday, 2009. A very readable reference for covering everything you would want to know about the Bible.

Hahn, Scott. *A Father Who Keeps His Promises: God's Covenant Love in Scripture*. Cincinnati: Charis, 1998. An accessible introduction to the Bible from a Catholic perspective.

____. *Understanding the Scriptures: A Complete Course on Bible Study*. Chicago: Midwest Theological Forum, 2005. A very accessible complete introduction to the Bible from a Catholic perspective.

Hahn, Scott, and Curtis Mitch, ed. *Ignatius Catholic Study Bible: New Testament*. San Francisco: Ignatius Press, 2010. A magnificent and easily accessible commentary on the New Testament from a Catholic perspective.

Sources on Biblical Topics and Specific Books of the Bible

Barber, Michael. *Coming Soon: Unlocking the Book of Revelation and Applying Its Lessons Today*. Steubenville, OH: Emmaus Road, 2006. An excellent commentary on the Book of Revelation.

____. *Singing in the Reign: The Psalms and the Liturgy of God's Kingdom*. Steubenville, OH: Emmaus Road, 2001. A great overview of the Psalms.

Bergsma, John. *Jesus and the Dead Sea Scrolls: Revealing the Jewish Roots of Christianity*. New York: Image, 2019. An excellent look at early Christianity in the New Testament within its Jewish context in light of the evidence for Judaism during Jesus's day coming from the Dead Sea Scrolls.

____. *Psalm Basics for Catholics: Seeing Salvation History in a New Way*. South Bend, IN: Ave Maria Press, 2018. An excellent overview of the Psalms.

Hahn, Scott. *First Comes Love: Finding Your Family in the Church and the Trinity*. New York: Doubleday, 2006. A great discussion of the Trinity and the family in light of Scripture.

____. *The Fourth Cup: Unveiling the Mystery of the Last Supper and the Cross*. New York: Image, 2018. An excellent look at the Eucharist in the Bible.

____. *Hail, Holy Queen: The Mother of God in the Word of God*. New York: Doubleday, 2001. An excellent look at Catholic teaching on Mary in light of Scripture.

_____. *Joy to the World: How Christ's Coming Changed Everything (and Still Does)*. New York: Image, 2014. An excellent discussion of the biblical nativity.

____. *The Lamb's Supper: The Mass as Heaven on Earth*. New York: Doubleday, 1999. An excellent look at the Mass in light of the Book of Revelation, and the Book of Revelation in light of the Mass.

____. *Lord, Have Mercy: The Healing Power of Confession*. New York: Doubleday, 2003. An excellent look at the Sacrament of Confession in light of Scripture.

____. *Many Are Called: Rediscovering the Glory of the Priesthood*. New York: Doubleday, 2010. A great look at the Catholic priesthood in light of Scripture.

____. *A Pocket Guide to St. Paul*. Huntington, IN: Our Sunday Visitor, 2008. A compact volume covering the basics of St. Paul's Letters from a Catholic perspective.

____. *Swear to God: The Promise and Power of the Sacraments*. New York: Doubleday, 2004. A great look at the Sacraments in light of Scripture.

____. *Understanding "Our Father": Biblical Reflections on the Lord's Prayer*. Steubenville, OH: Emmaus Road, 2002. A brief look at the Our Father in light of Scripture.

Hahn, Scott, and Emily Stimpson Chapman. *Hope to Die: The Christian Meaning of Death and the Resurrection of the Body*. Steubenville, OH: Emmaus Road, 2020. An excellent look into the biblical background of Christian teaching on death and the resurrection.

Hahn, Scott, and Leon Suprenant, Jr., ed. *Scripture and*

the Mystery of the Mother of God. Steubenville, OH: Emmaus Road, 2016. An excellent volume situating Catholic teaching on Mary in light of Scripture.

Pitre, Brant. *Jesus the Bridegroom: The Greatest Love Story Ever Told*. New York: Image, 2014. An excellent look at the bridal imagery associated with Jesus as he fulfilled Jewish messianic expectations.

____. *Jesus and the Jewish Roots of the Eucharist: Unlocking the Secrets of the Last Supper*. New York: Doubleday, 2011. An excellent look at the Eucharist in its biblical context.

____. *Jesus and the Jewish Roots of Mary: Unveiling the Mother of the Messiah*. New York: Image, 2018. An excellent look at Catholic teaching on Mary in its biblical context.

Sri, Edward. *God with Us: Encountering Jesus in the Gospel of Matthew*. Steubenville: Emmaus Road, 2019. A good overview of the Gospel of Matthew.

____. *No Greater Love: A Biblical Walk Through Christ's Passion*. West Chester, PA: Ascension Press, 2019. A great look at the passion accounts in the Gospels.

____. *Rethinking Mary in the New Testament: What the Bible Tells Us about the Mother of Messiah*. San Francisco: Ignatius Press, 2018. A good overview of Catholic teaching on Mary in light of the Bible.

Sources on the Historical Reliability of the Bible

Kaiser, Walter C., Jr. *The Old Testament Documents: Are They Reliable and Relevant?* Downers Grove, IL:

InterVarsity Press, 2001. Overall a very good discussion of the historical reliability of the Old Testament by a leading evangelical Protestant scholar. Unfortunately, the early chapter on the canonization process of the Old Testament is inaccurate and in favor of the Protestant perspective.

Morrow, Jeffrey L. *Jesus' Resurrection: A Jewish Convert Examines the Evidence.* Toledo, OH: Principium Institute, 2017. A brief but thorough treatment of the historical evidence supporting Jesus's resurrection.

Pitre, Brant. *The Case for Jesus: The Biblical and Historical Evidence for Christ.* New York: Image, 2016. An excellent look at the historical reliability of the New Testament portrayal of Jesus.

Williams, Peter J. *Can We Trust the Gospels?* Wheaton, IL: Crossway, 2018. A very good and readable introduction to the historical reliability of the Gospels by an evangelical Protestant scholar.